D1555274

TELEWORK

John Wiley
INFORMATION SYSTEMS SERIES

Editors

Richard Boland   **Rudy Hirschheim**
Case Western Reserve University **University of Houston**

TELEWORK: TOWARDS THE ELUSIVE OFFICE

Ursula Huws, Werner B. Korte
AND **Simon Robinson**
for Empirica

 John Wiley
INFORMATION SYSTEMS SERIES

JOHN WILEY & SONS
Chichester · New York · Brisbane · Toronto · Singapore

Published by John Wiley & Sons Ltd
Baffins Lane, Chichester, West Sussex
PO19 IUD, England

Other Wiley Editorial Offices

John Wiley & Sons, Inc., 605 Third Avenue,
New York, NY 10158–0012, USA

Jacaranda Wiley Ltd, G.P.O. Box 859, Brisbane,
Queensland 4001, Australia

John Wiley & Sons (Canada) Ltd, 22 Worcester Road,
Rexdale, Ontario M9W 1L1, Canada

John Wiley & Sons (SEA) Pte Ltd, 3 Jalan Pemimpin #05-04,
Block B, Union Industrial Building, Singapore 2057

Library of Congress Cataloging-in-Publication Data:

Huws, Ursula.
    Telework: towards the elusive office / by Ursula Huws, Werner B.
Korte, and Simon Robinson for Empirica.
        p.   cm.—(John Wiley information systems series)
    Includes bibliographical references.
    ISBN 0 471 92284 6
    1. Telecommuting. I. Korte, Werner B. II. Robinson, Simon,
1953– . III. Empirica. Wirtschafts- und Sozialwissenschaftliche
Forschungs- und Beratungsgesellschaft. IV. Title. V. Series.
HD2333.H88   1990   89-24830
331.25—dc20   CIP

British Library Cataloguing in Publication Data:

Huws, Ursula
    Telework: towards the elusive office.—(Wiley series in
    information systems)
    1. Work patterns. Effects of technological innovation in
    telecommunication systems
    I. Title II. Korte, Werner B. III. Robinson, Simon.
    1953–
    331.25'7

    ISBN 0 471 92284 6

Typeset by Photo·graphics, Honiton, Devon
Printed in Great Britain by Biddles Ltd, Guildford, Surrey

Contents

Series Foreword

In order for all types of organisations to succeed, they need to be able to process data and use information effectively. This has become especially true in today's rapidly changing environment. In conducting their day-to-day operations, organisations use information for functions such as planning, controlling, organising, and decision making. Information, therefore, is unquestionably a critical resource in the operation of all organisations. Any means, mechanical or otherwise, which can help organisations process and manage information presents an opportunity they can ill afford to ignore.

The arrival of the computer and its use in data processing has been one of the most important organisational innovations of the past thirty years. The advent of computer-based data processing and information systems has led to organisations being able to cope with the vast quantities of information which they need to process and manage to survive. The field which has emerged to study this development is *information systems* (IS). It is a combination of two primary fields: computer science and management, with a host of supporting disciplines, e.g. psychology, sociology, statistics, political science, economics, philosophy, and mathematics. IS is concerned not only with the development of new information technologies but also with questions such as: how they can best be applied, how they should be managed, and what their wider implications are.

Partly because of the dynamic world in which we live (and the concomitant need to process more information), and partly because of the dramatic recent developments in information technology, e.g. personal computers, fourth-generation languages, relational databases, knowledge-based systems, and office automation, the relevance and importance of the field of information systems has become apparent. End users, who previously had little potential of becoming seriously involved and knowledgeable in information technology and systems, are now much more aware of and interested in the new technology. Individuals working in today's and tomorrow's organisations will be expected to have some understanding of and the ability to use the rapidly developing information technologies and systems. The dramatic increase in the availability and use of information technology, however, raises fundamental questions on the guiding of technological innovation, measuring organisational and managerial productivity, augmenting human intelligence, ensuring data integrity, and establishing strategic advantage. The expanded use of information systems also raises major challenges to the traditional forms of administration and authority, the right to privacy, the nature and form of work, and the limits of calculative rationality in modern organisations and society.

The Wiley Series on Information Systems has emerged to address these questions and challenges. It hopes to stimulate thought and discussion on the key role information systems play in the functioning of organisations and society, and how their role is likely to change in the future. This historical or evolutionary theme of the Series is important because considerable insight can be gained by attempting to understand the past. The Series will attempt to integrate both description—what has been done—with prescription—how best to develop and implement information systems.

The descriptive and historical aspect is considered vital because information systems of the past have not necessarily met with the success that was envisaged. Numerous writers postulate that a high proportion of systems are failures in one sense or another. Given their high cost of development and their importance to the day-to-day running of organisations, this situation must surely be unacceptable. Research into IS failure has concluded that the primary cause of failure is the lack of consideration given to the social and behavioural dimensions of IS. Far too much emphasis has been placed on their technical side. The result has been something of a shift in emphasis from a strictly technical conception of IS to one where it is recognised that information systems have behavioural consequences. But even this misses the mark. A growing number of researchers suggest that information systems are more appropriately conceived as social systems which rely, to a greater and greater extent, on new technology for their operation. It is this social orientation which is lacking in much of what is written about IS.

The Series seeks to provide a forum for the serious discussion of IS. Although the primary perspective is a more social and behavioural one, alternative perspectives will also be included. The present volume, *Telework: Towards the Elusive Office* by Ursula Huws, Werner Korte and Simon Robinson, exemplifies the theme of the series by presenting a careful analysis of the economic, social and legal faces of telework from the perspectives of the individual worker and the policy analyst as well as the organisational manager. They report and interpret the results of an extended empirical study with important implications for understanding the present reality of telework and for intelligently guiding its future.

Rudy Hirschheim
Richard Boland

Acknowledgements

This book could not have been written without the support of the Commission of the European Foundation, which funded a great deal of the research on which it is based, through its Forecasting and Assessment in Science and Technology (FAST) programme, through its European Strategic Programme for Research and Development in Information Technology (ESPRIT) and through the European Foundation for the Improvement of Living and Working Conditions.

Since 1984, when Empirica began its work on telework, we have been helped by more officers of the Commission than it is possible to name here. However, we should like to single out for particular thanks, Ricardo Petrella, director of the FAST programme, and Werner Wobbe, head of its 'Technology Work and Employment' sub-programme, who assisted us with humour and understanding. Our work for the ESPRIT programme has been helped immeasurably by the analytical insights of Jan Roukens, head of the Information Technology Applications Division of ESPRIT and the concerned and patient involvement of project officer Johannes Machnik. We are also grateful for the enthusiastic participation and constructive suggestions of our two ESPRIT project reviewers, Niels Bjorn-Andersen and Bruce Christie. At the European Foundation, our thanks go to project manager Eberhard Kohler.

We should also like to acknowledge the support of our partners in ESPRIT Project 1030, Gerry Ryan, Richard Wynne, Kevin Cullen, Tom Romayne and Ciaran Dolphin of the Work Research Centre in Dublin and Mike Hopkins and Brian Ennis of Irish Medical Systems in Dublin.

For carrying out the fieldwork on our surveys of European managers and employees, our thanks are due to Infratest Germany, Infratest France, Burke Milano, Business Decisions of London and MIL of London.

We are also extremely grateful to all the employers and teleworkers, too numerous to name individually, who so cheerfully gave up their time to share their experiences of telework with us.

The production of this book has, in many ways, been an exercise in telework itself, with one author in London and two in Germany, one of whom is a part-time homeworker. Co-ordination would not have been possible without excellent administrative support. We were fortunate enough to be provided with this, together with a wide range of other support services, by the secretaries in our Bonn office, Christine Künkel and Maria Grünhage, who met all our demands, however apparently unreasonable, with unfailing efficiency and good humour.

In London, the lion's share of copy-editing and checking tables and references fell on Mandy O'Keeffe, whose support, both practical and psychological, was vital during the latter stages of producing the manuscript. Thanks are due too to Rebecca Flemming, who stepped in at short notice to produce the index.

At John Wiley, we would particularly like to thank Rudy Hirschheim and Dick Boland, editors of the Information Systems series, for their helpful suggestions, and Diane Taylor, for tolerating our delays and seeing the book through the press.

Last, but certainly not least, we should like to thank Wolfgang Steinle, Empirica's managing director and architect-in-chief of the Empirica telework programme. Not only did he bring us together, he also supported the work at every stage, and must claim a large part of the credit for any success it might achieve.

Ursula Huws
Werner B. Korte
Simon Robinson
December 1988

A Note on the Literature on Telework

Several sections of this book are based on a survey of the literature on telework carried out by Empirica during 1987. We preface the book with a note on the character of this literature because it differs markedly from what is usually to be found on the library shelves devoted to work organisation.

The literature on work organisation is generally fairly predictable: dry and analytical, written for the academic researcher; or concise and pragmatic, designed for the the busy manager who wants to produce results. If one wants answers to broad questions about the quality of life or speculations about future social forms, this is not the subject heading which usually springs first to mind.

Yet when it comes to the particular form of work organisation known as telework we find an utterly different situation. This subject has gripped the public imagination and become for many a symbol of the way in which a future society, making intensive use of information technology, will be radically different from the familiar past. So, although telework still accounts for only a tiny fraction of all employment, the literature on it covers an extraordinarily broad spectrum, from the panoramic speculations of futurologists to sensational accounts in the popular media.

The first publications on the subject emerged during the oil crisis of the early 1970s, and focused on possible tradeoffs between transportation and telecommunications, with the primary objective of identifying ways of saving energy. Foremost among these authors was Jack Nilles, the grandfather of telework research (Nilles *et al.*, 1976). But a number of other researchers addressed the same issues (e.g. Glover, 1974; Pye, Tyler and Cartwright, 1974; Pye, 1976; Metayer, 1981; Harkness and Standal, 1982; Kraemer, 1982; Kraemer and King, 1982; King and Kraemer, 1981; Dover, 1982a, b).

Next came various futurist publications taking a sweeping view of history, positing a future in which telework will become the dominant organisational form of work. Of these, Alvin Toffler's vision of the 'electronic cottage' (Toffler, 1981, 1985) is probably the best known, although it is by no means unique. Similar positive images of a future in which electronic commuting has become the white-collar norm can be found in such varied sources as the works of British industrialist Mike Aldrich (Aldrich, 1982, 1984), feminist Barbara Gutek (Gutek, 1983), and California academic Frederick Williams, who puts forward the notion that we are witnessing the dawn of an 'electronic renaissance' (Williams, 1983).

The optimists do not have the field entirely to themselves, however. Contrasted with these utopias are alternative visions of the future in which telework brings, not new freedoms, but isolation, atomisation and exploitation (Mehlmann, 1985; Gregory, 1983; Siegel and Markoff, 1985; Huws, 1983, 1984b).

During the early 1980s, such visions were reflected in a very large number of articles in the popular press in the USA and Europe. The majority of these articles project a positive image (e.g. Whitehouse, 1981; Wiegner and Paris, 1983; Beck, 1984; Brooks, 1982; Clinton, 1983; Voge, 1981) and most illustrate their point with photographs and interviews with one or two individual teleworkers drawn from the same small range of telework schemes.

In contrast with these were a smaller number of popular articles which emphasised the negative aspects of telework, with titles like 'Chained to the kitchen computer' (Wilson, 1982), 'Will new technology woman be a drudge?' (Park, 1982), 'Working at home: is it freedom or a life of flabby loneliness?' (Larson, 1985), 'Work-at-home trend could be two-edged sword' (Kleiman, 1983), 'Loneliness of the long-distance programmer' (Groom, 1984a), 'Plug into exploitation' (*New Scientist*, 1984) or 'Working at home: women's blackspot' (Else, 1982).

During the same period, serious research projects began to be set up to survey the reality and future potential of teleworking from a broader perspective than its mere potential to substitute for physical commuting. Surveys of teleworkers which were published included an analysis of such issues as the implications for organisational structure and job design (e.g. Olson, 1981, 1982, 1983, 1985a b; Pratt, 1983; Kawakami, 1983; Brandt, 1983; Craipeau and Marot, 1984), the equal opportunities implications (e.g. Huws, 1984a, b, c; Lie, 1985; Vedel, 1984, 1985, Vedel and Gunnarsson, 1985; Goldmann and Richter, 1987), attitudes towards telework (Haefner, 1983; DeSanctis, 1984; and the Empirica surveys described in chapters 10 and 11 of this book) comparisons with traditional forms of homeworking (Bisset and Huws, 1984) and the extent to which the employment needs of people with disabilities were satisfied by telework (Ashok, Hall and Huws, 1986; Empirica, 1985).

In-depth articles also began to appear in the specialist computing and management press which analysed the advantages and disadvantages of specific forms of teleworking and gave practical advice to managers and workers embarking on telework schemes (e.g. Gordon, 1984, 1985a, b; Romero, 1983; Sarson, 1986; Upton, 1984; Franklin, 1986; Lallande, 1984; Harvey, 1982; DeSanctis, 1983; Meyer, 1983; Miller, 1986). These were followed by 'how to' manuals aimed at managers and written by telework veterans (e.g. Gordon and Kelly, 1986; Edwards and Edwards, 1985; Judkins, West and Drew, 1985).

Other sources of information on the subject include policy overviews (e.g. US Congress, Office of Technology Assessment, 1985; Bureau of National Affairs, 1986); conference proceedings (e.g. National Research Council, 1985; European Foundation for the Improvement of Living and Working Conditions, 1984; Housing Associations Charitable Trust, 1984; Zimmerman (ed.), 1983; Steinle *et al.*, 1988) and various academic research reports (e.g. Pugh, 1984; Holti and Stern, 1984, 1985; Stern and Holti, 1986) which examine problems of definition and classification. The subject of telework is also touched on in some of the general literature on office automation (e.g. Hirschheim, 1985; Strassman, 1985; Bjorn-Andersen, 1983; Hebenstreit, 1983).

The interested reader will find all sources used in this research listed alphabetically under author in the Reference section of this book. It is a motley collection, in which the slight and sensational rubs shoulders with the serious and scholarly, where individual anecdote claims equal status with broad survey. Because of the level at which public debate on the subject has been carried out, we felt it appropriate to include the entire range, and proffer our apologies to those readers who find the resulting text too dense with references for ease of reading.

Chapter 1

INTRODUCTION—WHAT IS TELEWORK?

One of the most arresting images in the public imagination of our times is that of a lone figure at a computer terminal, perhaps in an isolated rural setting, linked, as it were umbilically, to employers and the rest of the world only by an electronic cable. This image has given rise to some of the most optimistic utopias, as well as some of the most pessimistic dystopias of recent years. Innumerable phrases have been coined to sum it up: the electronic cottage; telecommuting; flexiplace; remote work; distance work; networking; telework. And in many countries fierce controversy prevails as to whether it extends or diminishes individual freedom; whether it improves or degrades working conditions; whether it liberates or enslaves women; in short, whether it is overall a good or a bad thing. It is difficult to recall any other technological development affecting work organisation which has aroused so much moral passion since the introduction of the power loom.

Yet, for a concept which has been so hotly debated, telework—for such we will call it in these pages—is surprisingly elusive. In common speech there does appear to be some working consensus of opinion on what it means. The belief is that information technology has made it possible to decentralise many types of work involving the electronic processing of information, and telework is simply the term used to describe workers who have been dispersed in this way. It is only when one attempts to collect empirical data on telework, so that its development can be quantified and future trends extrapolated, that this consensus dissolves. As soon as we try to count the numbers of teleworkers or locate the industries in which they are situated, it becomes clear that we have no stable or concrete definition of what we mean by the term. In fact it is doubtful whether it is even possible to construct one using existing conceptual and statistical categories.

This is not to say that some of the definitions so far put forward have not been useful for the specific purposes for which they have been devised, merely that none is sufficiently universal or unambiguous to use as the basis for empirical investigation.

Interest in telework first arose during the oil crisis of the early 1970s, its impetus coming from the desire to save energy. It occurred then to some researchers, most notably Jack Nilles at the University of Southern California, that information technology provided the potential for substituting electronic

1

communication for physical travel, thus contributing to the minimisation of one of the most extravagant forms of fuel consumption—the daily commute to work by private car (Nilles *et al.*, 1976). The starting point of research was therefore the journey to work and its costs and benefits, which could, once quantified, be compared with the costs and benefits of staying at home and using a telecommunications link to communicate with the employer. In this context, the new verb 'to telecommute' was a perfect expression of the concept at issue—the substitution of IT-based remote communication for physical travel. Indeed this word, reputedly coined by Nilles, is still the one most commonly used in the United States for telework.

However, the concept of substitution which it embodies does create some problems for the analysis of telework. The idea that transport or telecommunications costs are a significant factor in the choice of whether or not to adopt remote working patterns has not been supported by research. As early as 1981, Margrethe Olson, as a result of her work for the Diebold Group and at New York University's School of Business Administration, concluded that organisational culture and managerial attitudes are the most important determinants of this choice (Diebold Group, 1981; Olson, 1982). This view has been corroborated by much of the subsequent research in the field. The desire to save on commuting does not figure at all in the eight motives cited by telework consultant Gil Gordon for the choice of telework by US employers (Gordon, 1988) or in the four quoted by Edwards and Edwards (Edwards and Edwards, 1985). In Empirica's survey of European employers of teleworkers, which is described fully in Chapter 9, about a quarter gave reduced commuting as a reason for choosing telework, but this was ranked below other factors in importance. The picture is similar when teleworkers themselves are asked why they have chosen this form of work. Survey after survey has shown that, although many see it as one of several advantages of telework, avoiding the daily journey to work is rarely a primary reason for the choice, being ranked below such factors as the need to combine working with family demands, the need for flexibility or the desire for autonomy (see for instance, Olson, 1985a, 1983; Huws, 1984a, and our own research, described in Chapter 9).

Of course it can be argued that although the substitution of telecommunications for travel is not the reason for the choice of telework, it is nevertheless a result of it. This may well be the case, but it is essentially unverifiable, for without a definition of telework which enables it to be readily identified by employers or by teleworkers themselves, it is impossible to collect the sort of empirical data which would make a quantitative analysis possible. The only situation where one is certain to get an affirmative answer to the question 'Do any of your employees work remotely as a substitute for travelling to work?' is one in which an employee who formerly travelled to work has now ceased to do so. A 'yes' could not be guaranteed in a number of other situations which might, on investigation, fall within most people's definitions of telework— for instance, a situation where an employee had been recruited as a remote worker, or where a company made regular use of home-based freelance workers, or sub-contracted work to a company employing homeworkers. The substitution process is unlikely to be visible to the employer unless it has actually physically taken place within recent memory. From the point of view of the teleworker, the substitution is likely to be little more apparent. Many remote workers perceive the choice they have made not as that between working remotely or travelling to a central office, but as that between working remotely or not working at all.

It is clear, then, that 'the substitution of telecommunications for travel' is not in itself an adequate definition of telework. What then are the alternatives? A definition which has gained some informal currency in common speech is one which perceives telework as a sub-category of homeworking, in other words it is 'work which is carried out at home involving the use of information technology'. However, on close investigation, this definition too becomes fraught with difficulties.

The first problem is that it excludes forms of remote working which are not home-based, such as neighbourhood offices and satellite work centres. For practical purposes this may not matter as much as it appears to, since these forms of remote working generally seem to have a stronger presence in the minds of commentators on the subject than in reality. Nevertheless, it does pose conceptual difficulties which cannot be ignored.

Another problem is to define what we mean by 'at home'. It is very common for workers who are normally office-based to take work home occasionally, perhaps because it requires concentration to complete, because it needs to be finished urgently or because the worker is ill or temporarily disabled. It is also common for workers who are primarily based at home to visit the office of their clients or employers and sometimes to work there for long periods. In between, there are a number of flexible arrangements which do not fall easily into either category. This difficulty can be circumvented in practice. It would be relatively easy to design a survey which, for instance, defined as homeworkers those who had spent more than 50 per cent of their working time at home over a given period. The danger is that any particular limit set is bound to be arbitrary.

However, that is not the only difficulty. It is also important to distinguish between people who work 'in the home' and those who work 'from home'. Here too there is a grey area, since there are some workers who work partly at home and partly elsewhere. Many current definitions of the term 'homeworker', exclude those working 'from' home, along with professional and artistic workers. For instance the Homeworkers (Protection) Bill, unsuccessfully introduced to the British parliament in 1979, defined a homeworker as:

> An individual who contracts with a person not being a professional client of his or hers for the purpose of that person's business for the execution of any work (other than the production or creation of any literary, dramatic, artistic or musical work) to be done in domestic premises not under the control of the management of the person with whom he contracts, and who does not make use of the services of more than two individuals in the carrying out of that work.

Adopting such a definition might exclude a large proportion of the workers currently described as teleworkers, including freelance computer programmers, mobile sales staff using portable computers, systems analysts, consultants of various sorts and some journalists, not only because of the professional nature of their work but also because it takes them out and about onto the premises of clients or other third parties, such as information suppliers.

This commonly-made distinction does not, therefore, appear to contribute a great deal to the construction of a definition of telework and it is necessary to seek other delineators—a task which becomes increasingly difficult the more closely one explores the data on people working at home.

From sources such as censuses of population it becomes clear that, even if we exclude those directly involved in manufacture, workers 'in' the home include such diverse categories as farmers, hoteliers, publicans and shop-keepers who live and work on the same premises as well as a variety of artistic and craft workers. Similarly, excluding lorry drivers, taxi drivers, building workers and other clearly defined groups from the category of workers 'from' home still leaves us with a motley collection of sales representatives, service personnel, agents and entrepreneurs across a broad range of industries.

In these days of cheap personal computers, many of these may make some use of information technology in the course of their work, but it would be unwise to assume that this factor alone is enough to identify them as teleworkers. Is it really useful to categorise in this way farmers, TV repair technicians, plumbers, architects or any other group of self-employed, home-based workers just because they make incidental use of computers for accounting, word processing or other administrative functions? and can they be said to differ in any significant way from others sharing the same occupations who use more traditional methods to organise their work, or who delegate these functions to a sub-contractor?

To take another example, what should be the designation of a married woman who is employed by her husband to keep the books and carry out secretarial duties for his home-based small business? She is, after all, a homeworker, but not working at a distance from her employer. If it is decided not to call her a teleworker, what happens if his business expands and he decides to work from an office or showroom elsewhere, although she continues to work from home—does she then change her status overnight and become a teleworker?

Such examples could be multiplied endlessly. They serve merely to point out that the simple fact of working from a home base and using information technology is not a good enough basis from which to construct a definition of telework which is likely to be useful for analytical purposes.

A third possible basis for a definition of telework lies in the technology itself. Could we, perhaps, define as telework all activities which require electronic communication between the central office of an employer and an employee working at a distance on a remote terminal? At first glance, this too may seem an attractive option; on closer investigation, however, it also raises major difficulties.

For one thing, it includes all organisations with branch structures which have internal electronic communications systems. Let us take the example of the insurance industry. Many insurance companies have had a branch structure almost since their inception. However, the introduction of new technology has brought changes in the division of labour between the high street branches and head offices. Computerised databases have given decentralised staff immediate access to information which formerly had to be retrieved by telephone or letter from a central office, allowing them to provide detailed comparisons between different policies and instant quotations for their clients. This has in turn enabled their employers to slim down head office staffing levels, since fewer staff are now required to process information requests from branches. Similar changes have taken place within other financial institutions with branch structures. It is a similar story in retailing, where sophisticated point-of-sale terminals have made automatic ordering possible, along with the automatic supply of information about stock levels to central offices. In so far as they make use of computerised information systems, public sector organisations such as social security offices, employment exchanges and libraries also fall into this category.

In addition to organisations which have branch structures in order to be near their customers, there are also organisations which have relocated certain functions at a distance from their head offices for other reasons, for instance to take advantage of certain local labour market conditions. These cover a wide spectrum from, at one extreme, companies which have moved back-office functions out of city centres into the suburbs of those same cities (Moss, 1984; Nelson, 1986) to those which have moved them across oceans from the United States to the Caribbean or Southeast Asia (Huws, 1985, US Congress, Office of Technology Assessment, 1985).

To define all the workers involved in these developments as teleworkers would be ludicrous since it would create a category so large as to be meaningless; a majority of workers in the finance industry would become teleworkers as would a substantial proportion of those in many others. We are thus left, once again, with the problem of delineating a sub-category which is useful for our purposes.

There are several possibilities. One could, for instance, draw distinctions on the basis of the size of the remote organisation. At one end of the spectrum are the huge unwieldy regional offices of state organisations, or national or transnational corporations; at the other are small suburban word processing pools or individual agents. The latter seem closer to what most people seem to mean by telework, but where along this spectrum should the line be drawn? And could it be anything but arbitrary?

Another possibility would be to include as teleworkers only those staff whose work involves the direct transmission of electronic data through telecommunications networks. But this again seems likely to produce arbitrary classifications. Should one distinguish, for instance, between someone accessing a computer in the next room and someone accessing a computer at the company's head office, using identical methods? Is it feasible to draw a distinction between data preparation operators involved in batch processing whose work is transmitted to head office at the end of the day by their supervisor and those involved in on-line processing who are directly linked to the main computer? If a new system is introduced into a local branch based on locally sited microcomputers, to replace an earlier system using a head-office mainframe, do all the workers using it suddenly cease to become teleworkers?

In some industries the distinctions to be drawn are even more complex. To use the insurance industry once again as an example, a continuum can be observed running between the individual insurance broker or 'financial adviser', paid by commission, operating from a home base and using a videotex-based network as an essential tool of the trade, and the office of a large insurance broking company: the difference is only one of scale; the relationship with the information provider and the technology used is likely to be essentially the same. The difference between the work carried out in the office of the insurance broker and that done in the branch office of a company which is itself an insurance provider will also be very similar. To confuse things even further, many of the jobs carried out in the branch office of the insurance-providing company may be identical to others carried out in the same company's head office. Is there any point in the web of relationships where it is possible to draw a line and state categorically that all the workers on one side of it are teleworkers and all those on the other are not?

Examples drawn from other industries lead us into parallel dilemmas. We are therefore left without any obvious point at which to place the boundary which separates teleworkers from their fellow workers. Should it depend on the size of their place of work? On its location? On the technology they employ to carry it out? Or on whether the network to which they are linked is provided by their employer or by some other, external organisation? Or should we simply decide that this factor is entirely irrelevant to the definition of telework? Whatever the answer to these questions, it seems that we shall have to look to other variables to find a conclusive definition.

One possible variable which we have not investigated so far is that of the worker's contractual relationship to his or her employer. Telework is often associated with the growth of sub-contracting, of self-employment and of various temporary or casual forms of work which are often grouped together under the general heading 'new ways of working', and information technology has certainly been intimately involved in these developments. One reason for this is that office automation facilitates the 'unbundling' or disaggregation of organisational structures by standardising processes, formalising decision-making structures and increasing the potential for quantifying and monitoring the performance of individual parts of an organisation (Brusco, 1981). The result has been a vertical disintegration of organisations and an increase in the sub-contracting of a wide range of services, often to companies started up by ex-employees of the contracting organisation (Mitter, 1986; Mattera, 1985). The famous Rank Xerox experiment which resulted in the coining of the word 'networking' was an example of telework being developed in the context of the honing down of the parent organisation and the sub-contracting of various activities which had previously been carried out in-house (Judkins, West and Drew, 1985). But whether work is contracted out to a sub-contracting company, an individual freelance or a temporary contract worker, we are still left with the problem of which types of sub-contracted work to classify as telework.

Even if we restrict the range of possible activities to office services, the dilemma does not disappear. A typical office might sub-contract such services as graphic design, typesetting, advertising, accounting, legal advice, data processing and overflow copy typing, all of which involve the processing of information to some extent. If they are not all to be classed as telework, how should distinctions be made? Should the designation be restricted only to those using computers? If so, at what level of technology usage is a worker reclassified? Let us say that a self-employed home-based copy typist trades in her ageing electric typewriter for an electronic typewriter with a memory. Is she now a teleworker, or must she wait until this has in turn given way to a word processor? If the graphic design studio acquires a personal computer for doing the accounts, are the designers transformed overnight into teleworkers?

An alternative approach ,might be to draw a demarcation around those using a direct telecommunications link with the contractor for the delivery of information. However, this too might lead to arbitrary distinctions between groups of workers whose location, method of work and relationship with the employer do not differ significantly in other respects. For instance, our copy typist, equipped with her new word processor, might find it more convenient to send the diskette containing her completed work to the contractor by messenger rather than using her modem. Does such a small difference justify a separate classification? Similarly, one could argue that the nature of a graphic designer's work is not fundamentally altered because the copy and rough sketches for a rush job happen to be delivered via a fax terminal, instead of through the post.

A distinction based on the size of the sub-contracting enterprise is also likely to produce arbitrary results. To take another example, there is rarely much real difference in the work carried out by a single freelance computer programmer, two who have got together to form a partnership, a programmer working for a small firm employing perhaps four or five, or one employed by a larger company. Such differences as do exist, for instance cost differences caused by the higher overheads of organisations which are not based in people's homes, or the additional reliability offered by an organisation, as against an isolated individual, in case of sickness, have no connection with the contractual relationship, the technology employed, or the nature of the work carried out.

It appears then that even a study of contractual relationships, although it may spread useful light on some aspects of telework, fails to provide us with the raw material for a definition of telework which can form a framework for empirical research.

These many difficulties facing the researcher attempting to produce a clear definition of telework prompt the question, why bother? If a concept is as nebulous as this, then wouldn't it be better to abandon it and develop a different framework for analysis, more amenable to precise categorisation? Perhaps, instead of focusing on telework, we should be concentrating on a study of the changing geographical organisation of work, of new travel patterns, of the use of information technology by home-based workers, of new forms of contractual relationship between employers and workers, or of changing patterns of work organisation.

We believe that this would be a mistake. Despite its lack of precision, the word telework has acquired a potent symbolic value. Quite independent of the extent to which it describes a measurable reality, the idea of the teleworker has become a representation of what the future of work might be. Aware that major upheavals are taking place in the organisation of work, though not quite able to pinpoint what these are, many people have seized on this image, and projected onto it many of their hopes and fears about the future. Recent employment trends have aroused considerable anxiety in some, and excitement in others. The notion of telework provides a concrete focus for these feelings.

It is no accident that the issue of electronic homeworking has become so politically loaded, and the debates surrounding it so polarised. It can be seen as the logical conclusion, the most extreme form, of many of the tendencies discussed above. Whether we like it or not, the image of the remote worker is now a highly-charged symbol. For some it is a symbol of liberation from the daily grind of living in a suburb, commuting into the city, working from 9 to 5 and wearing stuffy suits, a chance to get to know one's family and pursue new leisure interests. For others, it has become a symbol of isolation, exploitation and the end of any possibility of temporary escape from the drudgery of housework and childcare.

With attitudes so polarised, and debates so heated, it becomes a matter of direct public concern to discover to what extent this symbolic image matches the reality, the dynamics of its development and the extent to which it is likely to spread. Researchers thus have a responsibility to collect what empirical data they can and develop some sort of framework within which it can be analysed, however imperfect that framework may be.

Up to now, most of the researchers who have carried out empirical investigations into telework have tended to adopt a pragmatic approach. Faced with a very limited number of well-known examples of telework, and with few possibilities for identifying a larger sample, they have frequently taken these well-known examples as their starting point, analysed them, and developed typologies to fit which have then, in a circular fashion, formed the basis of their definitions.

The approach which we have followed in this book is based on a recognition that telework cannot be adequately characterised in terms which are solely technological, organisational, locational or contractual. It is not a monodirectional or a monodimensional phenomenon and cannot be defined along any single parameter. Even a definition which takes account of all of these factors in combination cannot, we feel, provide the basis for the accurate quantification of telework at any particular point in time. However, we also think that the main purpose of research into telework should not be to produce static measurements of its extent, but to produce information about the dynamics of its adoption. The answers we seek are therefore to such questions as: what are the factors which encourage or discourage employers from taking up telework? What are the incentives or disincentives from the point of view of the individual worker? How do these change under differing circumstances? What are the costs and the benefits of telework at the level of the individual worker, of the organisation and of society as a whole?

To answer such questions, what is needed is a definition which distinguishes telework from the alternative options available to a manager or an individual worker. We believe that this can be done by using a definition which focuses on three variables: the location of work; the use of electronic equipment; and the existence of a communications link to the employer or contractor. We define telework as work the location of which is independent of the location of the employer or contractor and can be changed according to the wishes of the individual teleworker and/or the organisation for which he or she is working. It is work which relies primarily or to a large extent on the use of electronic equipment, the results of which work are communicated remotely to the employer or contractor. The remote communications link need not be a direct telecommunications link but could include the use of mail or courier services.

While recognising the inadequacies of this definition in any absolute sense, we do feel that, at the present stage of technological development, it is a functional tool for examining the dynamics of the adoption of telework. In the rest of this book, this is what we propose to do, drawing on an extensive review of the literature on the subject, on several surveys we have carried out in this field and on Empirica's experiences in providing consultancy on telework.

Chapter 2

TELEWORK IN THE GENERAL CONTEXT OF OFFICE AUTOMATION

In order to develop an understanding of the dynamics of telework it is essential to view it in the overall context of general office automation. Although, as we will go on to show, there is little evidence that the introduction of telework necessarily follows from the existence of particular forms of technology within an organisation, it is nevertheless the case that it is information technology which has made feasible many of the changes in the location and organisation of work which are involved in telework. A degree of office automation can thus be said to be a precondition, even though it is not a determinant, of telework.

Today, there is still neither a universally accepted term to describe the application of IT and IT systems in the office nor a universally accepted definition of office automation. The most comprehensive overview of definitions which we could find in the literature was Hirschheim's (Hirschheim, 1985), and his is the definition which we found most useful in capturing the entirety of office automation. It is a definition which accommodates the concept of office systems as fundamentally social systems (Hirschheim, 1985; Checkland, 1986) and office functions as largely consisting of communication and information processing tasks (Morgenbrod and Schwärtzel, 1980) and succeeds in synthesising earlier definitions by Olson and Lucas (Olson and Lucas, 1982) and Zisman (Zisman, 1978). According to this definition:

> Office automation in its current form refers to the application of integrated computer, communication and office product technologies and social science knowledge to support the myriad activities and functions in an office or office environment. (Hirschheim, 1985, p. 16)

It has been estimated by various authorities that over half the working population in the United States and the European Economic Community economies already works in information-related activities (see, for instance, Dostal, 1985). In such activities information is captured, stored, processed, modified, communicated and used as a basis for decisions. These functions, some of which are capable of being automated, are carried out in conjunction with the human information-processing activities of seeing, hearing, speaking and writing.

Information transmission for the purpose of communication can be categorised along several parameters such as form, type (voice, data, text, image communication) and content, and by its geographical and organisational distribution. Figure 2.1 illustrates one way of categorising the information-processing and communication functions carried out in an office. Today, most offices have a number of systems for handling information, such as meetings, telephone, telex, mail, photocopier, fax, mainframe computer, individual personal computer and typewriter. Most of these systems are self-contained and independent, and a considerable amount of effort and cost is entailed in transferring information from one system to another and keeping records, many of which duplicate each other. Office automation provides the possibility of breaking down the barriers between these systems.

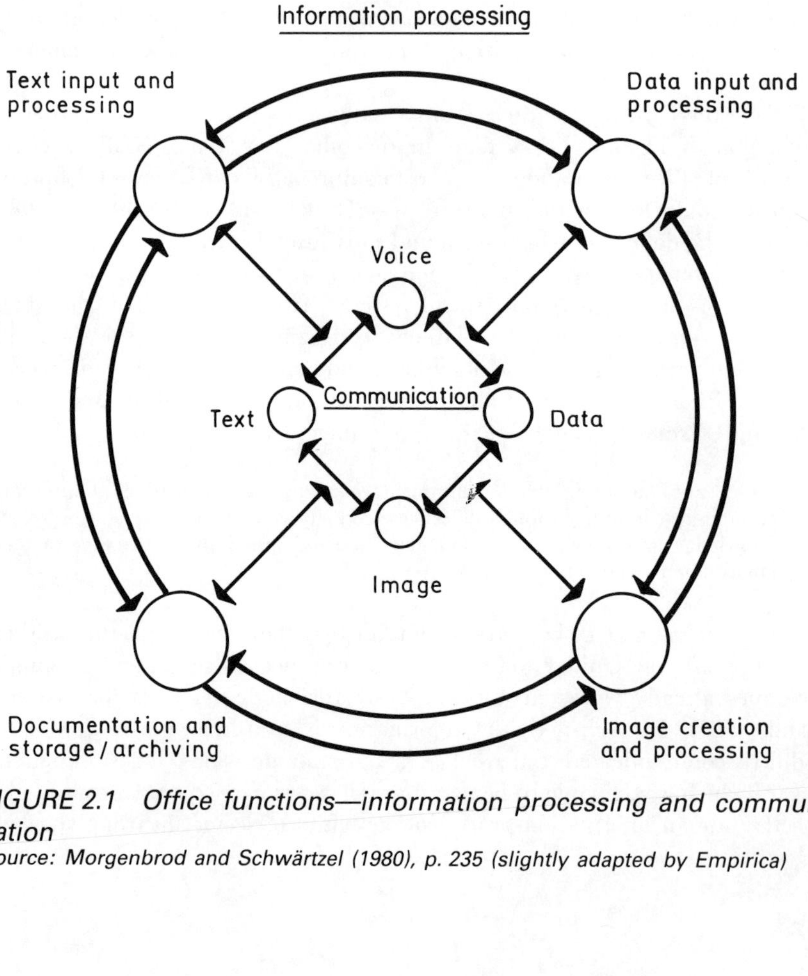

Information processing

Text input and processing

Data input and processing

Voice

Text   Communication   Data

Image

Documentation and storage / archiving

Image creation and processing

FIGURE 2.1   *Office functions—information processing and communication*
Source: Morgenbrod and Schwärtzel (1980), p. 235 (slightly adapted by Empirica)

All commentators agree that the introduction of new information and communication technologies into the office enables drastic changes in information processing and communication to take place. This is achieved by the integration of information-processing and communications technologies which were previously quite separate.

> The application of communication technologies in concert with the computer and new storage media, allows integration of communication, data management and recordkeeping functions. (Otten, 1984, p. 28)

> The revolution in office communications technology has two sides: one concerned with the production of organisational intelligence and the other with its distribution. What makes recent developments interesting and magnifies their potential impact is the fusion of two previously distinct aspects of the communication process. (Taylor, 1982, p. 4)

> The greatest changes, however, will lie in the convergence of these technologies with telecommunications, allowing the linking together of previously stand-alone products and the sharing of resources. (Hirschheim, 1985, p. 12)

Hirschheim describes an 'integrated information resource' function 'which is the confluence of three previously separate functions: data processing, telecommunications, and office services' (Hirschheim, 1985, p. 12). This convergence is depicted in Figure 2.2 which suggests how the four major means of information communication—voice, image, text and data—are evolving and converging into one integrated resource. In a fully integrated office, a work station could take voice input, paper or pictures, automatically file this information and transmit it in any of these forms, provided that the systems are designed to be technically compatible with each other, using standardised interfaces. According to Otten, electronic business communication, in which all information is digital, offers five distinct advantages over traditional forms of communication:

1. Overall cost reduction through savings in labour
2. Substantial acceleration of communication
3. Substantial reduction in paper handling
4. Integration of true instant data communication with record management for on-line retrieval at a later time
5. Improved communication effectiveness through practical two-way communication and efficient use of multiple forms of softcopy data representations in the form of printed text, graphics and synthetic speech. (Otten, 1984, p. 30)

The potential of such integrated office systems is beginning to be recognised, but they have by no means yet become a reality. To the extent that it is happening, the linking of different information-based communications systems is occurring in a piecemeal way in all but the most highly organised offices.

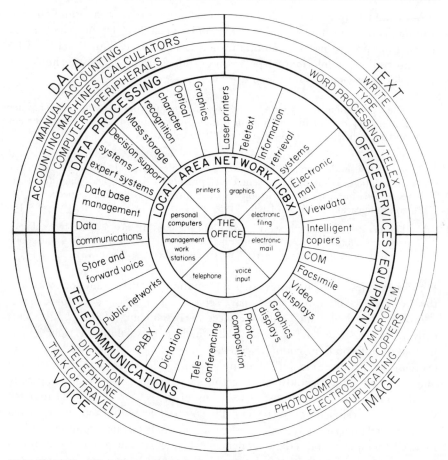

FIGURE 2.2   The integrated information resource
Source: Hirschheim (1985), p. 13

There are still serious bottlenecks to be overcome in the provision of a broad-band telecommunications infrastructure for communication between different offices, in hardware and in software development before it will be possible to have all the information-processing components of a typical organisation in effective, reliable, user-friendly, interactive dialogue with each other. Nevertheless, it is in the stumbling progress towards this ideal of the fully integrated office that the new forms of work organisation most conducive to the development of telework appear most likely to emerge. As James Taylor puts it:

> Two things are occurring here: first, the 'boundaries' of the traditional organisation are crumbling as fluid networks evolve to link people in the group

to those with similar interests outside; and second, even within the organisation, the pattern of message exchange increasingly diverges from the traditional organisation chart, with its well-defined hierarchy, in favour of a kind of 'all-channel', everyone-to-everyone network of links. (Taylor, 1982, p. 10)

Technical developments in the area of office automation and telecommunications are changing the locational as well as the temporal characteristics of office work. It is now possible for organisations to reconsider the assumption that all employees must go to one central location to work:

> The introduction of telecommunications and computer technology into the workplace has profound implications for the nature of work itself. In particular, the implementation of 'office automation' permits significant changes in the organisation and execution of office work. It is possible that the term 'office' may take on new meanings. Office automation provides the potential to alter the locational and temporal definitions of large numbers of office jobs. (Olson and Tasley, 1983, p. 1)

Rauch believes that increasing use of new information and communication technologies in organisations results in a widely dispersed office structure with a complex network of intercommunications. He has developed a model to illustrate his view of the impact of new information and communication technology on the organisational structure of a company, reproduced here as Figure 2.3. This model shows us a future in which organisations are much less spatially confined than at present, with their separate parts held together not by physical proximity but by an interactive web of communications networks. This physical decentralisation is reflected, according to this view, in a decentralisation of decision making.

In the 1970s, Nilles christened this the 'diffused work society', and speculated that in it, companies would maintain only a small core staff and workload peaks would be dealt with by delegating work to dispersed individuals working at home or from neighbourhood offices. Such work arrangements would depend for their effectiveness on telecommunications links for transmission of work and contact with fellow-workers and employers (Nilles *et al.*, 1976).

In contrast to the hierarchical co-ordination of office tasks which currently integrates workers into the structure of an organisation, some commentators have predicted that in the future, tasks will be co-ordinated much more strongly and directly through markets. Under a system like this, 'each worker acts as an individual entrepreneur who sells his or her performance to the highest bidder' (Williamson, 1980, quoted in Brandt, 1983, p. 3).

This analysis suggests that a decentralisation of decision making accompanies the geographical dispersal of work. While this trend may well be evident when work is externalised by means of sub-contracting, the pattern is not a universal one. Contradicting it in some respects is a trend for geographical decentralisation

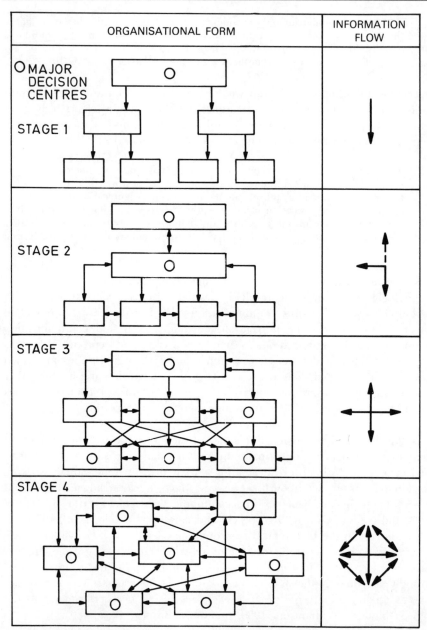

FIGURE 2.3 The effects of information technology on corporate
organisation
Source: McHale (1976)

MEDIA	FUNCTIONAL CHARACTERISTICS	PERSONNEL CHARACTERISTICS
Mainly written	Vertically oriented hierarchical bureaucracy. Organised by expertise. Written communications with fixed decision rules and chains of command with centralised decision points. Least horizontal communication.	People trained for highly specialised and limited functions. Little job mobility. Pyramidal authority structure with fixed procedures for access or appeal to higher levels.
Written Telephone Xerox	Horizontally organised by function areas Mixture of fixed decision rules and autonomous functional rules. Shorter chains of command with more decision points.	Transitional form of organisation sharing characteristics of stages 1 and 2. Mixture of line and staff functions with corresponding organisational roles well defined but flexibly adjusted to allow for more autonomy via both formal and informal access to higher levels of decision making. Job mobility more confined to upper level organisational tasks. Other workers tend to remain tied to stated work descriptions and rankings.
As above but significant introduction of computer use at each level speeds up feedback.	Network type of organisation with mission or objective foci which set flexible decision rules. Information flow includes critical man/machine interfaces (e.g. systems analysts programmers and comptrollers) which feed back from bottom to top. More autonomous decision making.	Skills less tied to specific sets of tasks within organisation. Worker less tied to a single work situation with developing competence and more flexible skills less attached to specific employing organisation. Organisations tend to arrange work to develop capacities of people rather than use the capacities to accomplish work. Growth of serial careers with multiple entry paths into different careers etc.
As above, plus more extended use of interactive communications modes, remote terminals, video conference techniques etc. enabling widely distributed decision centres to interact swiftly.	More diffuse and geographically separated network type, with a high degree of adaptability and change in organisational configuration. Information and decision flows evolve in response to perceived needs rather than predefined and preset objectives or programmes. Increased feedback at swifter rates enables previously autonomous decision-making to be integrated into whole system directions.	As above – mix of diverse specialities flexibly adaptive to changes in task and policy directions. The managerial executive becomes the prime interface and coordinator of temporary systemic clusters of specialised project groups – with multiple mobile and overlapping memberships. Ranking according to competence in flexible performance rather than by hierarchical position in organisation.

to be accompanied by a centralisation of control. There is some evidence that organisations employing remote workers are more likely to exercise close monitoring and tight control over their staff than those whose workforce is safely under their eye in a central office. As Brandt himself points out: 'Remarkably, the more dispersed the organisation's spatial structure, the more attention is generally paid to aspects of the organisation's formal structure, such as type of employment, mechanism of coordination and supervision' (Brandt, 1983, pp. 2–3).

Whether or not we accept such visions in their entirety, we are left—if we accept that some degree of office automation is a prerequisite for the development of remote forms of working—with the question of how they are likely to come about. What, in other words, is the process by which work reorganisation takes place as information technology is introduced?

Information technology is rarely introduced overnight. Office work which has been carried out for years on the basis of traditional communications and information systems is not usually switched over to new and innovative systems in a single sweep. There are normally several steps in between. A typical progression might be as follows:

Phase 1

The introduction of electronic systems into traditional office environments, such as the substitution of electronic memory typewriters or stand-alone word processors for electric or manual typewriters; the use of photocopiers instead of carbon paper; the extension of a telephone to a telephone system (PABX) with additional facilities such as number recall or automatic redialling.

Phase 2

The use of data and information from traditional data processing systems and the application of telecommunications networks and services such as fax, teletex or videotex.

Phase 3

The integration of stand-alone office systems into partly or completely integrated systems with (at least partial) use of electronic telecommunication services and networks.

This illustrates that the process of office automation is not characterised by disruptions but rather by a continuous flow of changes in the office environment.

A number of researchers in this field have developed phase models of office automation, or make distinctions between different 'stages in office automation growth' (Meyer, 1983) or 'cycles of investment in IT' (Maggiolini, 1986).

Meyer identifies four stages: conception, initiation, contagion and consolidation, which are summarised, together with their salient characteristics, in Table 2.1.

Maggiolini opts for a model in which investment in and assimilation of information technology is seen as passing through three cycles. This is illustrated in Table 2.2. In this model, the role of the technology changes at different stages of the assimilation process, progressing from 'operational' systems to 'coordination and control' systems and then to systems supporting 'transactions'. In the first stage it is a work tool, a means of raising productivity in the production process itself; in the second, it takes on the functions of co-ordination and control; while in the final stage it becomes a medium of transaction, an integral part of the means of communication in and between offices (Maggiolini, 1986).

Figure 2.4 is a graphic representation of this model, which shows how Maggiolini sees these stages as overlapping with and developing from each other. What all these concepts have in common is a characterisation of office automation as a continuous flow of changes in office environments. The introduction of telework can, in theory, form an integral part of this process. Nilles was one of the first researchers to examine how it might do so, looking particularly at the changes in the organisational structure of a company that

TABLE 2.1   Stages in office automation growth

Stage	Characteristics
1 Conception	
(a) Early	Cost-displacement applications (such as word processing, administrative telecommunications and records management)
(b) Advanced	Cost-displacement applications: plans to build first pilot of managerial and professional information tools
2 Initiation	
(a) Early	Use of pilot by information professionals
(b) Advanced	Use of pilot by managers and professionals
3 Contagion	
(a) Early	Use of limited set of office automation tools by multiple end user groups
(b) Advanced	Widespread use of limited set of office automation tools: pilots of advanced integrated systems
4 Consolidation	Widespread use of integrated office automation systems

Source: Meyer (1983), p. 53

TABLE 2.2   Cycles of investment in IT

1st cycle: COMPUTER TECHNOLOGY

- 'operational' systems (e.g. payroll)
- the computer as a 'work tool', informatics as 'production' technology
- added value: the computerisation of procedures
- benefits: the reduction of (information processing) 'production' costs

2nd cycle: DATA RESOURCE TECHNOLOGY

- 'coordination and control' systems (e.g. production planning and control)
- information technology as coordination and organisational control technology
- added value: the electronic storage of data
- benefits: the reduction of 'coordination' costs

3rd cycle: ELECTRONIC COMMUNICATIONS TECHNOLOGY

- 'transactional' systems (e.g. electronic mail, telematic services, external data bank services)
- Information technology as mediating technology (particularly on the market)
- added value: the computerisation of communication
- benefits: reductions in 'transaction' costs

Source: Maggiolini (1986), p. 80 (slightly adapted by the authors)

may occur as a result of the implementation of office technology and the introduction of remote working. The most significant change he predicted is that organisations will no longer be limited to a central office work environment operating within traditional working hours.

Historically, even in industries not dealing with the creation of physical goods in factories or the performance of a service which requires face-to-face contact with customers, it has been usual to locate work centrally, in the case of office work in downtown business districts. The explanation for this, according to Nilles and his colleagues, can be found in transport requirements:

> Until recently in the history of man, communication over any distance was dependent upon transportation, that is one had to travel physically or send written documents to another place to communicate with another individual or to transact business. To a large degree, the availability or varieties of transportation determined the location, growth and configuration of cities. (Nilles *et al.*, 1976, p. 1)

Before information technology became widely available, in the late 1970s and 80s, offices in central urban locations retained a number of advantages

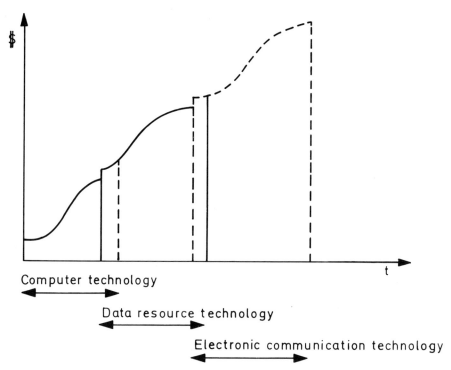

FIGURE 2.4   *Process of assimilation of IT*
Source: Maggiolini (1986), p. 81

over rural and more peripheral locations. These included economies of scale in the use of capital equipment, close supervision of subordinates, ease of communication with co-workers, and access to central files and reference materials needed in the work process (Kawakami, 1983).

The traditional form of company organisation, still the dominant form in the western world, is characterised by a hierarchical co-ordination of tasks that integrate workers into the structure of an organisation by employing them and paying them fixed salaries (Brandt, 1983, pp. 2–3).

Olson describes the traditional company as a place where it is 'assumed that a critical mass of employees will occupy a central work place a set number of hours a day, typically "nine to five". Work performance and organisational procedures are critically bounded by this place and these hours' (Olson, 1982, p. 80). The invention of the telegraph and telephone increased the possibilities for flexibility in administering office work but not to the extent that the daily commute to the central office could be abandoned. However information technology 'provides the potential for changing the definition of office work in terms of space and time' (Diebold Group, 1981, p. 1).

Nilles was the first to attempt to conceptualise the evolutionary development of organisational structures in terms of their geographical structure and corresponding telecommunications interfaces. In an analysis which influenced much subsequent work on the subject he and his colleagues identified four different phases: centralisation, fragmentation, dispersion and diffusion, which are illustrated graphically in Figure 2.5. According to this analysis, centralisation represents the mode which is currently dominant in most industries:

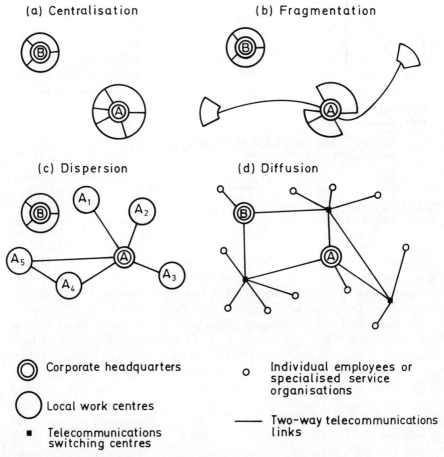

FIGURE 2.5   *The spatial evolution of organisations*
Source: Nilles et al. (1976), p. 12

All administrative operations are located at a single site, with workers divided into functional groups according to their primary information product. Where national organisations are divided into regional offices, the regional home office generally replicates this monolithic structure. (Nilles *et al.*, 1976, p. 11)

In the fragmentation phase, more or less coherent sub-units of the central organisation break off and relocate elsewhere. These coherent sub-units separated from the central core can either develop into a miniature replica of the parent (branching) or into a functional unit such as data processing, accounting, etc. (segmentation) which might no longer be located at corporate headquarters.

In the dispersion phase, a number of smaller decentralised work locations are established by the firm throughout the city or region where it is based. 'However, employees now report to the location nearest to their homes, irrespective of the department in which they work. The employees obtain their operating information through the central "computer", either directly or through local minicomputer or file storage' (Nilles *et al.*, 1976, p. 14). In a dispersed organisation, since each department now consists of a collection of employees whose work sites are physically scattered, a sufficiently sophisticated telecommunications and information storage system must be available to allow for an effective information transfer. Alternatively, the jobs of the employees must be redesigned so that they can still be self-contained at each individual location. During this stage, according to Nilles, face-to-face communication will only be necessary for managers and decision makers. In the dispersion phase, most employees are able to achieve substantial reductions in commuting and firms are able to tap labour markets that have not been available before.

The ultimate stage in this evolutionary process is diffusion, which allows firms to maintain a relatively small core staff either dispersed or at a single location. In the diffused work society, Nilles predicts, workload peaks or specialist types of work will be handled by individual workers who offer their services through a telecommunications network to several different firms and clients, the 'coordination of work by markets' posited by Brandt (Brandt, 1983). In the diffusion phase, information services could be offered in at least two ways: through the development of special organisations which provide specific business information services to their clients through telecommunications links; or by individual employees working from home, rather than at a local business centre, through a telecommunications network either for a single employer or for several different clients.

More empirical in its approach than Nilles's work was that carried out by Margrethe Olson in the early 1980s for the Diebold Group and independently at New York University (Diebold Group, 1981; Olson, 1982, 1983). Taking as her starting point the ways in which large organisations might feasibly take advantage of information technology to remove work from the spatial and temporal bounds of the central 9 to 5 office, she concluded that telework could take four possible organisational forms: satellite work centres; neighbourhood work centres; flexible work arrangements; and work at home. This classification has been widely followed in the serious literature on telework, although—or perhaps because—it does not imply a sequential development between these various forms, but suggests that they are equally valid alternatives available to any organisation with a sufficiently developed IT infrastructure and the will to decentralise.

According to this analysis, satellite work centres are relatively self-contained organisational units of a company which have been physically relocated and separated from the parent firm. The emphasis is on locating these centres within a convenient commuting distance for the greatest number of employees using the site. The number of employees working in a satellite work centre is determined by three factors: economies of scale in the use of equipment and services; the maintenance of a sufficient hierarchical structure for adequate management on site; and sufficient social interaction among employees. In order to benefit from economies of scale it may be optimal to relocate an entire function such as accounting or data processing. The supervision of work is generally by management staff on site.

Neighbourhood work centres are offices equipped and financially supported by several different employers. In these offices, employees of the founding organisations share space and equipment in a location close to their homes. While there are enough workers to provide necessary social interaction, hierarchical structures are generally lacking and supervision of work is carried out remotely. One of the principal motivations behind this concept is to reduce the time and expense of commuting. In addition, neighbourhood work centres enable firms to make use of lower office rents outside the city centre. These centres are, however, difficult to implement—particularly on a large scale—since they require extensive co-operation between different organisations. Figure 2.6 illustrates the difference between satellite work centres and neighbourhood work centres.

Flexible work arrangements provide employees with flexibility in the scheduling and location of work. This option recognises the need for occasional alternative work arrangements, especially for professional and managerial employees, and provides mechanisms to accommodate domestic as well as work responsibilities.

Work at home is the most decentralised form of remote work. Employees work at home on a regular basis and there is considerable flexibility in the choice of working hours. Work can be spread over 24 hours a day, seven days

Satellite Work Centres

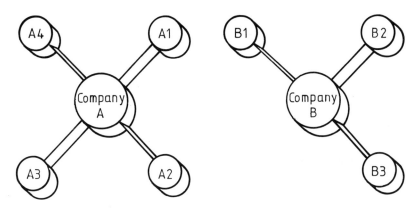

Neighborhood Work Centres

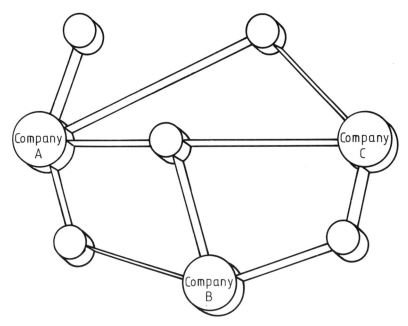

FIGURE 2.6 Two telework options: satellite work centres and neighbourhood work centres
Source; Diebold Group (1981), p. 4

a week, to suit the needs of the individual, the employer or the particular job in hand. In contrast with other forms of remote work, work at home does not provide opportunities for social interaction and relies exclusively on remote supervision.

The different combinations of these four organisational forms with various modes of task co-ordinations have been systematised by Brandt. His conclusions are summarised in Figure 2.7, which presents a range of possible forms of spatial concentration and work co-ordination, all of which he considers will be feasible with the use of advanced information technology. He believes that the present dominance of Field A, the hierarchical organisation of work in a central office building, will give way to a variety of different forms as shown in the figure. He does not follow Toffler (Toffler, 1981) in envisaging a total shift to Field B, the individual entrepreneur working at home, as the characteristic form of work, seeing it rather as one form among many (Brandt, 1983).

Such work has been valuable in providing a framework for the analysis of telework. However, as has already been pointed out, this is a subject in which the gap between what is technically feasible and what actually takes place is considerable. Whether or not any of these possible forms of telework are

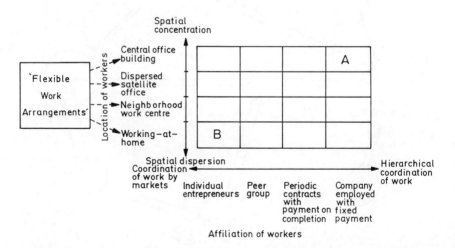

FIGURE 2.7   Organisational forms of decentralisation and work co-ordination
Source: Brandt (1983)

actually adopted also depends on many other factors, psychological, social, economic, legal and political. In the next few chapters we will be examining some of these, as well as looking at the experiences of telework schemes which have already been set up.

Chapter 3

THE ORGANISATION AND MANAGEMENT OF TELEWORK

We noted in Chapter 2 that the mere availability of information technology within an organisation is no guarantee that it will adopt telework, and that we must look to other factors to discover the constraints on its development. Many commentators believe that present organisational structures and managerial attitudes form a major barrier to the rapid spread of telework (e.g. Gordon, 1984, 1985a, b, 1988; Diebold Group, 1981; Sandiford, 1982; Judkins, West and Drew, 1985; Kawakami, 1983; Craipeau and Marot, 1984; Bureau of National Affairs, 1986). Olson goes so far as to state that resistance from managers and the strength of organisational culture are the main reasons why telework is still a comparative rarity (Olson, 1981, 1982, 1983, 1988).

She points out that the prevailing philosophy in large corporations in the USA is one of encouraging close identification with the company by its employees. The development of a strong corporate image and the provision of facilities based at the workplace inspire loyalty and discourage workers from venturing outside the building during the course of the working day. A dispersed and decentralised workforce, self-catering and out of contact with the corporation's visual identity, is in direct contradiction to this approach.

Furthermore, she argues, the management of remote workers is beyond the capabilities of many managers, who rely on frequent visual contact to reassure themselves that their staff are really working. Successful management of teleworkers requires trust and the development of new supervisory methods which are quite contrary to the management style currently practised in most organisations.

This conclusion is borne out by the results of other surveys. A Philips Business Systems survey found fewer than 10 per cent of managers in favour of telework, while 60 per cent were opposed, saying that they needed the interaction of individuals in offices to work effectively. In another survey carried out by the Management Sciences Department of the University of Minnesota, 53 per cent of managers said that they thought that telework was difficult to manage. This was perceived as by far the greatest problem posed by telework for organisations. No other negative factor was cited by more than 14 per cent of the sample (DeSanctis, 1984).

In Europe, the situation is similar. When Empirica carried out a survey of managers in four European countries, the results of which are described in detail in Chapter 10, it was found that their reservations about telework outweighed their willingness to explore the use of telework either to decentralise existing office workers or to sub-contract information-processing tasks to specialist outside companies using telecommunications links. Conservative attitudes and institutional inertia were confirmed as the major factor currently preventing European companies from making use of telework. More than half the sample felt that 'there is no need to change from the current situation', citing this as their main argument for not wishing to consider introducing telework. A high proportion also expressed the view that telework would bring 'organisational difficulties'. The general impression is one of resistance to change and fear of disruption to current organisational patterns.

The view that the introduction of telework involves organisational change is clearly not without foundation. Survey results support the approach taken in much of the 'how to' literature, which places great stress on the need to change organisational structures and management practices. Virtually all the authors in our literature survey who address themselves to managers considering setting up telework schemes emphasise the need to develop new management styles (Gordon and Kelly, 1986; Mertes, 1981; Upton, 1984; Heilmann, 1988; Miller, 1986; Webb, 1983; Lallande, 1984), and some (e.g. Harvey, 1982; Brandt, 1983) point out that structural reorganisation will also be required.

The keynote of most of the advice given on setting up a new telework scheme is caution. The need for careful preparation is reiterated. It is suggested that the initiator of a scheme prepares the ground carefully, discussing the project in detail beforehand with key managers in the organisation and with future teleworkers, as well as carrying out feasibility studies on the working methods and technology which it is proposed to use (Gordon and Kelly, 1986). Special attention should be paid to developing appropriate structural design and documentation (Batt, 1982).

Careful selection of staff is another prerequisite. Not all employees can adapt easily to telework, and tests may have to be devised to select those with the right personality type, as well as the right work skills and experience to make successful teleworkers (Olson, 1982; Gordon and Kelly, 1986; Judkins, West and Drew, 1985; Miller, 1986; Empirica, 1986).

Training is also considered extremely important, not only for teleworkers but also for their managers and future co-workers. For future teleworkers, this training should include personal skills, such as learning how to organise one's time, as well as task-related skills (Gordon and Kelly, 1986; DeSanctis, 1983). Where teleworkers are setting up their own companies, or changing to freelance status, then they should also be equipped with business skills, for instance in forecasting, marketing, book-keeping and negotiation (Gordon and Kelly, 1986; Judkins, West and Drew, 1985; Empirica, 1986). Some teleworkers from management grades may also require task training in areas of work where they have previously been able to rely on the services of support staff, for instance in data retrieval or keyboard skills (Mertes, 1981). In the case of teleworkers with disabilities, who may have no previous work experience, basic training in 'what it means to work' is necessary in addition to any specific training relating to telework (Ashok, Hall and Huws, 1986). Training for managers should also include negotiating skills where they will be required to deal with independent contractors. In addition, managers should be given an insight into the working situation of teleworkers, and coached in remote communication and management skills (Olson, 1982, 1988; Empirica, 1986; Drew, 1986; Judkins, West and Drew, 1985).

Even when extensive preparation and training has taken place, it is still considered advisable to start with small, experimental pilot projects and only gradually build up to a large-scale teleworking scheme (Meyer, 1983; Gordon and Kelly, 1986). In short, the introduction of telework is seen—at least at the setting-up stage—as making quite considerable organisational demands on the employer.

It is a similar story when we come to the day-to-day management of remote workers. It is nearly universally agreed that successful remote management requires a major change both in style and in attitude on the part of most managers. The most important component of this is a shift towards management by results (Gordon and Kelly, 1986; Judkins, West and Drew, 1985; Olson, 1988; Miller, 1986).

With some tasks, such as word processing or data entry, this can take the simplest form of payment by results—the piece-rate system (Geisler, 1985). With professional and managerial workers it may involve a more complex process of breaking work down into 'deliverables' (Gordon and Kelly, 1986). This is not purely a question of work organisation but also involves developing ways of encouraging a task-orientated motivation among teleworkers (Heilmann, 1988).

Where managers are themselves teleworkers, as in the UK companies ICL (now owned by the American-based STC) and the FI Group, many aspects of remote management are also facilitated. Both of these companies have developed considerable expertise and sophistication in the remote management of software development staff over two decades. In the case of ICL, it has been found possible to retain a time-based method of payment (Huws, 1984a). The FI Group, a company built on remote working with more than 75 per cent of its staff based at home, has developed a method of remote management which combines time-based payment with the setting of 'deliverables', in the form of fixed work targets. A good deal of work by specialist estimators is required to set these targets, which are monitored both qualitatively and quantitatively through weekly reports, team meetings, detailed record-keeping and monitoring of visits to clients and computer time usage. The FI Group's home-based 'panel members' are possibly the most closely monitored in the UK software industry. As a consequence, the company has a much higher ratio of managers to programmers than is the norm (Huws, 1984a; Shirley, 1979, 1985; Franklin, 1986).

Managers' lack of trust in the staff they supervise is frequently seen as a constraint on the development of telework (*Business Week*, 1982; Clavaud, 1981, 1982; Olson, 1982). Ann Lallande reports on the problems initially encountered in a telework experiment at Control Data, in the USA, when lack of trust led to unnecessarily complex reporting and log-in procedures and overly detailed instructions to home-based programmers. This resulted in resentment by the teleworkers concerned and management problems caused by the fact that 'the record-keeping system cost more money than it was worth' (Lallande, 1984). Miller argues that 'telework does not call for more trust; it calls for careful assessment and reapplication of the trust that is necessary for organisational performance in the first place' (Miller, 1986). Romero, on the other hand, suggests that the telework manager must accept a much more egalitarian relationship than in the past, becoming a 'facilitator rather than a dictator' (Romero, 1983).

As well as requiring different methods of monitoring, remote management also needs a much more formal pattern of communication. This in turn demands that managers are more disciplined in setting clear objectives and keeping records of instructions given and decisions made (Lallande, 1984; DeSanctis, 1983; Diebold Group, 1981), a development which some commentators welcome as leading to more thoughtful communication (Hirschheim, 1985), although others report that teleworkers regret the depersonalisation of communication which results (Craipeau and Marot, 1984). For effective performance, it is considered important that lines of communication are kept short (Diebold Group, 1981; Heller, 1981) and that managers give good feedback to their teleworkers (Gordon and Kelly, 1986).

It can be seen, therefore, that the introduction of telework is likely to place greater demands on managers than traditional methods of work, as well as demanding more organisational resources—at least in its early stages. But what of its long-term implications for organisational structure?

Some commentators believe that in order to maximise the benefits of telework from the employer's point of view, major structural reorganisation may be required. The model most often put forward is that of a central 'core' of full-time, permanent, office-based employees with a 'periphery' of other workers, of whom teleworkers comprise a sub-group, who can be deployed more flexibly (e.g. Gordon and Kelly, 1986; Upton, 1984). The ease with which such a reorganisation can take place will depend on the existing structure and organisational culture of the organisation (Olson, 1982, 1983, 1988; Brandt, 1983).

Despite the fact that the largest telework organisation we are aware of, the FI Group, has a hierarchical structure, with seven tiers of management (Franklin, 1986), telework is generally considered to be most difficult to implement in organisations with rigid hierarchies. Harvey considers that telework encourages lateral communication and that the use of electronic mail speeds up decision making, bypassing traditional lines of communication and actively breaking down hierarchies (Harvey, 1982). In this, he is in broad agreement with the ideas about the effects of decentralisation on organisational structures put forward by Taylor (Taylor, 1982) and Brandt (Brandt, 1983) which were quoted in Chapter 2.

Turoff and Hiltz go further, arguing that telework makes the concepts of centralisation and decentralisation outmoded, substituting a structure based on fluid 'networks' by means of which teleworkers become members of *ad hoc* groupings formed around particular projects (Turoff and Hiltz, 1983). This also implies a high degree of lateral communication and an erosion of vertical chains of command.

These commentators leave us with an impression that telework brings with it a breaking down of hierarchies and a loosening of centralised control over workers. However, others describe a very different tendency, whereby telework is accompanied by an intensification of Taylorian methods of control over the work process, by means of a routinisation of tasks and the imposition of discipline imposed by payment by results (e.g. Bjorn-Andersen, 1983; Gregory, 1985; Chamot and Zalusky, 1985). On the face of it, these two views appear to be incompatible.

In practice, however, it may be possible to reconcile them. A possible explanation for this apparent contradiction is that the organisational implications of telework are different depending on the nature of the tasks being decentralised and the seniority of the workers involved. This is a view supported by Kawakami who sees an increasing polarisation between professional and executive teleworkers, exercising a considerable amount of autonomy, and clerical teleworkers, who have little control over their work (Kawakami, 1983).

Our survey results substantiate this view to some extent, but suggest that the true picture is somewhat more complex. A UK survey which compared low-paid homeworkers in traditional manufacturing and clerical occupations with home-based computer professionals found a number of similarities between the two groups, including relative underpayment, close monitoring by the employers, and insecurity of employment (Bisset and Huws, 1984).

Empirica's telework survey, described in Chapter 9, also found unexpectedly high levels of dissatisfaction with pay and working conditions among home-based computer professionals compared with other teleworkers. This suggests that the differences between the two groups may not always be as great as might be supposed and leads us to look for further enlightenment.

A plausible hypothesis is that the greater freedom from central control experienced by some professional-level teleworkers may be based on an illusion resulting from an alteration in the mechanism used to exercise managerial control. Direct means of control have been replaced by indirect ones, with a greater emphasis on self-monitoring and measurement by results. The process of receiving instructions increasingly takes the form of a negotiating session, requiring the exercise of different skills by both parties and a different formal relationship from that which prevailed before, a change which is especially pronounced when teleworkers have been given the status of independent contractors. This may give both parties an impression of interacting as equals in an open marketplace. However, the underlying power relationship may remain fundamentally unaltered. It is still the employer who controls the specifications for the work, the delivery date, the manner in which it is to be executed and various other conditions, including the amount and method of payment. Where the teleworker's status is that of a freelance, the insecurity of employment and lack of the rights which accompany employee status may in fact increase, rather than decrease, the teleworker's dependence on the employer.

Although teleworking need not involve any real loss of central control over the workforce, it does, as already mentioned, invariably involve organisational changes, some of which do not flow so much from the telework arrangement *per se* as from the widespread adoption of electronic communications. These changes do not flow inevitably from the introduction of the technology. They are not predictable but will vary widely depending on the management approach which is adopted when these new technologies are introduced. Numerous commentators (e.g. Hirschheim, 1983; Ryan *et al.*, 1988; Peltu, 1980; Otway and Peltu, 1983; Bjorn-Andersen, 1983; Strassman, 1985; Meyer, 1983) have pointed out the widely differing outcomes of differing office automation policies on organisational structure.

It can be concluded that management and organisational problems do not form an absolute barrier to telework, in that workable solutions have been developed in several cases. However, they do constitute a major restraint on its development and have probably contributed more than any other factor to the cautiousness with which remote work has so far been taken up. The setting up of a telework scheme may place heavy demands on many organisational resources including technical, work study, personnel and training functions. Radical changes in management style and attitude would be required in most organisations before telework could become a feasible option. In many cases organisational changes would also be needed to make it function effectively.

In Chapters 8 and 9 we look in detail at how specific organisations have dealt with these changes, and how participants in existing telework schemes have reacted to them. Chapter 10 analyses managers' reservations about telework, showing how they vary between different countries, industries and types of organisation.

Chapter 4

THE ECONOMICS OF TELEWORK

The economics of telework are generally debated at two quite distinct levels—the macroeconomic, concerned with the costs and savings to society as a whole, and the microeconomic, concerned with the costs and benefits to a single organisation and its employees. There is, of course, a strong link between the two. In many respects, the former is simply the sum of the latter. However, in this book we have chosen to keep these two debates separate. The reason for this is that most individuals and organisations when making decisions do not base them on the expectation of benefits which will only accrue at the level of society as a whole. The costs they take account of are those which appear on their own balance-sheets; the benefits, those which are visible in the form of improved income, expanded turnover, a higher quality of work or some other tangible advantage.

If we wish to identify the factors which influence decisions about telework, it is therefore confusing to confound economic advantages (such as savings to a nation's total fuel bill) which are experienced at the societal level only with those (such as savings in rent) which are experienced at the level of the individual organisation. The first may well influence the decisions of planners and politicians but they are highly unlikely to affect those of a company or an individual considering whether telework is a feasible option.

In this chapter, we examine the economic costs and benefits of telework both to the employer and to the individual teleworker. It must be appreciated that it is not always possible to draw an absolute distinction between these. There are in practice wide variations in which expenses are incurred by whom, for instance who is responsible for the purchase of equipment or which party pays for the delivery of work, depending on such variables as the contractual status of the teleworker, or the structure of the particular industry involved. The wider economic impact of telework at a macroeconomic level is discussed in Chapters 12 and 13.

The literature on telework pays great attention to the costs and benefits of telework to the employer. It also—in contrast with most other literature on work—looks in some detail at the costs and savings to the individual worker. However, few studies make an overall assessment of the balance of gains and losses, probably for the good reason that so many variables are involved that such an estimate could not be meaningfully applied to any real-life situation.

The subject is most easily examined by breaking it down in separate cost categories.

OFFICE OVERHEAD COSTS

One of the most frequently cited economic advantages of employing teleworkers is the saving on office overhead costs. This was given as a major justification for setting up the Rank Xerox networking scheme in the UK (Drew, 1986; Sarson, 1986). The authors of a book about the scheme (Judkins, West and Drew, 1985) report that as individual staff members were moved out of the company's central London premises, it was possible to vacate a building, formerly housing 42 staff, allowing continuing total overhead savings of some £350,000 per annum.

Gordon and Kelly estimate that in the United States it may cost $4000 to $6000 to house a single worker in a downtown office, excluding the costs of electricity and real estate and other taxes (Gordon and Kelly, 1986). Presumably this sum also excludes service costs such as cleaning, decoration, provision of furniture and fittings and other overhead costs such as canteen facilities, and a proportion of the salary costs of 'overhead' staff such as security staff, receptionists, clerical support staff and so on.

It should be pointed out, however, that savings in office overheads do not automatically follow from the decision to allow some staff to work from home some of the time. If the organisation is still maintaining the same building, with the same amount of floorspace, the fact that some desks are unoccupied for part of the time may make very little difference to the size of the bills. Appreciable savings accrue only when a sufficiently high number of staff are teleworking to allow for an identifiable part of a building to be vacated or sub-let, or to avoid a move to larger and more expensive premises which would otherwise be necessitated.

Even when costs are saved at the office, they may not disappear altogether. If telework takes the form of work from a satellite or neighbourhood office, they may reappear, albeit in a scaled-down form, as overhead costs for the decentralised office. Because of the loss of economies of scale, some costs may even be higher for these local offices; however, such extra costs are likely to be offset by savings resulting from lower rents and other advantages of being away from the city centre.

Even in the case of home-based telework, office overheads may not disappear altogether. Some costs may be transferred to the teleworker, who may be faced, for instance, with higher energy costs for heating and lighting a part of the home which would not otherwise be used during the day. There is also often a hidden cost involved in allocating space in the home for work use. The teleworker might otherwise choose to live in a smaller, cheaper home or to let out the extra room to a lodger. Other costs to the homeworker may include extra maintenance and cleaning, and in some cases, additional insurance on the home and its contents. Thus this factor which is a credit for the employer, may become a debit—albeit a relatively unimportant one—for the worker.

EQUIPMENT COSTS

There are so many variables in relation to equipment costs that it is impossible to make meaningful generalisations. Depending on the type of work carried out and the quality of communication required, the necessary technology can vary from a simple telephone to elaborate teleconferencing facilities. Between these two extremes lies a wide range of permutations and combinations of various types of computer terminals, printers, messaging systems, modems, fax machines, photocopiers and other equipment. In a US survey of 14,000 female homeworkers, by Kathleen Christensen in conjunction with *Family Circle* magazine, it was found that three out of four clerical workers used only conventional tools—typewriter, telephone and pencil—to perform their homework (Bureau of National Affairs, 1986).

A US survey of employers who had set up telework schemes found that the equipment put into employees' homes ranged from $700 for a terminal to over $16,000 for a stand-alone word processor, printer, continuous belt dictation unit, modem and extra telephone line, but that in most cases work in the home and in the company was performed on equivalent equipment (Pratt, 1983).

Again, the question of cost allocation arises. When work is carried out in a central office, the employer is the undisputed owner of the equipment and is expected to bear the cost. However, when workers are based at home, there is no such automatic assumption, and a number of different ownership and payment options exist. In some cases, companies make arrangements to hire their machines to teleworkers. In others, they provide loans so that individual teleworkers can purchase the equipment, thus ensuring that it becomes the legal property of the teleworkers and does not threaten their status in law as self-employed contractors (Kawakami, 1983; Geisler, 1985). In other cases, employers simply expect the teleworker to supply whatever equipment he or she requires to carry out the work effectively. In all these cases, equipment costs are effectively allocated to the teleworker. On the other hand, there are reports of teleworkers billing their employers for equipment which then becomes in effect their own personal property (Romero, 1983). A final option which is occasionally followed is for employers to give away, or sell at a very low price, obsolescent equipment from the office which is due for replacement.

We have not come across any organisations which have been deterred from embarking on telework schemes by the capital cost of providing hardware. This is hardly surprising given that often these workers would need similar equipment if they were based in a central office. However, it is quite possible that individuals considering the possibility of setting up independently as teleworkers may have found the initial capital outlay prohibitively expensive. As hardware and software prices continue to fall, this problem will diminish in importance.

The variations in the allocation of the capital costs of equipment between employer and teleworker are reflected in variations in the allocation of running costs. Here it is more usual to find employers bearing such costs as telephone bills, maintenance costs and the costs of computer supplies such as diskettes and stationery used in the course of work. Sometimes employers who are not prepared to pay the capital costs of purchasing an expensive item of equipment are willing to pay a smaller recurrent hire charge for it. This may encourage some teleworkers to lease equipment as an alternative to buying it. In some countries, there are also tax advantages to choosing this option.

START-UP COSTS

Most of the 'how to' literature on telework aimed at managers (e.g. Romero, 1983; Judkins, West and Drew, 1985; Gordon and Kelly, 1986; DeSanctis, 1983; Edwards and Edwards, 1985) emphasises the importance of careful preparation. Their proposals include conducting feasibility studies; setting up and evaluating pilot schemes; screening potential teleworkers and providing adequate training for them and for their managers; and in some cases carrying out a major job redesign exercise as well.

Unless external consultants are used, these activities need not involve much cash outlay. Their main costs will be in staff time, and this may be appreciable. However, Strassman does point out that one of the advantages of telework to employers is that much of the training costs can be transferred to the employee's free time (Strassman, 1985).

Other start-up costs include the installation of telecommunications links, the purchase or in-house development of suitable software, and any necessary adaptations to the remote work site to make it suitable for telework. For individuals setting themselves up independently as teleworkers, additional start-up costs would be incurred, for such items as advertising, the printing of stationery and other expenditure associated with setting up a new business. If satellite or neighbourhood offices are being set up, then other start-up costs might be incurred, such as the cost of acquiring the premises.

Depending on the circumstance, therefore, start-up costs may be a significant expense. For telework to be viable they will have to be met either by the employer or by the individual teleworker. Where the arrangement involves the relocation of existing employees, the most usual pattern is of give-and-take, with putative teleworkers contributing free time while their employer foots many of the bills.

Freelance teleworkers generally have to find the time and meet the costs of setting up themselves. However, in many cases, these costs will be lower than they would be for a large organisation, since individual contractors need not be concerned with organisational or management questions.

TRANSPORTATION COSTS

Just as the saving on office overhead costs is presented to managers as one of the greatest advantages of telework, the saving on travel time and costs is frequently perceived as its main attraction to workers. This is reflected in many articles about telework in the popular press. For instance a typical article in an American magazine is headed with the question:

> Do you love the idea of saying good-bye to freeway traffic jams or crowded commuter cars and doing your job at home? (Wiegner and Paris, 1983)

While a British women's magazine aimed at middle-class working women opens with the words:

> Soon we'll be able to go to work without even leaving our front doors. Word processors, computer terminals and cable television will link us to central offices, and commuting on crowded trains . . . will be horrors of the past. (Woodham, 1983)

This impression can, to some extent, be substantiated. One study of homeworkers carried out by the Diebold Group found that the primary advantage of telework to the employees was the reduction in commuting (Diebold Group, 1981) and a similar finding in relation to industrial homeworkers is reported by Markusen (Markusen, 1983), although other surveys (e.g. Huws, 1984a; Vedel, 1984; Pratt, 1983; Goldmann and Richter, 1986) as well as our own most recent survey, which is described in Chapter 9, have consistently found that other advantages take precedence.

The first attempt to quantify this saving in financial terms was by Nilles and his colleagues. Using 1972 prices, and basing his estimates of the distances involved on those actually travelled by the employees of a California-based insurance company, he concluded that commuting by private car cost on average $1573 annually for someone using their car only for commuting to work and $651 when half the car's use was for other purposes. Applying cost-benefit analysis techniques, it was calculated that the break-even trip-to-work distance at that time was 5.33 miles. A typical employee commuting further than this would receive a net benefit from becoming a teleworker, but there would be a net cost if a shorter journey to work was saved (Nilles *et al.*, 1976).

A decade later, the Lanier corporation, promoting an audio dictation system designed for use by teleworkers, was claiming that the transportation costs which would be saved for each worker averaged $145 a month (Lanier, 1982).

No detailed comparisons are available for European countries, but it is clear that substantial sums of money are spent on the daily journey to work by many white-collar workers. With rare exceptions (such as transportation authorities which give free travel to their own staff, or a few London employers who give interest-free loans to their employees for the purchase of season tickets), this is an expense which is entirely borne by the worker, even though it may be indirectly reimbursed in the form of higher salaries in metropolitan areas where commuting distances are longer.

It would be rash, however, to assume that transportation costs disappear altogether when telework is introduced. Firstly, most teleworkers are expected to travel into the office at regular intervals, typically once or twice a week. Secondly, there is generally a need for some work to be physically transported to and from the remote work site, however sophisticated the electronic communications system (Huws, 1984a; Gordon and Kelly, 1986). Some telework schemes may involve visits by safety officers or managers to the remote sites (Evans and Attew, 1986; Ashok, Hall and Huws, 1986).

Thus, while it would be fair to say that telework involves a reduction in transportation costs, it does not lead to their elimination. However, many of the new transportation costs involved in telework, such as delivery of work by messenger, or travel to meetings by teleworkers, their co-workers or managers, may now be claimed by the teleworker from the employer as business expenses. The net effect of this may be that transportation costs become a credit factor for teleworkers, but a debit, albeit a relatively small one, for their employers.

MANAGEMENT COSTS

In order to determine whether the cost of managing teleworkers is greater or less than that of managing on-site workers it would be necessary to make some systematic comparisons. This, on the whole, has not been done, making this too an area of speculation. Most researchers into telework are agreed that managing teleworkers requires different techniques and a different style from the conventional over-the-shoulder method still in use in most offices where managers share the same physical workspace with their staff (e.g. Olson, 1981, 1982, 1985a; Gordon and Kelly, 1986; Craipeau and Marot, 1984;

Meyer, 1983). However, nowhere has a detailed costing of these new management methods been undertaken.

A central element in the new approach to management is for teleworkers to be monitored by results. The emphasis is on 'deliverables' which might be the production of reports or other documents in the case of professional or managerial staff, or take the form of the payment of piece-rates for clerical-grade teleworkers. This effectively involves a greater degree of self-management by workers and might therefore be expected to lighten the workload of managers. However, the UK software company, the FI Group, which has developed a considerable expertise in the remote management of projects over the two and a half decades since it was founded, uses a much higher degree of supervision than is the norm for comparable on-site workers in the industry. Manager/staff ratios within the company are 1 : 5 for programming (1 : 4 for programming on a bureau basis); 1 : 6 for specification writing; rising to 1 : 8 for systems design, 1 : 10 for systems analysis and still higher ratios for senior consultancy staff (Huws, 1984a). Each manager is supervising less than half the number of staff managed by his or her counterparts in most other UK data processing departments and software companies.

To what extent this greater intensity of management is a function of individual company style, and to what extent it is necessitated by the specific nature of telework is a matter of speculation. In the lack of any firm evidence, we must conclude that the extra costs or savings in management should not be discounted, but require further research. It is likely that they will vary considerably depending on the nature of the work involved, the structure of the employing organisation, the basis on which teleworkers are paid and other factors. Whatever they turn out to be, it will obviously be the employer, rather than the individual teleworker, who will bear these costs, although teleworkers may find themselves with extra tasks to perform connected with self-monitoring, such as filling in time-sheets.

COMMUNICATIONS COSTS

One of the major expenses incurred in telework is, of course, the cost of communication, both between the teleworker and his or her employer and between the teleworker and any clients of the employing organisation with whom he or she has to deal. The question of how much this communication costs is addressed in the literature on telecommunications/transportation tradeoffs (Nilles *et al.*, 1976; Harkness and Standal, 1982; King and Kraemer, 1981; Kraemer, 1982; Kraemer and King, 1982; Pye, 1976; Pye, Tyler and Cartwright, 1974). While most of these studies conclude that there are many situations in which the cost of communications is much less than the equivalent transportation cost, all are agreed that this saving is dependent on a number of factors, several of which are variable.

One variable is the mode of communication used. While postal delivery, telephone communication and electronic mail may be comparatively cheap, full video teleconferencing facilities are expensive, and at present prices only become cost-effective under quite special circumstances. Other important variables are the existing telecommunications infrastructure, the number of people involved in a particular meeting, its duration, and the distance which would have to be travelled if physical transportation were used.

Except where packet-switched networks, broad-band cable networks or private land-lines are used, most electronic communication in telework still involves the use of telephone networks designed for voice transmission. Since these are generally charged by distance, the distance of the teleworker from the employer's office becomes critical for telework applications where the worker is expected to be on-line for a significant part of the working day. In one teleworking experiment involving remote word processor operation, American Express discovered that the scheme was only cost-effective within the local call-charge area (Moore, 1985).

Whether or not tariffs for services other than the telephone are distance-related depends on the national legal framework a PTT operates in. Whereas charges for fixed links often have a distance component, packet-switched data networks generally have a tariff structure based on volume only. Thus the choice of service and the vagaries of telecommunications regulation may serve to encourage, or deter, the telework option. In one instance, a telework scheme proposed by a group of small businesses in the rural South-West of England foundered on this issue. The scheme would have depended for its effectiveness on the provision of a landline to London, enabling subscribers to the scheme to connect up to London clients for a local call-charge. In the event, it was ruled impermissible for British Telecom to supply the service without imposing a distance-related charge (Holti and Stern, 1984). A review of the literature undertaken in 1982 found that high telecommunications costs were a major disincentive to the development of on-line telework applications for clerical-level staff, and that the need to provide a more cost-effective means of electronic communications was a major factor in the UK government's plans for the development of broad-band cable systems (Huws, 1984a). However, a more recent survey carried out by Empirica, described in Chapter 10, found that this factor was overshadowed by others in organisations' reasons not to adopt telework.

Communications costs are not only likely to be a major factor in the operation of telework, they are also an ongoing one, unlike the initial outlay on installation and equipment which can generally be amortised over the first few months of a telework scheme. The level of these costs will therefore play an important role in determining the decision of an organisation whether or not to decentralise staff, or of an individual freelance whether it is feasible to set up as a teleworker.

WELFARE BENEFITS

Although this is not always the case, it frequently happens that the decision to decentralise workers is accompanied by a change in their status to that of independent contract workers (US Congress, Office of Technology Assessment, 1985; Kawakami, 1983; Mazzonis, 1984; Judkins, West and Drew, 1985; Gordon and Kelly, 1986).

Where this takes place, there is a considerable saving to the employer in health insurance, paid leave for sickness, maternity or holidays, pensions contributions and other welfare benefits. Telework consultants Gordon and Kelly assert that in the long run it is damaging to morale and staff loyalty 'to cut corners on the employer/employee relationship'. Nevertheless, they point out the attractions of a number of different contractual options which enable employers to shed some or all of these costs (Gordon and Kelly, 1986). In this instance, what is a credit item for the employer becomes a debit for the teleworker.

PAY

It would be reasonable to expect a tradeoff between some of the increased costs transferred to teleworkers, such as office overheads and welfare benefits, and higher pay. This does indeed appear to have occurred where senior executive staff are concerned (Judkins, West and Drew, 1985; Kawakami, 1983) and in some cases with professional staff (Kawakami, 1983).

However, in many cases the opposite has occurred, and teleworkers have found themselves not only with fewer benefits but also with lower earnings than their counterparts who commute physically to work (Bureau of National Affairs, 1986; Huws, 1984b). In the case of women workers with family commitments, telework may not be perceived as an alternative option to going to work in an office but as an alternative to having no paid employment at all.

Such findings have given rise in a number of quarters to fears that telework may lead to exploitatively low levels of pay (e.g. New Scientist, 1984; Else, 1982; Gregory, 1983, 1985; Chamot and Zalusky, 1985; Lie, 1985; Vedel, 1985; Goldmann and Richter, 1987; Taylor, 1982; Technology, 1984; Bisset and Huws, 1984). Some commentators have noted that the low pay levels may be compounded by other financial disadvantages of which teleworkers are initially unaware. In the words of the US House Committee of Government Operations report on home-based clerical work:

> Homeworkers may be aware of some tradeoffs they make, such as accepting lower wages, loss of health and pension coverage, and lack of vacation and sick leave, in exchange for the chance to remain at home and earn some income. But they may not realize other drawbacks, such as their having to pay Self-Employment instead of lower FOICA taxes, if they are bona fide contractors, having no income tax withholding, the lack of coverage by workers compensation and unemployment insurance to help them in periods of no work, and the absence of protection against discrimination based on race, sex, religion, handicap or age. They may not be aware or adequately informed about their right to deduct from their income taxes the expenses associated with working at home. (Bureau of National Affairs, 1986)

Others have argued that the benefits to the teleworker of being home-based, in terms of savings on clothes, meals and transportation, justify cutting back the pay of teleworkers by 5–15 per cent in comparison with on-site staff. This position is rejected by Gil Gordon and Marcia Kelly who consider that it undermines the basic logic of telework which in their view is that workers should be paid by results (Gordon and Kelly, 1986).

Whatever the morality of the question, the fact remains that for a number of employers, substantial savings in salary are being made as a result of telework schemes, and a minority of teleworkers, mainly in professional and managerial occupations, are also better off as a result of their situation. In the case of pay, it is generally true to say that one party's gain is another's loss, so these savings to employers can be regarded as costs to their remote workforce, and *vice versa*, although they may be offset against other advantages in some cases.

The subject of teleworkers' pay is a complex one, in which variables such as employment status, sex, age, number of dependants, occupation and educational qualifications all play a part. The 1987 Empirica survey of teleworkers has produced the most detailed comparative information on teleworkers' pay to date. Its findings are described in Chapter 9.

PRODUCTIVITY

There is a surprising degree of unanimity in the literature on the extra productivity of teleworkers compared with on-site staff. This has been variously reported at 20 per cent, rising in some cases to 100 per cent (Kelly, 1985), 25–30 per cent (Huws, 1984a), 'an aggregate average for those whose work was quantifiable of 43 per cent' (Walters and Evans, 1984), as much work as a full-time employee in five hours a day (Heller, 1981) and numerous other, similar, estimates.

The reasons given for this extra productivity are many: teleworkers give their 'best' hours, working in tune with their bodily rhythms (Heller, 1981; Craipeau and Marot, 1984); they underestimate the amount of time they have actually worked because of feelings of guilt or inadequacy (Woodham, 1983); the employer does not pay for 'downtime' including coffee-breaks, social chats, times when equipment is not working etc. (Huws, 1984a); teleworkers are free from interruptions (Strassman, 1985; Gordon and Kelly, 1986); in some cases, employers get 'two minds on the payroll for the price of one' where teleworkers draw on the advice and information of other household members to help them with difficult tasks (Turoff and Hiltz, 1983).

A major problem with this area of research is that for many types of white-collar work no reliable instruments have been developed for measuring productivity. Except in the case of lower-grade staff paid on piece-rate systems, most of these reports are based on subjective estimates of productivity increases either by the teleworkers themselves or by their managers. It is possible that, because the introduction of telework has coincided with a different system of management based on 'deliverables', some of this productivity increase may in fact be a function of the reorganisation rather than of the telework arrangement *per se*. A further possible difficulty is that this method has led to a concentration on those aspects of the job which are easiest to quantify, at the expense of those which are less easy to measure, such as informal training or various qualitative factors. This would serve to overestimate the actual increase in productivity. Finally, some schemes may be demonstrating a 'Hawthorne effect', with the productivity increase being partly attributable to the publicity attracted to teleworkers because of the novelty of their working methods.

John King and Leslie Kraemer are virtually alone in sounding a cautionary note in this respect. They conclude that:

> The current claims for decentralising potential and productivity payoff from implementation of telecommunications technologies rest on only the loosest understanding of the social, technical, and organizational dynamics that surround actual technological adoption and routinization. A much more serious look at how things really work (or don't) is called for. (King and Kraemer, 1981)

Despite this warning, the overwhelming conclusion to be drawn from cases studied so far is that telework brings substantial productivity increases which, well-publicised as they are, constitute a good measure of the attraction of this method of work for many employers, an attraction which is emphasised in the publicity materials of telework equipment suppliers. The Lanier Corporation, for instance, states that the home-based 'transcriptionists' using their equipment are 'using "drive" time as productive time' and are *paid only* for production' (Lanier's emphasis), adding, for good measure, that 'Business does *not* pay for coffee breaks, lunch, or other non-productive activities. The wages paid versus work received ratio changes in favour of the *employer!'* (Lanier's emphasis) (Lanier Business Products, 1982).

The financial advantages of this extra productivity accrue to teleworkers only when they are paid by results at a rate which is genuinely comparable (allowing for the value of other benefits) to that paid to equivalent on-site workers.

OTHER SAVINGS TO EMPLOYERS

A number of other financial savings to employers are mentioned in the literature on telework. They include:

- savings on shiftwork, unsocial hours or overtime payments
- off-hour utilisation of mainframe computers
- savings on redundancy payments to permanent staff (where teleworkers are used as a casual pool to protect against downswings in demand)
- lower rates of staff turnover
- savings on disability benefits payable to employees
- savings on relocation expenses (Gordon and Kelly, 1986; Diebold Group, 1981; Rifkin, 1983; Pratt, 1983).

OTHER SAVINGS TO TELEWORKERS

Telework may also bring additional financial savings to teleworkers. These include:

- child-care costs
- the need for an extensive wardrobe of business clothes
- parking costs (these are estimated by the Lanier Corporation respectively at $172, $30 and $66 per month for a clerical-level worker)
- where the teleworker did not previously enjoy subsidised canteen facilities, the cost of buying a pre-cooked lunch
- for self-employed home-based teleworkers, the cost of leasing office space outside the home (estimated at up to $1,000 a month by Joanne Pratt) (Lanier Business Products, 1982; Gordon and Kelly, 1986; Pratt, 1983; Diebold Group, 1981).

CONCLUSIONS

As already noted, with such a large number of variables, it is not possible to quantify the overall financial losses or gains from telework either to the employer or to the teleworker with any degree of precision. The literature reveals a degree of consensus—albeit largely unsubstantiated—that the benefits to employers considerably outweigh the losses. However, no such consensus exists in relation to teleworkers, where there is an ongoing debate on the subject. Generally speaking, it is probably true to say that senior staff, unencumbered with child-care commitments or disabilities, are most likely to do well out of the arrangement, while low-level clerical staff, especially women with young children, are likely to be poorly rewarded compared with their office-based counterparts. However, the results of the Empirica telework survey indicate that the relationship between occupational status and cost benefit is complex and even such generalisations are fraught with difficulty. For instance, the group of teleworkers which felt most strongly that it was underpaid was made up, not of clerical staff but of female data processing professionals. In Chapter 9 we examine this issue in greater detail.

Chapter 5

TELEWORK AND THE LAW

The subject of telework touches on many different areas of law, some of which are extremely complex, and will, it seems, require test cases to be brought before they are unambiguously clarified.

CONTRACTUAL RELATIONSHIPS

Current practice reveals a number of different types of contractual relationship between teleworkers asnd their employers or clients. The most straightforward of these in many ways is that of employee/employer, whereby the teleworker has exactly the same legal status, rights and obligations as other employees of the organisation working on-site.

In the United States, many of the telework experiments which have been set up involving professional or executive staff have involved a retention of employee status (Mazzonis, 1984, National Research Council, 1985). However, this is by no means universally practised, and corporations often shift employees to independent contractor status when they become home-based workers (US Congress, Office of Technology Assessment, 1985). This seems particularly to be the case with lower-grade keyboard workers whose output is amenable to payment by piece-rates (Mazzonis, 1984). In fact, as in other countries, the vast majority of people working from home in the United States are, or are considered to be, independent contractors (Olson, 1988). If these workers contract with only one organisation they may in the eyes of the law be employees even though both they themselves and their clients consider them to be independent contractors (US Congress, Office of Technology Assessment, 1985). US case-law suggests that the critical factor in deciding whether or not a worker is an employee is the degree of dependence on the supplier of work. Criteria used for assessing this can be summarised as: the degree of control over the work; opportunities for profit and loss; whether risk capital is supplied; the degree of permanence of the relationship and the amount of skill and initiative contributed by the worker (Elisburg, 1985).

Some employers have gone to elaborate lengths to circumvent the provision of employee status, for instance by obliging their workers to pay a hire charge for the equipment they use, so that it is legally their property (Kawakami,

1983; Geisler, 1985). In only two reported cases have teleworkers taken legal action in an attempt to establish employee status. In one, eight home-based claims examiners sued the California Western States Life Insurance Company, charging that the company's claim that they were independent contractors was incorrect. This case had yet to be resolved when it was reported. In the other, where the Department of Labor brought suit against DialAmerica Marketing, the US Court of Appeals for the Third Circuit found that the home-based telephone number researchers were not independent contractors but employees subject to the minimum wage and record-keeping requirements of the Fair Labor Standards Act (Bureau of National Affairs, 1986).

In the UK, the situation is similar, with some employers granting employee status to their teleworkers, while a greater number do not (Huws, 1984a). Again, the law regards some homeworkers as employees even when they and their employers do not. Test cases have established the employee status of homeworkers in manufacturing occupations (Ewing, 1982; Davies, 1984). As in the USA, however, there is no simple rule-of-thumb which can be applied to determine whether a particular worker is an employee. A study of British case-law suggests that it depends on a number of different factors including the method and frequency of payment, the regularity of hours of work, the availability of welfare benefits, the degree of supervision, the number of employers worked for and the provision of capital and equipment (Leighton, 1983). At least one British employer, the FI Group, has made loans to its teleworkers for the purchase of company-supplied equipment in order to preserve their status as self-employed contractors.

In West Germany, we find an additional legal status category affecting employees who work outside a conventional office environment: the home-worker, covered by the Homework Law (Heimarbeitsgesetz, HAG). People working as homeworkers as defined by this law are not classified as employees but as a category of people enjoying employee-equivalent status covered by special legal provisions. Although there are many similarities with employees, there are also some differences. In particular, there is no general protection against wrongful dismissal. Remuneration usually takes the form of payment by results, subject to binding conditions (though rarely on the basis of collective agreements) and operating risks (e.g. lack of orders) are not borne solely by the employer (Kappus, 1984; Pfarr, 1984; Kilian, Bosrum and Hoffmeister, 1986, Müllner, 1985, 1986; Kufner-Schmitt, 1986). Because the law on homework was originally developed to cover only industrial work, it is generally considered inadequate as a basis for contracts of employment for telework. As one commentator remarks: 'The Heimarbeitsgesetz definitely needs revising if it is to cope with the technical and societal developments which are currently transforming work, work environments and contractual arrangements' (Kilian, Bosrum and Hoffmeister, 1986, p. 372).

It is possible that a general lack of clarity about the legal status of teleworkers may have acted as a deterrent to the setting up of telework schemes in some cases. A survey of teleworkers in the UK (Huws, 1984a) found that, except in a small minority of cases where teleworkers were genuinely freelance (those who had worked for more than three employers since becoming teleworkers), self-employed contract workers were worse off than comparable teleworkers with employee status, with lower average earnings and fewer welfare benefits. Their lower incomes were attributable not to lower hourly rates of pay but to the fact that they had less continuity of employment.

Self-employed status can offer some advantages to the teleworker, however. In some cases, it may make it easier to claim tax concessions for the teleworker or, where married couples are taxed jointly, his or her spouse. Most benefits of self-employed status accrue only when a teleworker is working for more than one organisation. This is not without reason the crux of much legal discussion about teleworkers' status.

Where several different clients are involved, there is often a greater variety of work and cross-fertilisation of ideas. Teleworkers with scarce skills may be able to negotiate higher rates of pay than they would receive as employees, although in many cases these do little more than compensate for the loss of welfare benefits and job security. Finally, some teleworkers welcome the chance to exercise choice about which projects to take on.

With the exception of trade unions and professional associations representing genuinely freelance, multiclient professionals, such as freelance journalists or film technicians, trade unions and other organisations campaigning on behalf of home-based workers are convinced that the advantages of employee status more than outweigh the disadvantages. In Europe and the United States, the fear of the loss of employee status occupies a central place in trade union arguments against telework (Trades Union Congress, 1985; Chamot and Zalusky, 1985; Trade Unions Group, 1984a,b; Peles, 1985; Empirica, 1986). In the UK the right to employee status has been formally included in its 'Homeworkers' Charter' by the National Homeworking Campaign (Greater London Council Industry and Employment Branch, 1985), and there have also been attempts to give statutory force to this right (Bisset and Huws, 1984).

To employers, there are many advantages in shedding the responsibility for providing permanent employee status to teleworkers. Self-employed contractors can provide a highly flexible workforce which can be taken on as needed to cope with peaks in workload. Making a clear distinction between permanent 'core' staff and temporary contractors makes it possible to develop a 'no lay-offs' policy for the core staff, giving them greater stability (Gordon and Kelly, 1986). Using contractors makes it possible to avoid the cost of sick pay, holiday or maternity leave, pensions contributions and other overheads associated with permanent employees. The employer only pays, so to speak, for what is actually used. Finally, freelance contractors may be able to provide a service too specialised and too rarely required to warrant its development or retention among the permanent staff. For decades, specialist freelance staff have been available to supply occasional needs such as translation, indexing or graphic design. The development of information technology has spawned new specialisms, such as database searching (Mazzonis, 1984; Wiegner and Paris, 1983), systems development, or even advice on the setting up of telework projects (Gordon and Kelly, 1986).

However, just as the advantages of employee status for teleworkers are tempered by some disadvantages, so too the use of freelance contractors may also bring some disadvantages to their employers. These may include higher hourly or weekly rates of pay than would be payable to employees, and lack of dependability or loyalty (Gordon and Kelly, 1986). In some industries, security of confidential commercial information may become a problem if contractors are also working for competitors. However if the flow of information is two-way, some may construe this as an advantage as well as a disadvantage of the arrangement.

Direct employment or self-employment are not the only contractual options for teleworkers, although they remain so in practice for most lower-grade workers. Professional and managerial level staff frequently take up telework under other arrangements. They may be directing their own limited companies or operating under a variety of contracts which could be related to output or to a fixed period of time, varying from a few hours to a year or more. These contracts may be negotiated directly with the final client, or indirectly, with a sub-contracting organisation or agency (Judkins, West and Drew, 1985; Franklin, 1986; Sarson, 1986; Groom, 1984b). Partnerships and co-operatives are other possible legal forms, although these are not mentioned in the literature, with the exception of a prototype 'community data workshop' project which was never implemented (Greater London Council Industry and Employment Branch, 1985). In the UK, there has been a considerable growth in recent years in the number of small businesses carrying out sub-contract work for larger organisations (Curran, 1986; Ganguly, 1985). This growth seems likely to continue. In a situation of high unemployment, mostly of a structural nature, a sluggish economy, and rapidly changing markets, organisations place a high priority on their ability to keep abreast of these changes by responding quickly and flexibly. Breaking up large unwieldy organisations into smaller units and externalising as many functions as possible are vital components of this strategy (Steinle, 1988b).

There is no evidence that the advantages or disadvantages of any of these contractual forms *per se* act as a constraint on the development of telework. However, it may well be that the time and legal costs involved in investigating the various possibilities and negotiating the final contract may provide a disincentive in some cases. Lack of negotiating skills may also be a deterrent. At Rank Xerox it was found that when future teleworkers were given training in negotiating skills but their managers were not, this resulted in contracts which were extremely favourable to the teleworkers (Drew, 1986; Groom, 1984b). Presumably, when managers are equipped with these skills and teleworkers are not, the reverse situation applies.

INSURANCE

The question of insurance is closely connected with that of contractual status. Employees can expect their health insurance (in the USA) and National Insurance (in the UK) contributions to be paid by their employers, who also become responsible for employee liability, personal injury and other types of insurance. In cases of self-employment, these become the responsibility of the individual teleworker (Silver, 1985; US Congress, Office of Technology Assessment, 1985).

The responsibility is less clear-cut in other cases, and much depends on individual contracts and the smallprint of particular insurance policies. For instance, who should be responsible for the loss or damage of data or equipment used in telework? Or injury to third parties caused on the teleworker's premises? Who is insured for delivery and pick-up of work? (Gordon and Kelly, 1986; Elisburg, 1985). There is no case-law in these areas, so the answers must remain speculative. In only one case, involving telework for the US Army, have insurance problems appeared sufficiently serious adversely to affect the outcome of the scheme. Here, government liability, protection of government property and workmen's compensation were all perceived as problems. Along with security difficulties, these led to the discontinuation of the project, despite the development of a 'hold harmless' agreement absolving the government of responsibility, which all teleworkers were obliged to sign (McDavid, 1985).

HEALTH AND SAFETY

As with insurance, legal responsibility for the health and safety of teleworkers will vary according to their employment status. In the UK, employers have a statutory duty to ensure a safe workplace for their employees 'as far as is reasonably practical' and to provide them with information about the potential hazards of the equipment and substances they are working with. However, no procedures have been laid down for the implementation of this legislation in relation to home-based workers. Some draft regulations were issued by the UK Health and Safety Executive in 1979 which proposed that work 'of a type normally carried out in an office' should be excluded altogether from the scope of the Health and Safety at Work Act when carried out in the home. However, these regulations were subsequently withdrawn (Huws, 1984a).

The most detailed document on the health and safety of teleworkers discovered in a search of the published literature was a policy statement issued by the US-based computer manufacturer DEC 'designed to provide health and safety protection for employees who conduct office-type work in their homes' in the UK. This clearly spells out the company's obligations as an employer under the relevant British legislation, the Health and Safety at Work Act and the Offices, Shops and Railway Premises Act. It accords to homeworkers the status of 'controllers' of their working premises, placing on them the obligation to take reasonable precautions to ensure their own safety and that of other users of the premises. The company has the right to inspect the premises to ensure that they are safe, and provides a detailed safety questionnaire which the teleworker must complete annually (Evans and Attew, 1986).

The situation in the USA is similar to that in the UK. Homeworkers are covered by the Occupational Safety and Health Act but it is in practice virtually impossible for it to be implemented effectively (Bureau of National Affairs, 1986). There is no evidence that the fear of becoming liable for industrial injuries or diseases is currently a deterrent to the employment of teleworkers. However, in the United States there is a fear that if legislation to regulate the use of Visual Display Terminals to minimise health hazards is enacted this might restrict the development of telework since it would become very difficult for employers to ensure compliance at remote sites (Gordon and Kelly, 1986).

COLLECTIVE REPRESENTATION RIGHTS

Neither the USA nor the UK—the two countries where telework is most widespread—gives an automatic right to collective representation to any group of workers. Trade union bargaining rights in these two countries usually follow a process of recruitment by the union, which has to show—generally by means of a ballot of the relevant group of workers—that it has majority support before the employer enters into negotiation with it. This is not the case in many other European countries where there is a clearly-defined legal framework for the collective representation of workers, often through works councils or committees. After surveying the employment legislation of the EEC countries, Yota Kravaritou-Manitakis came to the conclusion that it should be amended to give certain rights to teleworkers: teleworkers should be taken into account when calculating the number of workers required for setting up representative bodies such as works councils, safety committees or union councils; teleworkers should have the right to stand for election to these representative bodies; and they should be entitled to vote in these elections. She believes that, compared with traditional homeworkers, teleworkers will be well placed to take an active role in the organisations which represent workers because they will be able to use the technology to set up interactive networks for lateral communication amongst themselves and to access databases to gain up-to-date company information (Kravaritou-Manitakis, 1987).

At present, representation of teleworkers by trade unions is the exception rather than the rule. In the USA, a group of home-based teleworkers employed by the University of Wisconsin hospital to transcribe medical records joined the public-employee union, the AFSCME, as a result of which they now receive the same wages and benefits as on-site colleagues, instead of piece rates (Foegen, 1987). The teleworkers employed in the UK by ICL are represented by the managerial union, the MFS (formerly known as the ASTMS). They too, in contrast with most other British teleworkers, have been granted the full status of employees, with the same wages and welfare benefits as their on-site colleagues (Huws, 1984a).

PLANNING REGULATIONS

The deterrent effects of zoning regulations on telework are difficult to quantify. In both the USA and Europe, planning regulations tend to be extremely complex, varying considerably from one locality to another both in their content and in the degree to which they are enforced (Holden, 1984; Bureau of National Affairs, 1986; Gordon and Kelly, 1986). While some organisations, such as the US National Association for Cottage Industry (Wolfgram, 1984) and authors (Postgate, 1984) are vehemently in favour of the lifting of any restrictions on the use of homes as workplaces, the literature supplies only two examples of situations in which zoning rules have posed problems in practice. One occurred during the 1970s when Steve Shirley, the founder of the FI Group, the UK software company, was found to be in breach of planning regulations for using her home as the company's head office. The situation was remedied by 'cosmetic changes such as moving a registered office to a "commercial" location' (Shirley, 1988). In the other, a particularly strict Chicago zoning ordinance was invoked to stop a teacher and his wife from writing a textbook or developing software programs on their home computer (Rubins, 1984, cited in Baer, 1985). Should telework become widespread, then changes in zoning laws will undoubtedly be required. In the meanwhile, these cannot be regarded as a major constraint on its development.

REGULATION OR BANNING OF HOMEWORK

In some states of the United States and in some European countries, there exist partial or total bans on the employment of home-based workers to carry out certain types of work, frequently garment-making or other forms of manufacture associated with the traditional 'sweated trades'. Even where these are not prohibited, they may be governed by regulations concerning minimum wages, leave provisions and health and safety practices. In recent years, a highly polarised debate has grown up over the question of deregulation.

On the one hand, the AFL–CIO and the Service Employees International Union in the United States and some European unions such as IG Metall in West Germany have called for a total ban on electronic homework for clerical-level workers (National Research Council, 1985; Peles, 1985; Deutsches Gewerkshaftsband, 1986), while others have favoured increased regulation (Mumme, 1983; Trades Union Congress, 1985; Trade Unions' Group, 1985b). On the other hand, there have been various attempts to repeal what legal restrictions currently exist, accompanied by a vociferous commentary in the popular media almost universally in favour of deregulation (e.g. *Wall Street Journal*, 1984; Wolfgram, 1984; Wiegner and Paris, 1983). Particular controversy surrounded the celebrated 'Vermont Knitters' case, when a group of would-be home knitters who had successfully applied to the Labor Department to have the proscription on homework lifted found themselves opposed by the International Ladies' Garment Workers Union, supported by unions and some state labour officials (Beck, 1984). In August 1986, the Department of Labor itself proposed lifting the ban on homework, a proposal which was opposed by the garment industry unions. In the same year the state of New York moved in the opposite direction by instituting a new law designed to crack down on sweatshops and illegal industrial homework. White-collar homework would, however, be unaffected (Bureau of National Affairs, 1986).

In the present deregulatory climate, it seems unlikely that legal prohibitions will be brought into effect which will restrict the growth of home-based telework. It is possible, however, that this situation may change, at least in some European countries. If it does so, the future development of homeworking will be profoundly affected. In addition to the prospect of a slow-down or reversal of its spread, there is a possibility of a major deflection of decentralised work out of individual homes into alternative sites. Not to be discounted is a further possibility, that without effective enforcement, attempts to regulate homeworking could simply lead to a growth in the illegal economy (Hirschheim, 1985).

Chapter 6

HOW IT FEELS—THE HUMAN ASPECTS OF TELEWORK

In all the media attention which has been given to telework, it is inevitably the human aspects which have attracted the most comment, both positive and negative. Sometimes, telework is presented as unproblematically good or bad from the point of view of satisfying individual human needs such as those for autonomy, social integration, family contact and job satisfaction. However, most serious commentators in varying degrees recognise that complex tradeoffs are involved for each individual teleworker in evaluating the relative advantages and disadvantages of remote versus office-based work.

There are a number of variables involved in this calculation. One is the type of remote work which is envisaged. In 1981 Bo Hedberg and Marilyn Mehlmann contrasted the different human effects they thought would result from two very different types of telework, home-based work and work carried out from a neighbourhood office. The neighbourhood office scored high on social contacts, a good learning environment, flexible work organisation and compatibility with local institutions (such as shops, day care centres, etc.) and trade union organisation. Homeworking achieved a low score in all of these areas, doing better only in the ambiguous advantage of achieving a closer integration between work and private life (Hedberg and Mehlmann, 1981). However, by 1988, Mehlmann was pessimistic that neighbourhood offices which were life-enhancing in this way could be set up without intervention to deflect the effects of market forces (Mehlmann, 1988).

Another variable is the gender of the teleworker. Several commentators (e.g. Monod, 1985; Lie, 1985; Vedel, 1984, 1985; Vedel and Gunnarsson, 1985; Cronberg, 1982; Goldmann and Richter, 1987) have pointed out that the human advantages and disadvantages of telework are generally quite different for men than for women. When work is carried out in the home, male teleworkers will generally be provided with a separate room to work in and may be shielded by their spouses from distractions by children or stray callers. In contrast, women are likely to work in a communal area, such as a kitchen, playroom or living room, and to be simultaneously responsible for keeping an eye on young children or other dependants. They are also responsible for the general running of the household which is therefore less likely to be experienced as a relaxing environment (Monod, 1983; Lie, 1985; Chalude, 1984). In addition, the pattern of occupational segregation is such that women are more likely to be carrying out routine work with less intrinsic job satisfaction and involving less social interaction (Gregory, 1985; Huws, 1983). This is a factor which is examined in some detail in Chapter 9, in the context of our own survey of teleworkers in fourteen organisations.

The psychological experience of telework is also affected by the type of work being carried out and the teleworker's motivation. In this context, Margrethe Olson identifies four main types of full-time remote work: exploitation, autonomy, trade-off and privilege. *Exploitation*, stereotypically, refers to a low-skilled clerical worker, usually female, who is working from home because she has no choice. Desperate for work, she is prepared to accept low pay and work for piece-rates. The second category, *autonomy*, describes the motivation of a teleworker who has chosen to work from home because of a need to be independent. This type is usually a self-employed entrepreneur, prepared to sacrifice security for autonomy and is more often male than female, but by no means exclusively so. The third category, *tradeoff*, describes the situation of teleworkers who have a genuine choice about where to work, but have chosen to be based at home because, in their own personal circumstances, this arrangement has the fewest disadvantages. This type of teleworker is most commonly a professional worker, who has chosen to be home-based because of family commitments or relocation and is more likely to be female than male. Working from home in this way is often seen as a temporary solution to a passing problem. As its name suggests, the final category, *privilege*, refers to a small elite of teleworkers whose bargaining position with their employers is strong enough to allow them to dictate their own working conditions. Olson found a prevalence of this type in her 1983 survey of computer specialists in Silicon Valley. 'Typically', she says, 'they were male, with someone else at home full time to "keep the children out of Daddy's hair while he is working". To date, there are few indications that this type of arrangement extends much beyond those employees whose skills are unique and in extreme undersupply (Olson, 1987).

Another variable is whether or not the teleworker is disabled. Telework is often thought to be particularly appropriate for people with disabilities (Raney, 1985; Lewis, 1984a; *New York Times*, 1981; English, 1984; Tippmann, 1985). However, there are indications that people with disabilities are more likely than other groups to seek work for social reasons. In one survey in the UK, disabled teleworkers were asked what they looked for in a job and given seven factors to number in order of importance. Their first choices were 'the satisfaction of being able to use my skills, given my disability', 'companionship and a good working relationship', 'meeting new people' and 'learning new skills'. Of these, at least two are extremely difficult to satisfy in a homeworking situation. Other motivating factors requiring less social interaction to satisfy and therefore more appropriate to telework, such as 'financial rewards' and 'creativity' received much lower priority (Ashok, Hall and Huws, 1986). Sylvie Craipeau and Jean-Claude Marot describe the social isolation of a disabled teleworker in Paris who, because of the hours during which he was required to work, had to drop most of his previous daytime social engagements (Craipeau and Marot, 1984). However, a US survey found that handicapped people became less isolated as a result of becoming teleworkers. This was because it enabled them to meet new people, which was achieved by making special efforts to visit the office regularly (Pratt, 1983).

Empirica has been involved in setting up a number of pilot schemes involving people with disabilities which have the twin objectives of creating economically viable employment opportunities while facilitating the social integration of problem groups on the labour market. By 1988, 135 people with physical or mental disabilities or with a history of long-term unemployment were employed in five 'telework enterprises' in various European countries under this scheme. Social isolation is avoided by basing the work in neighbourhood offices. Initially, the projects are given support and advice with the aim of motivating and training participants eventually to manage their own self-financing independent enterprises.

Experiments such as these have shown that it is possible to minimise the effects of some types of physical and mental disability as a handicap on the labour market. Nevertheless, disability remains an important variable. Taking this and other variables into account, the human factors generally considered important in any evaluation of the advantages and disadvantages of telework can be grouped under a fairly small number of headings.

CHILD CARE

One of the most frequently cited advantages of telework is that it allows the parents of young children to combine work with parenting (e.g. Pratt, 1983; Schiff, 1983; Wiegner and Paris, 1983; Nilles, 1982, 1985b). Sometimes there is also a need to care for other household members, such as dependants with disabilities (Shirley, 1985) or elderly parents (*New York Times*, 1981).

A majority of permanently home-based teleworkers are believed to be women with young children. In a survey carried out for the UK Equal Opportunities Commission in 1982, 95 per cent of respondents were mothers of school-age or pre-school children (Huws, 1984a). Steven Kawakami, who carried out a survey of homeworkers in the USA, found that 'virtually all of the clerical homeworkers were women, and that most of these personnel had children at home'. He also describes a US-based software company in which 97 out of 115 teleworkers were women with children at home (Kawakami, 1983). A survey of 250 North Carolina firms also came up with the finding that 'women with children at home' were the type of employee most likely to choose telework (Risman and Tomaskovic-Devey, quoted in Gordon and Kelly, 1986). Other surveys have produced less clear-cut results. In a readership survey of *Datamation* and *Personal Computing* magazines in the US, Olson found that 84 per cent of respondents sometimes working at home were male. However, this proportion fell to 66 per cent when those working exclusively from home were considered separately (Olson, 1987). By contrast, the response to a companion survey of 14,000 readers of *Family Circle* was 100 per cent female (Christensen, 1987). Such differences can probably be put down to the differing characteristics of the readerships of these journals and the different types of work in which they are likely to be involved. The *Family Circle* readers fell mainly into Olson's 'exploitation' category, while the computer professionals were more likely to be teleworking for reasons of 'autonomy', 'tradeoff' or 'privilege'.

This general picture of telework dominated by women with responsibility for children was confirmed in Empirica's survey of teleworkers, described more fully in Chapter 9. Here, 73 per cent of the 119 teleworkers surveyed were female, 86 per cent were married and 78 per cent had at least one child. Of the children in the teleworkers' households 55 per cent were six years and under, and 35 per cent were under three years of age. The overall majority (82 per cent) of female teleworkers in the sample worked part-time and more than 90 per cent were not the main earners in the household and could be described as secondary wage-earners.

Surveys in Norway (Lie, 1985), Sweden (Vedel, 1984) and Germany (Goldmann and Richter, 1986) have all focused on female teleworkers with young children, though it is not clear to what extent this has been a by-product of the sampling methods used.

However difficult precise quantification is, it is apparent that a substantial proportion of teleworkers have adopted this form of work because of their caring responsibilities. In some cases, the motivation is a straightforward desire to spend more time with children (Brooks, 1982). However, the situation is often more complex with mothers showing considerable ambivalence towards having their children always present while they work. This was exemplified by one respondent in a 1982 UK survey, who when asked what was the main advantage of working from home replied 'being with the children all day' but when asked the main disadvantage of telework gave the same reply—'being with the children all day' (Huws, 1984a)!

In the same survey, a number of respondents described the guilt they experienced as a result of their dual role, sometimes feeling—even when it was recognised as an irrational response—that they were carrying out neither their work nor their parenting as well as they might, leading them to overcompensate (Huws, 1984a), a reaction which has been described in some detail by other commentators (Kleiman, 1983; Woodham, 1983).

In other cases, the choice of telework by parents of young children is seen not as a positive one, but as a necessary evil, caused by the unavailability or excessively high cost of daycare facilities (Kleiman, 1983; Mumme, 1983; Vedel, 1984; Clinton, 1983; Christensen, 1987).

Attempting to combine child-care with home-based employment may be stressful, described by one US homeworker as 'doing two jobs at once', and many teleworkers are only able to work while their children are asleep (Clinton, 1983; Huws, 1984a). Professional and executive-level teleworkers whose work involves concentration generally find that they need to make use of paid childminders to enable them to work effectively (Gordon and Kelly, 1986; Webb, 1983; Whitehouse, 1981). In the FI Group, perhaps the largest employer of teleworkers in the world, this is in fact made a condition of employment (Franklin, 1986).

After carrying out a series of interviews with home-based programmers with child-care responsibilities, Kathleen Christensen concluded that:

> This research challenges two important assumptions underlying the promotion of home-based work for mothers: (1) *the assumption that working at home gives the women control*, and (2) *the assumption that women simultaneously can care for their children and do their work*. The first is more illusory than real. These women define their hours in response to the schedules of other family members as well as of their employers, thereby constraining their control. The second is simply false. Few attempt to concentrate on their work and tend their children at the same time. Most work split shifts that can extend their days anywhere from 4. a.m. to 3. a.m. (Christensen, 1987—Christensen's italics)

Most mothers expect to spend a large proportion of their time caring for their children. However, many men who work away from the home see comparatively little of them. For them, the desire to spend more time with their children may be a motivating factor in the choice to take up telework and some report improved family relationships as a result (Judkins, West and Drew, 1985; Wiegner and Paris, 1983). However, others see the presence of children as a distraction from work, against which careful preventive action must be taken, such as rules forbidding children from entering the work area (Gordon and Kelly, 1986). One male teleworker interviewed by the *New York Times* in 1981 explained that his daughter was cared for by neighbours when he was working at home because 'I was there to work, not to babysit' (*New York Times*, 1981).

Perhaps the main advantage of telework to parents of young children is not so much that it allows work and child-care to be combined (which is only possible in a minority of cases) but that it creates a greater flexibility in the distribution of working time. It allows work to be fitted in around child-care commitments and makes it possible to recover working time lost due to such eventualities as children's illnesses. 'Flexibility in work schedules' was cited as an advantage by 53 per cent of teleworkers (second only to 'permits child/ family care', at 56 per cent) in a survey of US teleworkers carried out by the Diebold Group (Diebold Group, 1981), a finding which was echoed in the UK Equal Opportunities Commission survey the following year in which 'flexibility' was cited as an advantage by 55 per cent, while 'child-care' was cited by 70.5 per cent of respondents (Huws, 1984a). In the Empirica survey of teleworkers, the full results of which can be found in Chapter 9, the proportions were even higher. Over 90 per cent of the respondents cited 'flexibility' as an important or very important advantage of their current work arrangement. This advantage was given significantly higher ratings by women than by male teleworkers. Although absolute percentages vary according to the question method used, it is clear that flexibility in its various forms is a significant advantage to a large number of teleworkers.

CAREER ADVANCEMENT

In general, a lack of career advancement possibilities is seen as one of the disadvantages of telework to the individual teleworker (English, 1984; Renfro, 1985; Huws, 1984a), although this may in some cases be one which he or she is happy to trade off against other advantages (Gordon and Kelly, 1986). This can be attributed to the teleworker's lack of visibility in the office and fewer opportunities for informal social contact. An exception is the FI Group where the majority of the workforce, including senior managers, is home-based, thus creating a career structure for the company's teleworkers (Huws, 1984a; Franklin, 1986).

In a survey carried out for the Xerox Corporation, Joanne Pratt found no teleworkers who felt that their career prospects had improved, and a number of women workers who described the effects on their promotion prospects as 'suicidal' (Pratt, 1983).

Mobile executive-level teleworkers, whose work involves numerous face-to-face meetings, may not be disadvantaged in this way (Judkins, West and Drew, 1985) and the 1981 Diebold survey found that, although 22 per cent felt that their career would be disadvantaged by the fact that they were teleworkers, 13 per cent believed that their promotion prospects would be enhanced (Diebold Group, 1981). As will be seen in Chapter 9, in the Empirica survey of teleworkers, 35 per cent thought that their current chances of promotion were disadvantaged while 11 per cent believed them to be enhanced by telework. Webb quotes Margrethe Olson as speculating that less face-to-face communication might mean that physical attractiveness becomes a less important factor in promotions, thus leading to more equal opportunities for minorities, older women and the handicapped (Webb, 1983).

The general consensus seems to be that for those leaving or thinking of leaving a full-time office-based job to become a teleworker with the same employer, the lack of career prospects is a negative factor, creating a disincentive to working remotely. However, for people setting up independently as teleworkers, or using telework to gain some independence from their current employer, career prospects may seem to be improved (Korte and Robinson 1988a). In such situations, teleworkers are operating in an entrepreneurial mode with their career advancement in their own hands, determined by their own skill and judgement. This contrasts with the attitude of the employee, who perceives his or her career advancement as determined by the employer, and who therefore places a high value on being seen by the employer to be performing well.

SOCIAL CONTACT

Social isolation is generally considered to be the greatest disadvantage of home-based telework from the human point of view, and is the main reason given for opposing telework by those who do so. The Diebold survey found that 56 per cent of teleworkers surveyed mentioned social isolation as a disadvantage, a proportion which rose to 70 per cent among the women in the survey (Diebold Group, 1981). In the UK Equal Opportunities Commission Survey, 60 per cent complained of isolation, while 51 per cent said that they would welcome contact with other homeworkers. Indeed 22 per cent of the sample said that they would prefer to be working in an office, giving the need for more social contact as their main reason (Huws, 1984a).

Confirmation and amplification of these findings come from the results of the Empirica survey reported in Chapter 9. These show with some precision that the higher the proportion of their working time teleworkers spend at home, the more dissatisfied they are with their contacts with others in similar work. More than half of the teleworkers spending nearly all their working time at home mentioned the lack of social contacts as a disadvantage of telework. These conclusions are echoed in numerous other reports and illustrated in most press interviews with teleworkers (e.g. Groom, 1984a; Phelps, 1985; Manning, 1985; Larson, 1985).

One reason for the greater isolation experienced by female teleworkers may lie, not in any intrinsic gender difference, but in the different types of work which women are likely to be doing, with a tendency to be concentrated in more routine, lower-level work in which little or no social contact is involved in the job itself, and where fewer meetings are necessary (Kawakami, 1983).

Some commentators have suggested that diminishing social interactions with work colleagues may be compensated for by increased social activity in the community (Toffler, 1981; Aldrich, 1982; Craipeau and Marot, 1984;

Blanc, 1988). However, the Diebold survey found that teleworkers who were involved in community and other non-work-related activities felt no less isolated than those who were not, and that those who did not complain of isolation in their work tended to participate in solitary social activities as well. This suggests that family and community activities are not effective substitutes for the social world of the office (Diebold Group, 1981). The conclusion drawn by Olson is that need for social interaction may in part be a function of personality type, with wide variations between individuals (Olson, 1982). In her report for the Diebold Group, she suggests that there is a sub-group, comprising 22 per cent of the sample surveyed, consisting of people with a low need for communication. This sub-group also has fewer problems in concentrating on their work than the rest of the sample, but suffers more from stress (Diebold Group, 1981). Heilmann concurs with this view, pointing out that computer professionals tend to be of a personality type with low communication needs, and therefore particularly well suited to telework (Heilmann, 1988). Pratt also identified a substantial minority—25 per cent of her sample of teleworkers—who described themselves as 'loners', 'antisocial' or 'introverts'. All of the teleworkers in her survey were over 28 and had been married. Younger, single teleworkers had dropped out because of their need for the social interaction provided in the office environment (Pratt, 1983).

It might be thought that teleworkers in Olson's 'exploitation' and 'tradeoff' categories would be the most likely to suffer from social isolation, being the two groups most conscious of the disadvantages of the arrangement, while those in the 'autonomy' and 'privilege' categories, having actively chosen it without reservation, would be least likely to feel cut off from human company. However, even here there is some doubt. It is possible that these self-motivated types may be carried along for a year or two on the euphoria of being on their own and in control of their working lives, but that later, when their old work contacts have become out-of-date and the novelty has worn off, a reaction sets in which is very similar to that of the less privileged housewife, isolated with her children within the too-familiar boundaries of her home as she works. Tom Forester, a writer on office automation who was previously something of an enthusiast for telework, describes his own experience, in these words:

> An initial honeymoon period of two to three years, which was accompanied by feelings of elation and high productivity, was followed by a less satisfactory period which was accompanied by feelings of loneliness, isolation and a growing desire to escape the 'same four walls'. (Forester, 1988)

He also describes other problems in almost identical terms to those used by the women teleworkers in surveys by Christensen, Huws, Goldmann and

Richter and Vedel but assigns them not to teleworkers themselves but to their wives, illustrating once again the importance of gender difference in any analysis of the human experience of telework.

> The 'problems', which can become a serious drain on families, tend in my experience to include: explaining to the children that daddy is not available because he is 'at work'; explaining the same to friends, neighbours and other callers; and keeping the children quiet and rearranging the vacuuming so as not to disturb daddy. For the homeworker himself, there is the guilt and feelings engendered by hearing the children crying or arguing and not being able to intervene; hearing young children happily playing and not being able to join in; and the general problem of dividing 'work' from 'home' life. How do you explain to a two-year-old that daddy in the kitchen making a cup of coffee is thinking about his next paragraph and is not to be interrupted? (Forester, 1988)

Although not based on any representative sample, Forester's views are interesting for several reasons. Firstly, they illustrate that psychological problems are not confined to teleworkers involved in repetitive and uncreative work and, incidentally, by implication that, acute as they may be for 'daddies' they are considerably more stressful for those who have to combine serious work at home with being a 'mummy' as well, with no wife to act as gatekeeper. Secondly, they suggest that the six months or so which is normally allowed for evaluating the success of a telework pilot is much too short to pick up such psychological problems.

Forester also describes the experience of five other teleworkers similarly placed to himself (all, one presumes, male).

> Of the five, two divorced, one became seriously depressed and one returned to working in London. For only one of the five did homeworking appear to be an unmitigated success—and even in that case there were serious question marks over·aspects of the domestic situation which could lead to problems later. (Forester, 1988).

These problems are all attributed to homeworking by Forester, who quotes William Atkinson, the author of a popular American book about homeworking, as being convinced that the psychological problems of working at home are paramount:

> *It is very difficult—psychologically—to work at home.* Almost without exception, 'cottage industrialists' and 'telecommuters' alike report a host of problems, including lack of motivation and discipline, inability to organise work and manage time effectively, loneliness, family tension, fear of failure, burnout, stress and hypochondria. Essentially, these problems stem from an inability to be *self-managers*. In other words, the problems most often associated with working at home are triggered not so much by economic, legal, or technological factors as

by the failure of these pioneers to manage themselves and their work. (Atkinson, W., author of *Working at Home—Is It for you?*, Dow Jones-Irwin, 1985, quoted in Forester, 1988—italics in the original)

Here, isolation is regarded more as a symptom than as a problem in its own right, but it does nevertheless seem to be widespread among the entrepreneurial types of teleworker, among whom Atkinson is described as having carried out 'scores' of interviews (Forester, 1988).

That teleworkers are likely to become socially isolated appears to be accepted within most organisations which employ them, at least where they are in professional or managerial grades. It is widespread practice to test individuals for appropriate personality traits before agreeing to their becoming remote workers (Judkins, West and Drew, 1985; Gordon and Kelly, 1986). Many also go to some lengths to minimise teleworkers' sense of isolation by organising social get-togethers, circulating newsletters and other, less formal, means (Empirica, 1986a; Franklin, 1986). Further evidence of the need for social interaction is provided by the sporadic attempts among self-employed homeworkers, who are out of reach of such company-initiated schemes, to set up their own newsletters and networks. The British *Ownbase*, set up by an enterprising individual homeworker, Chris Oliver, is an example of this. It provides subscribers with a chatty newsletter, access to a database of contacts and, through its regional groups, informal gatherings at which members can meet and compare notes.

These experiences suggest that workers' desire for social contact may be a major restraint on the development of full-time, home-based telework. Rather than leading to its being abandoned altogether, this could have the effect of increasing the relative attractions of part-time, home-based telework (whereby the worker is based at home for only part of the working week) and of telework based in neighbourhood or satellite offices. Full-time, home-based telework is likely to be attractive only to a minority of the workforce—those who have low needs for communication and social interaction, probably people in professional jobs requiring concentration who are at a stage in their life-cycles when social needs can be met adequately within the household (typically these might be computer professionals or writers in stable partnerships with growing children).

AUTONOMY

Closely related to questions of social interaction are those of autonomy and control over the work process. As has already been noted, the Diebold Group survey of US teleworkers found a correlation between a low need for communication and a high level of concentration (Diebold Group, 1981). It seems likely that for some workers at least—those for whom the need for social interaction is high—the physical presence of colleagues may provide an external form of discipline which, however informal, makes it easier to structure the working day and concentrate on the task in hand.

This is an area in which survey results are ambiguous. The Diebold survey found that 31 per cent of teleworkers experienced motivation as a problem, including a higher proportion from those who did not have a strict work schedule, suggesting that self-discipline was the main difficulty. Only 22 per cent of the sample felt that motivation and productivity had improved as a result of becoming home-based. However, 66 per cent felt that their concentration had increased, compared with only 16 per cent for whom it had diminished (Diebold Group, 1981). In the UK Equal Opportunities Commission survey, 26 per cent of respondents said that they found self-discipline a problem (Huws, 1984a), while 21 per cent of the teleworkers in the Empirica survey of teleworkers mentioned this as a difficulty (see Chapter 9).

A lack of self-discipline does not necessarily lead to less work being done. It can take the form of 'workaholism'. Commentators describe teleworkers (generally male) who find it almost impossible to leave their terminals alone, sometimes just logging on 'to see who is on the network' or working late into the night to finish a particular piece of work or solve a nagging problem, often to the detriment of their personal relationships (Nilles, 1982, 1985b; Turoff and Hiltz, 1983). The need for external sources of discipline is felt in other areas of personal life too. Compulsive eating is a problem for a number of teleworkers (Huws, 1984a; Phelps, 1985; Gordon and Kelly, 1985; Lewis, 1984; Nilles, 1982) and has in fact been a reason why some have gone back to working full-time in an office (Phelps, 1985).

Sylvie Craipeau and Jean-Claude Marot conclude that the degree of autonomy experienced by a teleworker is dependent on the type of work carried out, low autonomy being associated with a high degree of fragmentation of the work process and the payment of piece-rates, while high autonomy accompanies professional work (Craipeau and Marot, 1984).

Because of the wide variations both in individuals' experiences of control over their own work and in their attitudes to it, it is difficult to determine whether this factor is likely to be a constraint on the future development of telework or an encouragement to its expansion. It seems likely that—in the short term, at least—some freelance and professional workers thrive on the self-motivating, self-disciplining approach to work which telework necessitates, and feel restricted by external controls. For them, one of the main attractions of telework is the autonomy it offers.

Other workers, however, prefer to operate within limits determined by a wider social group. It is sometimes argued that the collective control which can be exerted by a group of workers in a central workplace may in practice confer greater autonomy than individual choice exercised within the parameters laid down by indirect forms of external control such as those imposed by schemes for payment by results (Mumme, 1983; Trade Union Group, 1984).

Once again, it is likely that the worker's occupation and skills will play a critical role in determining which form of employment status confers the greatest control over his or her working life. At one extreme, the clerical worker on piece-rates will almost certainly gain greater room for manoeuvre from within the protection of a secure permanent contract of employment, while at the other the entrepreneur with rare skills will gain from being free from any long-term contractual obligations to a single client.

The results of the Empirica survey indicate that a substantial minority of professional-level teleworkers see themselves at least potentially in the latter category, with approximately a third regarding their situation as a good training ground for developing the self-starting skills of the entrepreneur. Of the teleworkers surveyed 34 per cent indicated that the options telework offers for developing skills of use in setting up one's own business were an important reason for starting telework. Moreover, self-employed status was felt to be an advantage by more than half of the respondents. However, this preference for self-employment was expressed in the main by those whose skills were in high demand (see Chapter 9).

PERSONAL RELATIONSHIPS

Little research has been carried out on the effects of telework on personal relationships within the home. Except for Forester's catalogue of failed marriages among his immediate acquaintance mentioned above, the literature includes little apart from one anecdote about a teleworker who reverted to working in an office because his wife felt that she was being spied on when he was at home all day (Webb, 1983). However, other observers report on improved relationships between husbands and wives, especially when both are teleworkers (Judkins, West and Drew, 1985; Turoff and Hiltz, 1983). Any scientific study of the effects of telework on relationships within marriage would have to take a long-term perspective and would be extraordinarily difficult to set up. Most intelligent couples would, presumably, take evasive action if they saw that their relationship was beginning to deteriorate because one or both partners were based at home, and one would probably be left with a survivor population of couples who were able to make telework work for them. The alternative scenario which Forester suggests—a sample of miserable home-based divorcees—would be extremely unlikely to perpetuate itself for long.

When it comes to the effects on personal relationships, it seems likely that the gender of the teleworker is a significant variable, since the place of work is not normally regarded as gender-neutral. According to the prevailing stereotype, going out to work is experienced as a 'masculine' activity, while staying at home is seen as 'feminine'. This gives the act of going out to work, or not going out, quite a different meaning for men than for women. For a woman, going out to work feels masculine, and carries with it various other notions associated with masculinity—she feels more independent, more capable, more in control of her life and so on. Staying at home, on the other hand, confirms her in her femininity. While this may have some advantages, it also connotes some negative feelings associated with being a woman, such as lack of confidence, dependence and restriction of movement. For a man, going out to work confirms him in the role of breadwinner and provider and reinforces the separateness of the public world of his work from the private domestic sphere. Working at home, on the other hand, brings these two worlds into close proximity and confuses their boundaries. It is, in effect, a feminising experience. One is struck, reading Forester's account of the problems he experienced as a homeworker, by the fact that what he is describing is in essence that common female experience, the 'trapped housewife syndrome'. In conversation with male teleworkers, the authors have also been surprised by the frequency with which those working at home have expressed fears connected with the loss of their visible role as breadwinners, for instance, the fear that 'the neighbours don't think I've got a real job anymore'. The loss of the masculinity-confirming buddy-world of the workplace is a further threat to male identity. The effects on male sexuality of such an undermining of masculine identity through unemployment are well known. It would not be entirely surprising if the effect of prolonged telework on some male egos were to produce a similar crisis, the first casualty of which might be their sexual relationships. Where the sense of identity is strong enough to withstand such an onslaught, and a man is capable of stepping outside the traditional stereotype of the absent breadwinner, then the effect could well be a liberating one, resulting in the relationship being strengthened.

For a woman homeworker, the problem is the opposite one: not how to break out of her traditional role as the stay-at-home, but how to survive within it, with the added stress of her paid work. Whether this leads to an improvement or a deterioration in her sexual relationships will depend as much on the personal qualities which are brought to those relationships as on any factors intrinsic to the situation. Perhaps the situation can best be summed up in the words of Gil Gordon—'telework makes good marriages better, and bad ones worse' (Gordon and Kelly, 1986).

CONCLUSIONS

It can be concluded that the costs and benefits of telework from a human point of view are not easy to assess. Many depend on the individual personalities concerned, and others vary according to the type of work in question and the particular domestic situation of the worker concerned.

When weighing up the psychological advantages and disadvantages of remote work, it is worth remembering that going out to work also has its penalties in human terms. Depending on the circumstances, these may include stress, alienation from children and other family members, exposure to racial or sexual prejudice or harassment, or the company of colleagues or superiors whom one dislikes or finds irritating, to name but a few. As with other aspects of telework, the choice to become a remote worker involves a tradeoff.

In weighing up the pros and cons, the greatest human benefit is undoubtedly the flexibility telework offers, which makes it much easier to integrate work with domestic life. The greatest problem, for a majority of teleworkers but not all, is undoubtedly social isolation. However, this can be minimised by the use of neighbourhood work centres in preference to home-based telework, by structuring jobs so that workers spend part of their working week in the office, and by organising regular social gatherings and providing good communication links between teleworkers and their colleagues.

Chapter 7

THE TASKS INVOLVED IN TELEWORK

In the last chapter, we looked at what types of people are the most suitable candidates for telework, and which groups are most likely to find themselves working remotely. Here we examine the types of work they are likely to be doing and the criteria for deciding which tasks are most appropriate for telework. This is an area where much of the popular literature about telework is surprisingly vague. Often, when it comes to defining what types of work are appropriate for decentralisation, only the most general phrases are employed, like 'most white-collar work' or 'work involving information processing', sometimes with a cautionary qualification to remind the reader that even in the most high-tech office some tasks still require face-to-face contact. Alvin Toffler, for instance, has this to say on the subject:

> An unmeasured but appreciable amount of work is already being done at home by such people as salesmen and salewomen who work by phone or visit, and only occasionally touch base at the office; by architects and designers; by a burgeoning pool of specialised consultants in many industries . . . and by many other categories of white-collar, technical and professional people . . . While it would be a mistake to underestimate the need for direct face-to-face contact in business, and all the subliminal and non-verbal communication that accompanies that contact, it is also true that certain tasks do not require much outside contact at all—or need it only intermittently. (Toffler, 1981)

Where researchers have been more specific than this, it has often taken the pragmatic form of producing lists of activities which are deemed especially suitable for decentralisation. Table 7.1, for instance, shows us the list developed by Lange and co-workers. Rather than focus on specific activities in this way, Lohmar identified 17 broad areas of work which he considers suitable for telework:

- word processing
- software documentation
- data bank information retrieval
- clerical work
- data entry
- translation (Lohmar, 1984)

TABLE 7.1   Activities suitable for telework

	Public administration	Private sector administration	Information-related services
Generally low qualification requirements	Data entry and editing Text entry and editing Simple clerical work (e.g. order processing) Dealing with simple telephone queries)	Data entry and editing Text entry and editing Simple clerical work (e.g. order processing)	Data entry (e.g. for market research) Text entry (especially typing services) Dealing with simple telephone queries
Generally high qualification requirements	Documentation and archiving tasks Qualified clerical work (e.g. checking applications) Preparatory planning Programming in dialogue with a computer	Documentation and archiving tasks Analysis and calculation in computer dialogue Preparatory planning Programming in dialogue with a computer Translation	Documentation and archiving tasks Database query services Analysis and calculation in computer dialogue Programming (software house) Translation (in specialist service)

Source: Lange *et al.*, 1982, p. 252 (translated and slightly adapted by Empirica)

- computer programming
- construction (CAD, CAM)
- writing of manuals
- systems analysis
- remote maintenance
- book-keeping
- consultancy
- distance learning/education
- remote control
- estate agency work
- estimation/accounting

In practice, up to now, when office work has been relocated, four main types of work have predominated, whether this has taken the form of resiting of back-office functions, the setting up of a telework scheme, or the establishment of sub-contract office services by individual entrepreneurs: data entry, text processing, programming and sales support.

Interestingly enough, these areas more or less coincide with the occupations of the people who expressed most interest in becoming teleworkers in the attitude survey of the general population in four European countries carried out by Empirica and described in greater detail in Chapter 11. Here, those showing most interest were mainly either in data processing professions like computer programming or systems analysis, or in other occupations involving data processing such as secretaries, clerical workers, typists and administrators. Engineers and scientific personnel also showed great interest in being employed remotely.

The apparent suitability of these areas was confirmed in another Empirica poll, this time of decisionmakers in Europe, which is described more fully in Chapter 10. Here, the areas which emerged as most appropriate for telework in the eyes of managers were, on the one hand, data input, data amendment and word processing, for which mass markets were foreseen, and on the other, tasks specifically tailored for particular clients, such as programming and senior administrative work.

The first systematic investigation of the tasks appropriate to telework was carried out in the USA by Margrethe Olson for the Diebold Corporation. She identified eight categories of jobs which could feasibly be carried out remotely:

- clerical and data entry
- word processing
- administrative and secretarial
- technical professional (e.g. programmer, systems analyst)
- business professional (e.g. financial analyst, engineer)
- field professional (e.g. field sales representative, inspector)
- manager
- executive

Heilmann compresses the spectrum of applicable office tasks to only six categories:

- word processing and software documentation
- programming and systems analysis
- data entry
- consultancy (e.g. sales representatives, mobile insurance agents)
- clerical work
- management (Heilmann, 1987)

In addition to identifying the types of work broadly suitable for telework, serious investigators have also felt it necessary to identify the specific characteristics of a particular job which make it feasible to decentralise it. Basing her analysis on close observation of existing telework schemes, Olson was the first to do this, in 1981 (Diebold Group, 1981). She concluded that there are six characteristic traits which are essential for remote work to be a success, a conclusion with which many subsequent researchers have concurred (Kawakami, 1983; Heilmann, 1987; Dostal, 1985). These traits can be summarised as follows.

1. Minimal Physical Requirements

Telework is unlikely to be successful where the job requires a great deal of equipment or storage space. Many teleworkers can function effectively with just a terminal and a telephone hook-up. Except where there are overriding social reasons for the telework arrangement, for instance to create employment for someone with a severe disability, the costs of any equipment required should be justifiable in terms of the value of the work produced by the teleworker.

2. Individual Controls Own Pace of Work

In her research in 1981, Olson found no teleworking jobs which were driven externally by short-term deadlines. Except for data entry jobs, all were project-orientated with long-term completion dates (Diebold Group, 1981). This feature of current telework practice contributes to the flexibility in the disposition of working hours which constitutes one of the main attractions of remote work.

3. Defined Deliverables

In most cases, effective management of telework is only considered possible where output can be controlled in terms of well-defined deliverables. This often implies payment by output, for instance where data entry clerks are paid by the transaction, or where contract programmers work on fixed price contracts for a delivered system or a completed program. However, there are successful schemes in operation where teleworkers are paid on a time basis, with work monitored according to carefully defined targets.

4. Need for Concentration

With the exception of data entry clerks, all the teleworkers surveyed by Olson characterised their jobs as requiring a degree of concentration for at least part of the time (Diebold Group, 1981).

5. Defined Milestones

It appears to be difficult for teleworkers to cope with planning long periods of uncharted time. Successful schemes typically involve the breaking down of long-term projects into manageable chunks, with easily definable intermediate deadlines so that progress can be monitored.

6. Low Need for Communication

Telework is not usually regarded as suitable for workers whose jobs require a great deal of communication with a variety of different colleagues. Some work, such as data entry or word processing, has a very low inherent need for communication. With other types of work, the most important requirement is that communications needs can be partitioned so that the teleworker can work for relatively long periods of time with little or no communication with the central office. What communication is required should be capable of being 'batched' during the time the employee is in the office or handled easily by telephone. Where the type of telework in question is based in a neighbourhood or satellite office, rather than in an individual home, then of course this stipulation only relates to remote communications with the central office, not to interchanges with fellow-workers at the same site.

This requirement exposes the limited capabilities of information and communication technologies to substitute for face-to-face contacts. Musiol has pointed out that this makes telework inappropriate for professionals in occupations which require a high degree of personal information exchange (Musiol, 1986).

This six-fold characterisation of jobs deemed suitable for telework, first developed by Olson in 1981, has been adopted in most of the American literature on the subject. Five years later in Germany, it was systematised by Heilmann, who developed a classification of tasks in five dimensions:

- work in groups/individual work
- materials
- location (centralised/decentralised)
- timing (cycle time, deadlines)
- quantifiability (Heilmann, 1987)

Figure 7.1 demonstrates how this classification system can be used to determine whether a particular office task is suitable for telework, using the example of a computer programming job. The lower ratings in this classification (1–3) apply to those elements of an office task which need to be carried out in central office buildings. The higher ratings (5–7) indicate task elements which can be decentralised easily. The overall decentralisation potential of a task is not a single value, but a combination of different evaluations along these dimensions. According to this classification system, tasks can either be defined as 'presence-orientated' (1–3) or 'results-orientated' (5–7) with a zone of transition in between (4) where telework can still take place provided certain precautions are taken (Heilmann, 1987).

Other researchers attempting to identify the characteristics of work which can be decentralised have drawn similar distinctions. Judkins, West and Drew concluded that jobs can be broken down into two broad categories: the 'continuity mode' in which being personally present at the point where the work is done is an essential feature of the job, and the 'output mode' in which the achievement of defined objectives is the main function of the job, and the place where the work supporting that achievement is carried out is incidental (Judkins, West and Drew, 1985, p. 25). Typical of a 'continuity mode' job is that of a receptionist whose work requires a continuous presence at the front desk. 'Output mode' can be exemplified by a computer programmer whose geographical location is immaterial provided the output—the completed program—is produced adequately and on time.

Into the 'continuity mode' category, Judkins and his colleagues place personal service work (tasks which can only be carried out by face-to-face contact with individuals), and 'managerial continuity work' (e.g. decision-making tasks). In the 'output' category, they put 'output service work', by which they seem to mean any task with specified outputs, in other words tasks which can be defined as the supply of a specific piece of work, and nomadic work, jobs—such as marketing jobs—which involve a good deal of travelling or meetings in other peoples' offices but which nevertheless need back-up from central support staff.

In practice, very few jobs fall completely into either of these two modes. Most embrace a range of tasks and roles and accordingly a mix of continuity and output modes. From the point of view of efficiency, the optimal telework task would be one which could be performed mainly in the output mode with the possibility of structural reorganisation to transfer any outstanding 'continuity' tasks to office-based colleagues.

In setting up the existing telework schemes, most of their initiators have erred on the side of conservatism when selecting tasks for decentralisation. The vast majority of teleworkers are doing jobs which fall well within these definitions of 'results-orientated' or 'output mode' tasks, and comply with

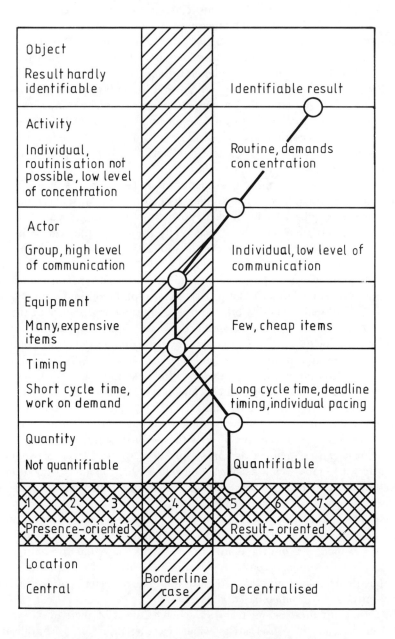

FIGURE 7.1   Suitability of tasks for telework
Source: Heilmann (1987), p. 355 (translation by Empirica)

TABLE 7.2 *Summary of existing telework projects*

Country[a]	Company	Type[b]	No. of workers	Occupation/tasks	Comments
FRG	Integrata Tübingen	S/TH	20	Dp professionals	
FRG	ICR Neustadt	H	2	Data entry	
FRG	Pilot project Baden-Württemberg	H/TN/TS/TF	7/2/7/1	Word processing	Pilot project funded by public sources
FRG	Siemens AG	H	2	Word processing	
FRG	Programmier Service GmbH (PSG)	E	80	Programmers	Handicapped people
FRG	Lufthansa AG, Hamburg	H	50	Data entry	
FRG	GWK, Cologne	E	20	Data entry	Handicapped people
FRG	ÖVA, Mannheim	H/TF	300	Insurance agents	
FRG	Bausparkasse Wüstenrot	S/TF	800	Insurance agents	
FRG	RWG GmbH	H	5	Programmers	
FRG	TastSatz Lulay GmbH	H	15	Word processing	
FRG	Odenthal Texterfassung	H	18	Word processing	
FRG	Bonner Übersetzungsbüro	E/TH	5	Translating, word processing	
FRG	Fotosatz Company	H	20	Word processing	
FRG	Research Company	F	2	Researcher	
FRG	Rehabilitationsprojekt 'Externe Datenverarbeitung'	E	15	Various tasks	Handicapped people
F	DGT—Pilot Project	H	14	Various tasks	Handicapped people
F	Telefonservice	H	37	Switchboard tasks	
F	Teleboutique/Sales agency	S	?	Salesmen, professionals	
F	Research Institute	H	1	Researcher	Pilot project for a handicapped person
F	Insurance company	S	700	Insurance agents	
F	Insurance company	H	1	Word processing	
F	Bank	H	2	Professionals	
F	Telephone marketing	F	84	Sales people	
F	Sports articles company	F	15	Sales people	Introduction of mobile terminals
F	Dp consultant	F	3	Programmers	
F	Telework Centre (Marne la vallée)	N	15	Various tasks	

(continued on p. 78)

TABLE 7.2 (Cont.)

Country[a]	Company	Type[b]	No. of workers	Occupation/tasks	Comments
UK	The FI Group	H/TF	1100	Dp professionals	'Panel members'
UK	Rank Xerox	H	55	Middle and senior executives	'Networkers'
UK	ICL	H	250	Programmers	
UK	Department of Trade and Industry	H	58	Typists, accountants	Pilot project for handicapped people
UK	ICL	H	100	Various tasks	
UK	Systime	H	150	Technical staff	
UK	Nottingham Building Society	H/TF	1/10	Dp professionals	'Associates'
UK	Business Information Company	H	6	Videotex editor/Technical dp staff Journalists	
I	Olivetti Software	F	1000	Programmers	
I	ENI (Chemical Industry)	F	50	Managers and professionals	
I	University of Milan	F	5	Various tasks	Pilot project
I	O. Group	H	?	Dp professionals	
NL	Telework Groningen	E	10	Various tasks	Handicapped people
NL	Telework Enschede	E	10	Various tasks	Handicapped people
SWE	SIGA Service-Centre (North Sweden)	N	40	Word Processing	Model for economically depressed regions
SWE	Nykvarn Work Centre	N	10	Various tasks	
USA	Heights Information	H	180	Dp professionals	
USA	Lift	H	?	Dp professionals	Handicapped people
USA	IBM	H	60	Sales reps, managers, Dp professionals, professionals	Additional terminals at home
USA	Tymshare Cupertino	F	40	Managers, Dp professionals	
USA	Interactive Systems	F	100	Dp professionals	
USA	AWS-Program (CDC)	F	27	Various tasks (consultants, programmers)	Alternate Work Site Programme

Country[a]	Company	Type[b]	Number	Tasks	Remarks
USA	Continental Illinois Bank	H	4	Word processing	
USA	Blue Cross/Blue Shield	H	200/14	Programmers/data entry	
USA	American Airlines	S	200	Data entry	Utilisation of low labour costs in the Caribbean
USA	Satellite Data Corp.	S	?	Data entry	
USA	Mountain Bell	H	8	Middle management	Terminated work-at-home trial
USA	American Express Company	H	10	Word processing	Handicapped people
USA	US Army (ALMSA)	H	4	Various tasks	Computer-based office support system
USA	Hewlett Packard Laboratories	F	1000	Programmers, engineers	Equipment at home for after hours work use
USA	Equitable Life	H	5	Programmers	
USA	Blodgett Computer Information Systems	H	100	Data entry	
USA	The Kemper Group	H	?	Word processing (insurance agents)	'Loss Control Consultants'
USA	Pacific Bell Telephone	H	?		
USA	Southern California Association of Government (SCAG)	H	15	Various tasks	
USA	Major Colorado Bank	H	3	Word processing	
USA	Aetna Life and Casualty	H	3	Dp professionals	
USA	Chase Manhattan Bank	H	4	Dp professionals	
USA	Ford Motor Company	H	3	Word processing	
USA	Investors' Diversified Services	H	3	Word processing	
USA	Manufacturers' Hannover Trust	H	4	Dp professionals	
USA	New York Telephone	H	12	Various tasks	
USA	Travellers' Insurance	S	76	Dp professionals	

[a]Country:
FRG: West Germany
USA: United States of America
F: France
UK: United Kingdom
I: Italy
NL: Netherlands

[b]Type:
S Satellite Work Centre
F Flexible Work Arrangement
H Work at Home
N Neighbourhood Work Centre
E Electronic Service Office

Sources: Various

Olson's six rules for success. As Table 7.2 shows, they are mainly data processing professionals or word-processor operators with a sprinkling of insurance salespeople, journalists and managers. This table summarises the available information on 70 telework schemes in six European countries and the United States, and is based on Empirica's own survey of teleworkers in combination with a review of the literature on the subject. More detailed information on the survey will be found in the next chapter.

It might be expected that telework schemes involving a neighbourhood work centre, satellite office or electronic service office might involve a wider range of tasks and occupations than those restricted only to home-based work. However, this seems not to be the case. When they are categorised according to the type of work arrangement, it is the homeworking category—admittedly by far the largest group in the sample—which covers the widest range of both tasks and occupations. A possible reason for this might be the fact that a large proportion of the non-home-based telework schemes have been set up with public subsidies for disadvantaged groups, with an emphasis on developing the types of skills and products for which they perceive the possibility of a mass market.

This table, of course, describes the world of telework as it is. If we attempt to discover the tasks and occupations which would be involved in telework as it might be, the picture would probably be very different. As information technology permeates more and more areas of the economy, so more and more work processes become systematised in ways which permit their being carried out using a computer, thus adding to the pool of tasks which can be successfully carried out remotely. The restructuring of industries also generates new types of occupation, some of which can be carried out by individual entrepreneurs, local agents or other staff for whom telework is a possible mode of work. Some possible future scenarios are discussed in Chapters 12 and 13 of this book.

Chapter 8

THE EMPIRICA TELEWORK SURVEY—I. TELEWORK IN 14 EUROPEAN COMPANIES

In 1987, Empirica carried out a survey of telework in 14 companies in Germany and the UK. Several research instruments were used, developed during the course of Empirica's earlier analytical and empirical work in this field. There were two questionnaires: one to be administered to teleworkers; the other designed for their managers. Both are reproduced in Appendix A of this book.

The main object of the survey was not to gather further impressionistic data on teleworkers' views of the advantages and disadvantages of their work situation but to investigate how their work is structured and to assess the relative importance of the many different factors which had already been identified in earlier research as shaping their individual situations. Therefore, the teleworker questionnaire was designed as a standardised instrument, the majority of questions being provided with pre-formulated answers. A small number of open-ended questions and, more importantly, interviews with individual teleworkers, served to colour in the picture gained from the statistical analysis.

The procedure adopted for the managers was somewhat different. The number of managers it is feasible to contact as sources of information on current telework schemes is considerably more limited than the number of teleworkers reachable for this purpose, so that statistical methods of structural investigation could not usefully be applied. Furthermore, telework schemes are organisationally very diverse, demanding a more flexible approach. Personal interviews therefore played a crucial role in the investigation. Information from standardised questionnaires supplemented these by providing a central core of detailed information comparable across all the schemes in the survey.

One problem which arose in some of the management interviews was a reluctance to admit the difficulties which had been encountered in the setting up and running of telework schemes. This was because in a number of cases the teleworking scheme had had to be 'sold' to other members of the organisation, to shareholders and to external bodies such as the press, political parties and the unions. Managers therefore had a strong vested interest in showing the telework scheme in as positive a light as possible, demonstrating it to be a success for all concerned. However, it was possible to correct much of this imbalance by comparing the management perspective with that of the individual teleworkers in these schemes.

After an initial approach to a number of German and British companies known to be involved in telework, a positive response was received from 14 companies. Questionnaires were distributed to the managers responsible for the telework arrangements in these organisations. In compliance with data protection legislation, Empirica asked the managers to select the teleworkers for inclusion in the case studies, and we have their assurance that they all complied with our request to avoid systematic dissemination of the questionnaires.

Because the sample of organisations was biased in favour of highly qualified staff, we compensated for this by selecting for inclusion in the survey larger numbers of teleworkers from those organisations which employ teleworkers in other occupational groups. Personal interviews with decision makers and teleworkers in these companies were conducted at this initial stage and again after the questionnaires had been returned. Table 8.1 gives an overview of the types and quantities of questionnaires which were distributed and returned. As can be seen, 100 per cent of the managers' questionnaires and 83 per cent of the teleworkers' questionnaires which were disseminated were suitable for inclusion in the analyses. This high response rate was achieved partly as a result of careful formulation of covering letters and reminders and the co-operation of project managers, but it seems also in part to be a reflection of the interest many teleworkers have in communicating to others about their unusual work situation.

It should be noted that the sampling method used does not of itself permit generalisation of the results to a universe of teleworkers or potential teleworkers

TABLE 8.1   Response rates in the telework survey

| | Types and quantities of questionnaires: | | | |
| | Managers | | Teleworkers | |
Country	Disseminated	Returned	Disseminated	Returned
West Germany	10	10	62	39
United Kingdom	4	4	82	77
Total	14	14 (100%)	144	119 (83%)

in Europe. However, the case studies do cover all the major activities currently known to be involved in telework schemes.

Despite our efforts to compensate for this in our sampling, typing and word processing tasks are still somewhat underrepresented. This is mainly due to the fact that those companies using telework for typing are often less than eager to publicise what they are doing, not least because of fears of union reaction.

A complete list of the companies involved in the survey is set out in Table 8.2. To our knowledge, this survey constitutes the most complete and detailed survey of teleworkers and teleworking companies anywhere in the world. It encompasses a broad range of the tasks which are generally considered suitable for being decentralised and reflects the diversity of the organisational forms which are involved in telework arrangements both in Europe and in the United States. Demographic characteristics can be found in Appendix B.

THE TELEWORK PROJECTS IN THE SURVEY

In the remainder of this chapter, we give thumbnail sketches of the 14 companies involved in our survey. Unless otherwise stated, all information in this section is derived from the questionnaires or from personal interviews with company personnel.

1. The United Kingdom

The Software Services Company

The FI Group, formerly known as F International, is a British consultancy and software house founded by Steve Shirley in 1962. Since its beginnings,

TABLE 8.2 *Companies involved in the case studies*

West Germany	United Kingdom
1. Consultancy company	1. Software services company
2. Accountancy services company	2. Computer manufacturer
3. Scheme for the disabled (programming)	3. Office equipment manufacturer
4. Phototypesetting company	4. Business information company
5. Insurance company	
6. Typesetting company	
7. Typing services company	
8. Scheme for the disabled (clerical work)	
9. Translation agency	
10. Research company	

the company has been distinguished from its competitors by a work system whereby the majority of its workforce, known as 'panel members', operate from home on a self-employed basis. It is characterised by 'its virtually ^'. female management and staff, and the charismatic leadership of its founder whose ideas still permeate the company's culture' (Franklin, 1986, p. 1). Over 25 years, the company has expanded steadily, rising—in terms of personnel— to over 1000 in 1985, of whom 261 were salaried and 817 self-employed. By that year, the company had developed into the 20th largest software house in Britain with annual sales of £7.5 million and an annual growth rate of 30 per cent.

Until recently, the FI group did not make much use of information technology for its own internal communications. Projects were largely co-ordinated and controlled by post and telephone, although in some cases clients installed on-line dial-up terminals and modems in the homes of the team members, to make it easier to test programs.

In 1984, the company underwent a major structural overhaul. As one commentator put it:

> Faced with the need for continued growth and with a changing industry that required new skills and centralised planning which would be difficult to achieve under the company's current decentralised structure, the FI Group's management realised it would have to make some changes in the company's organisational structure and bring in some outside managerial talent in areas which had formerly been the province of internally-grown managers. (Franklin, 1986, p. 1)

A new information systems manager was hired to draw up a strategy for upgrading the company's technological base and improve internal communications by means of an electronic mail network (Franklin, 1986, p. 7). The primary purpose of connecting panel members to this network was to make management more effective. However, it was also envisaged as a means of enabling work to be spread more evenly across regions. By the end of 1986, 125 of the group's 1100-odd workers were connected to this network via personal computers in their homes, but there was still some need for work on clients' premises.

According to its founder, the company was set up out of a desire to combine working with the care of her child, and a realisation that there were far more experienced female dp professionals prepared to work on this basis than conventional employers were prepared to use. The arrangement was seen as benefiting these women by enabling them not just to continue earning money without giving up their family responsibilities but also to continue developing their skills in an industry where an absence of more than one or two years would make it extremely difficult to return.

The present composition of the company's workforce suggests that this initial assessment of where the likely demand for this type of work would come from was largely correct. At the end of 1986, 96 per cent of the workforce were women, and over 90 per cent had children, while 82 per cent worked part-time, a proportion which rose to 90 per cent among the 'panel members', the self-employed teleworkers who made up 76 per cent of the company's workforce at the time.

The Computer Manufacturer

International Computers Ltd (ICL) is a wholly-owned subsidiary of STC plc, the European communications and information systems group, and specialises in providing integrated solutions to meet the information technology needs of specific markets. A major multinational with over 35,000 employees, STC has operations in 70 countries and a turnover in 1987 of £2 billion.

The ICL homeworking scheme was set up in 1969, at a time of skill shortages in programming, with the object of retaining the services of women programmers who had left their full-time, on-site work to have children. There are currently 300 women employed under this scheme, in two departments: Product Maintenance Sector (PMS), and CPS Professional Services (CPS). PMS has 90 home-based programmers who provide support for ICL software. CPS provides professional services internally to ICL, and externally to customers and third party distributors, employing 210 home-based systems analysts, designers, programmers, technical authors, project managers and consultants. It was the CPS unit which was chosen for inclusion in the Empirica survey and future references to the ICL telework scheme concern this group of workers.

About 50 per cent of these home-based workers are ex-ICL full-time employees who have transferred to PMS or CPS. The remainder previously worked for ICL's users, competitive manufacturers and their customers, or were freelance.

ICL homeworkers visit sites to varying degrees depending on the work they undertake. Site visits can range from once a month to four times a week. Most of these teleworkers are part-time, with a contracted number of weekly hours ranging from 16 to 37. The average working week is 21 hours.

In contrast with the FI group, all staff are full employees of ICL and are therefore entitled to the same company benefits as on-site colleagues working the same hours. Periods of time spent within the scheme are included in calculations of length of service, thus contributing towards holiday, pension, sickness and maternity leave and other service-related benefits. Hourly pay is the same as for other ICL staff doing the same work and there are opportunities for career progression.

Managers claim that staff training and updating is considered very important and distance learning techniques are used in addition to specially tailored courses. All staff who require a home terminal are provided with it by the company.

The Office Equipment Manufacturer

Rank Xerox International is a British company, of which 51 per cent is owned by its US parent, Rank Xerox. From its UK headquarters, the company controls 26 directly-owned operating companies in Europe and the third world, with distributors in another 40 countries. Until the late 1970s, it held a strong position in the photocopying equipment market, its main product until the mid 1970s. With the advent of competition from Japanese companies using advanced technologies, the company had to diversify into other office products: electronic typewriters, word processors, microcomputers, executive work stations and electronic network systems (Huws, 1984a; Judkins, West and Drew, 1985; Judkins and West, 1984; Empirica, ADR and the Tavistock Institute, 1986).

This company is undoubtedly the principal United Kingdom example of an organisation restructuring to operate with a peripheral workforce of sub-contractors, or, as they are called in this company, 'networkers', working at a distance with a telecommunications link to the Central London headquarters. So far, the experiment has not been extended beyond staff formerly based at the head office and is limited in scope.

With the primary aim of reducing overhead costs at the Central London office, the experiment began in 1982 with 21 'networkers', a number which grew slowly to reach 59 by the time of our survey in 1987. From the outset, it was decided that these teleworkers would be self-employed sub-contractors whose work for the parent company should be less than half their total turnover. Their work for this organisation should also involve the use in their homes of microcomputers manufactured by the company, communicating via telephone lines with a sophisticated local network, connecting microcomputers and executive work stations at the London headquarters.

This system has now been upgraded to provide a complex range of communications options which permit rapid and easy information interchange with remote electronic printing, a graphics capability, and high-volume photocopying. Experiments have also been carried out with other types of equipment—electronic typewriters with communicating capabilities, telecopiers and portable microcomputers (Judkins, West and Drew, 1985).

The underlying philosophy of the personnel department is that networkers should run independent small businesses, but also perform a substantial amount of work for their parent company. Tasks performed by the networkers from their homes as self-employed people cover a wide range of managerial and technical fields including finance, marketing, personnel and data-processing. To provide mutual support in setting up and sustaining these new businesses, an organisation called Xanadu was founded. All the networkers are members of Xanadu, which also acts as an information exchange and provides trading opportunities.

The Business Information Company

Fintech is part of FT Business Information, a subsidiary of the *Financial Times*. It was set up on a telework basis in 1984 and consists of a central office and four individual home-based workers, each of whom is a self-employed consulting editor, responsible for producing a twice-weekly newsletter in a specialist subject area relating to business uses of information technology. Two further Fintech editors work from their own offices, employing their own journalistic staff.

All six editors work on personal computers connected to the public telecommunications network which provides for the transmission of text and data to the central office where the publications are produced. They are also used for other purposes such as accessing and updating data bases.

2. West Germany

The Consultancy Company

INTEGRATA is a rapidly expanding German consultancy and software company. It was founded in 1964 and by 1985 it was the 6th largest software company in Germany with annual sales to a value of 42 million DM. The workforce expanded rapidly in the mid 1980s, from 121 in 1983 to 350 five years later. Most of these employees are involved in management consultancy, systems development, software development or training.

Telework at INTEGRATA began in a small way in 1983 when two women programmers, who would otherwise have stopped working altogether because of their desire to be at home with their children, were provided with personal computers and modems in their homes to enable them to communicate remotely with the company. In 1987, one of these two programmers was still in post, working part-time at home with full employee status, receiving the usual pay for this type of work in the company and entitled to the same holiday, sickness and other benefits as on-site colleagues.

In 1984, the company also set up a satellite office in Tübingen, to meet the requirements of one major client, an insurance company. This scheme was also still in operation at the time of our survey, with INTEGRATA reporting numerous advantages to the arrangement. The most obvious of these was that it was no longer necessary for workers to travel from other parts of Germany to carry out work on the client's premises. Instead, a specialist staff could be recruited locally and managed remotely. In addition, according to INTEGRATA management, there was improved motivation and productivity, an optimal retention of scarce skills and a greater capacity to cope with peaks in workload as a result of the existence of the satellite centre.

The Chartered Accountancy

RWG is a chartered accountancy company linked with co-operatives, mainly co-operative banks, by a telecommunications network. Each company within this network operates as an autonomous unit with RWG performing a central function by taking care of the interconnections between all the partners, ensuring a smooth flow of data and information, providing access to software requested by the members, developing new software packages when appropriate, providing access to a wide range of hardware located in their headquarters and developing software standards for co-operatives (Empirica, ADR and the Tavistock Institute, 1986).

Employment in RWG grew from 50 in 1967 to 223 in 1985 with a high proportion of young workers, 43 per cent being under 30 years of age (Geschäftsbereich, 1985, p. 31). Because of the nature of its work, RWG is a heavy user of information technology, communicating via a number of different telecommunications networks—the public telephone network (PSTN), the packet-switched network (PSDN), the Circuit-switched Data Network (CSDN), Digital leased lines (DLC) and videotex as well as internal networks. There was therefore an unusually good technological base for the introduction of telework.

Telework was first introduced into the organisation in 1983, when two highly qualified professional women left full-time work at the central office to have babies. Because it needed their scarce skills, RWG decided to re-employ them as part-time homeworkers under freelance contracts, using the PSTN for data transmission. Apart from this, they communicate with the organisation by telephone, letter and occasional meetings. In 1985, the telework scheme was expanded to five—all women involved in programming and software development. In each case, it was the birth of a child which triggered the change in employment status.

Insurance Company

This German-based company offers a wide range of insurance packages mainly aimed at the private individual. In 1985, the company employed a staff of

286 in its central office, 266 mobile insurance agents and 6500 part-time workers spread all over the country.

In 1978, the company equipped all its mobile insurance agents with portable terminals to allow for remote data entry, word processing, information retrieval, and accounting. The terminals are used by the insurance agents by connecting them via the telephone network to a central mainframe at the head office either from their own homes or directly from their customers'.

This strategy had a number of aims, the primary objective being to rationalise the field work, especially in relation to acquisition and customer service. By ensuring that data entry was carried out by the field force, there was also a saving on head-office staff time. Other advantages of the system were the fast information exchange it made possible between the central office and the scattered field staff, the ease with which data could be updated and an optimisation of data transmission costs. The agents found the terminals easy to operate and accepted them readily.

The Translation Agency

The translation agency was founded by a journalist and freelance translator who, in 1983, realised that his turnover and profits were rising steadily and that a point was rapidly approaching when he would have to increase his capacity to cope with his ever-expanding workload.

Until that time, he had been working primarily with conventional typewriters and making use of the services of a freelance secretary to help him out with the typing work. One of his regular customers had introduced a word processor in 1980 and encouraged him to work in his offices. This was advantageous for the customer because texts did not have to be retyped. However, by 1983, this customer, who had in the meantime purchased another four word processors and introduced teletex transmission, was no longer in a position to let the translator use the equipment during the daytime as it was needed by his own staff. At this point, the translator started thinking of opening his own office.

He therefore began considering the option of purchasing his own word processing system with teletex and, because it could not be installed in a private flat, of setting up an office. Such a step would enable him to offer his other customers texts prepared on a word processor, giving him a competitive advantage over his rivals. Texts would be clean and free of correction fluid, they could be translated and edited in the word processor thus saving time and rewriting costs, they could be transmitted to customers by teletex thus saving rewriting costs for the customer, and new markets could be tapped via teletex. At the time of our survey, the company's annual turnover was 100,000

DM and it employed ten freelance translators in addition to the founder and one other full-time employee.

In 1986, the company began to employ the translators as teleworkers, working from their homes using electronic typewriters and word processors. Besides translating texts, they also carry out typing, documentation and editing for the company's clients. At the time of our survey, there were plans to introduce electronic data and text transmission between their homes and the central office using acoustic couplers. This was principally to achieve compatibility between their personal computers and the system used in the office without incurring the expense of re-equipping all the teleworkers. This solution also opened up the possibility of communicating directly with clients by the same method. Figure 8.1 is a graphic illustration of communication patterns within the company.

The Typesetting Company

The photo typesetting company in our survey was established in 1972. Since it was set up, it has been almost entirely composed of self-employed people working from home. In 1987, when the company's turnover was 700,000 DM, there were 20 such freelances, together with four direct employees.

Most of the work is carried out on personal computers, using word processing software, although some work is still done on key-punch machines. The company does not transmit completed work electronically because of the high cost, but delivers it on floppy disk or punched tape.

The use of homeworkers is perceived by the company as a way of minimising costs in a highly competitive market. In contrast with the computer professionals in some other telework schemes, the housebound mothers who work for the company do not have scarce skills and see their work for the company as their only opportunity to earn.

The company cites several advantages to the arrangement. As well as saving on social benefits and tax payments because of the self-employed status of its staff, it has been able to avoid the high costs of central facilities which would occur if work were done in a central office. In addition, it claims that telework has made it easier to retain and recruit staff, reduced turnover and absenteeism and made it easier to deal with peaks in demand. Without the use of telework, there is some doubt whether the company could survive in such a competitive environment.

The Typing Services Company

The founder of this company set up as a freelance typist in 1971 and continued on her own until the early 1980s when, becoming aware of her steadily rising

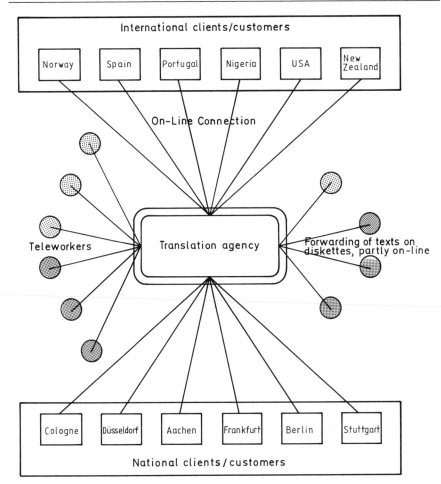

FIGURE 8.1 The translation agency

workload, she increased her capacity by employing an assistant on a freelance basis and introducing word processors. By 1982, expansion had been so rapid that she had taken on a further ten workers. By 1986, when annual turnover had risen to 200,000 DM, there were 18 people working regularly for the company, with up to 36 part-timers at peak times. Staff are almost exclusively part-time housewives working on a freelance basis, paid by piece-rates. All of them work from their homes.

The company uses 23 personal computers which have been specially adapted and modified for the company's purposes. So far, no PTT networks or services have been used. Data and text are stored on floppy disks and either sent by mail or delivered personally to the central office, to be forwarded to clients who are scattered all over West Germany.

The company is located in a rural area in the south of Germany where there are hardly any employment opportunities for women looking for part-time work. This factor has undoubtedly contributed to the success and stability of the enterprise which has been able to survive in a very competitive market. The fact that staff are freelance and home-based has enabled the company to achieve considerable savings in overhead expenses and in the cost of social benefits. Moreover, freelance work contracts with a piece-rate payment system permit a degree of flexibility which is seen by the company as particularly useful for dealing with fluctuations in workload.

The Photo Typesetting Company

The photo typesetting company, which was founded in 1930, carries out typing and photo typesetting for the production of magazines, journals, brochures, books and other printed materials. The work is carried out in a variety of ways: by employees based in the main company office; in decentralised service offices and sub-contracting companies; and by individual workers in their own homes, for the most part doing typing and word processing. With a turnover of 8 million DM, the company had, in 1987, 48 employees, 6 freelances and two sub-contracting offices working for it.

The company makes use of a variety of information technologies in its central office as well as in the decentralised units. It operates a mini computer system with two workstations and has 18 terminals connected to a Linotype host. The teleworkers operate either a personal computer or a remote terminal from their homes. Very little work is transferred electronically between the central office and the teleworkers or sub-contracting service offices and companies. The public telephone network is used routinely in only one instance: to receive about 100 pages of copy a day from a single regular client. Figure 8.2 illustrates the company's communication patterns in a graphic form.

The growth of telework within the company has been a gradual process stretching back to 1968 when it was introduced to retain the services of former key-punch operators who had left to have children. Equipment of the type they were used to was installed in their homes and they continued as part-time homeworkers. Today almost all home-based workers work with either a personal computer or a terminal.

Management cite other advantages of the telework arrangement: it makes it easier to cope with peaks in workload; it has reduced the costs of long-term employee welfare; it has facilitated rationalisation within the office; and it has led to reductions in central facilities and overhead expenses. However, not all

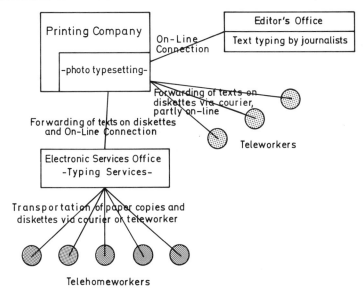

FIGURE 8.2   The printing company

work is regarded as suitable for being carried out by homeworkers. About 40 per cent of the company's work will, it is thought, continue to be carried out in-house because it contains complicated tables or formulae, because the amount of text is too small or because deadlines are too tight.

In the future, the company expects to receive an increasing amount of copy from its clients already keyed in, either transmitted electronically over the PTT network or on floppy disk or tape.

The Programming Scheme for the Disabled

This programming scheme is run by a limited company which provides sheltered work and more advanced employment options for people with disabilities. It is one of four associated companies established by a single foundation. The other three companies are involved in such varied activities as data entry, graphics services, the production of rehabilitation tools, office services, crafts, and home economics.

The activities now carried out under the programming scheme originated in 1971, when SIEMENS AG offered computer programming work to a number of suitably qualified handicapped residents of the foundation's rehabilitation centre. As contracts and the amount of work had steadily increased, it was decided in 1973 to establish a limited company.

The idea of the scheme is to offer employment and training options to physically handicapped people by means of telework. All handicapped people employed under the scheme live and work on the same site so commuting problems are not a constraining factor. They are all salaried staff, employees of the company.

A certain minimum level of qualifications and skills is a condition of employment in the scheme. Most of the employees were employed in skilled occupations before becoming disabled by illness or accident and have since been trained to become computer programmers in a special 18–36-month training course.

In 1987, the company employed 89 workers, primarily on software development for mainframes or personal computers. Annual turnover was just under 6 million DM and clients included many large companies in banking and manufacturing including SIEMENS, BMW and the Bavarian Bank, Bayerische Sparkassen und Giroverband.

Such has been the success of the scheme that the company has now established two additional offices in other parts of the country, offering the same spectrum of services. At the time of our survey, these employed thirteen workers between them.

All three offices in the scheme can be described as electronic services offices, being independent firms which carry out data processing and certain other computer-related services for other companies from a distance. It was the largest and longest established office which was selected for inclusion in our survey. Here, access to client computers is primarily gained via the Public Data Network for Fixed Connections (HfD) which offers dedicated digital lines between two units. Only minor use is made of the Public Switched Telephone Network.

The Clerical Scheme for the Disabled

Like the programming scheme for disabled people, the clerical scheme was set up by an association which was already running a workshop for people with disabilities. It was established in 1969 with the object of providing vocational training, useful employment options, medical treatment, and social integration and contacts for 700 disabled people.

In a special unit of the workshop, 40 severely disabled people are employed in a telework arrangement which can be described as an electronic services office. This unit carries out data entry, typing, word processing and some computer programming for a wide range of clients in the area.

The idea of the scheme is to use telework as a means of offering employment and training to people with physical disabilities. These employees either live and work on the site or commute to it daily. Recruitment is restricted to the immediate locality, so commuting distances are short. Nevertheless, the journey to work is still a problem for some of the disabled people in the scheme.

The unit makes use of a variety of equipment. Most workers use terminals, some of which are connected to hosts on the clients' premises via a modem. In other cases, work is carried out on stand-alone electronic typewriters. Considerable use is also made of videotex. However, the most usual arrangement is still for work to be entered from handwritten originals and stored and delivered on floppy disk.

The Research Company

The research company's field is social and economic science. It operates in an international market, providing research and consultancy services to national and international organisations, many of them in the public sector. The company was founded in 1977 and now has 16 employees, the majority of whom are graduate social and economic scientists. Reflecting the international nature of the company's activities, the employees are of many nationalities—including German, British, Irish, Italian, Greek, French and United States Citizens.

In 1986, the research company set up a telework scheme to enable one newly recruited senior researcher to work part of the time from a home base. The management saw this arrangement as an opportunity to recruit qualified staff whose skills would otherwise not be available. This teleworker lives some 200 km from the main office site and works on average three days a week at home and two days a week in the central office.

The advantages of the arrangement were soon realised and the scheme was subsequently expanded to include another senior researcher working part of the time from home. Both are full-time employees, and are equipped with a personal computer in their homes. At the time of the survey, PTT networks and services were hardly ever used as a means of data and text transmission between the teleworker and the central office, though acoustic couplers were used to some extent. Texts were usually stored on floppy disks and carried to and from the central office by the teleworkers in person. Earlier, the company had experimentally used a packet-switched link to the EEC EUROKOM electronic mail system, but had stopped doing so because of its high costs. It was hoped that this might change in the future with the introduction and implementation of ISDN.

In addition, the company was considering expanding the scope of its telework scheme further, to allow more of its research staff to work at home on alternate days. Apart from accommodating employees' wishes, this was seen as a way of avoiding the many distractions and disruptions of the central office environment.

Chapter 9

THE EMPIRICA TELEWORK SURVEY—II. RESULTS OF THE SURVEY

In Chapter 7 we looked at the range of tasks carried out in the telework schemes described in the literature on the subject. We were interested to find out the extent to which the schemes in our survey reflected this range, feeling that this would be one measure of the representativeness of our survey. As can be seen from Table 9.1, the survey managed to capture quite a diverse range of tasks. The table shows the number of organisations with teleworkers performing each task, the total number of teleworkers involved in each of the tasks and the number of teleworkers performing each task covered by the survey. Of course the representativeness of this sample of teleworkers cannot be determined in any absolute way because definitive information on the total population of teleworkers and the tasks they perform is not currently available.

Table 9.2 shows the age and sex structure of the teleworkers sampled. As can be seen, the majority, 72 per cent, are women, mostly concentrated in the 30–40 age range. It is also in this age group that the highest proportion of male teleworkers is to be found. Teleworking men are also present, in

TABLE 9.1 Telework schemes and teleworkers studied by task

| Major tasks performed in telework | Organisations *n* | Teleworkers | | Sampling fraction % |
		Total *n*	Sample *n*	
1. Computer programming (incl. dp-project managers)	5	867	77	8.9
2. Typing and word processing	3	49	7	14.3
3. Clerical work	1	40	4	10.0
4. Translating	1	10	2	20.0
5. Consultancy and research	2	60	12	20.0
6. Writing and editing (journalists and technical authors)	1	65	7	10.8
7. Sales/Business professionals	1	290	9	3.1
8. Other			1	
Total	14	1 282	119	9.3

TABLE 9.2   Age and sex structure of teleworker sample

Count	<30 years	30–40 years	40–50 years	>50 years	Row total
Male	7	13	8	3	31
	22.6	41.9	25.8	9.7	27.4
Female	11	53	17	1	82
	13.4	64.6	20.7	1.2	72.6
Column total	18	66	25	4	113
	15.9	58.4	22.1	3.5	100.0

slightly higher proportions than women, in both older and younger age groups. For both sexes, teleworking is rare in the over-50 age group. Despite the large cluster of women in mid-career, this is obviously not a homogenous group in age or gender.

HOW TELEWORK WAS INTRODUCED

One of the questions which interested us most about our sample was how and why they had become teleworkers. This is of course a question with two sides, that of the employer and the employee, since telework can only take place when there is sufficient convergence of interest for both parties to agree to it.

We turn first to the employers' side. There is in fact a wide range of reasons companies might have for considering the introduction of remote work. Most of the research which has so far been carried out in this area has been in the United States, where Gil Gordon, a telework consultant, identified eight common motivations: improved recruitment; improved retention of staff; curiosity to experiment; space savings; hiring the disabled employee; increased productivity; response to demand from employees; and the need to improve customer services (Gordon, 1988).

Edwards and Edwards suggest that employers' motivation can be condensed into four broad categories: to reduce turnover and retain valued employees; to overcome staff shortages; to keep growth up and costs down; and to increase productivity (Edwards and Edwards, 1985). Olson, referring again exclusively to the USA, states that 'organisational interest in telework experiments is spurred primarily by short-term needs and the most pressing need is to attract and/or retain qualified employees' (Olson, 1987). She also considers that the desire to improve productivity is an important incentive for some employers while others are motivated simply by faddism.

When designing our survey, we felt that it would be interesting to find out whether these conclusions were valid in a European context. We also wanted to discover the relative importance of these different motivations. Table 9.3 summarises our findings in this respect, giving for each possible reason the proportion of managers who found it important when setting up their own telework schemes. As can be seen from the table, two factors emerged as clear front-runners among most managers' stated reasons for introducing telework: an improved ability to cope with work peaks; and the retention and recruitment of scarce skills.

Three other motivations were also described as important by many managers: the reduction of employee turnover; the opportunity for staff to combine work and child care; and improved staff motivation and productivity. Next in importance, cited by about a third of the managers, were a reduction in central office and overhead costs; flexibility in working hours and a reduction in commuting. Despite the inclusion in the sample of a number of schemes involved with software production and despite numerous mentions

TABLE 9.3   Organisations' reasons for introducing telework

	Unimportant reason and n.a.	Important reason	Rank order
• Reduction in central facilities costs and overhead expenses	10	4	3
• Off-peak utilisation of the computer	14	—	7
• Improved motivation and increased productivity of employees	9	5	2
• Retention and recruitment of scarce skills	8	6	1
• Reduction of employee turnover and absenteeism generally	9	5	2
• Improved coping with surplus work (work peaks)	8	6	1
• Flexibility in determining conditions laid down in work contract	13	1	6
• Reduced costs for long-term employee welfare	12	2	5
• Rationalisation effort	11	3	4
• Flexibility in location of work	12	2	5
• Flexibility in working hours	10	4	3
• Skill upgrading of employees	11	3	4
• Possibility for employee to combine work and non-work activities (e.g. child care)	9	5	2
• Reduced commuting efforts and costs for employees	10	4	3
• Employment of the disabled	12	2	5

in the literature, savings due to off-peak use of a computer did not feature at all among the important reasons for introducing telework schemes.

In addition to these reasons, elicited from the management questionnaires, interviews with the managers uncovered some other motives for adopting telework. Some of these have more limited applicability than those given above but, for the schemes they refer to, were critical in the decision to take up telework. They include: the opportunity to increase a company's capacity at minimal expense; the opportunity to set up a new business; and the possibility of creating employment opportunities for disabled people.

There are two criteria on which the importance of motivating factors can be judged: firstly, how widespread the factor is, in other words, to how many organisations and teleworking schemes it applies; and secondly, how critical a given reason is for the decision to adopt telework. The results of our survey suggest that attempts to summarise the main reasons for the introduction of telework too schematically may unwittingly conceal considerable and important variations between different types of organisation.

One important variable is the extent to which the telework arrangement represents a physical relocation of an existing job. The literature on the subject often focuses exclusively on internally-led changes in the work organisation of existing companies. However, our survey found that a major factor in the generation of new telework schemes is in fact external, arising from new business-creation initiatives by individual entrepreneurs or organisations concerned with employment creation for disadvantaged groups.

Another variable is the type of work involved. A detailed breakdown of the reasons given for introducing telework on a case-by-case basis (which is presented in Appendix C of this book) shows a systematic coupling of certain motivations with particular types of activity. In the software development sector, for instance, the companies which decentralised computer programming did so in the main in order to retain the scarce skills of people who could not work in a conventional office environment. Some of these companies also thought that telework was a good way of offering greater autonomy to staff who wanted more control over their work. An added incentive for introducing telework in many of these software companies was the potential for reducing office overhead costs. Indeed, in some cases this was a major reason for adopting it.

By contrast, companies decentralising typing and word processing tasks (and to some extent clerical work) seemed mainly to be aiming at the minimisation of costs, including the expense of office space and other overheads (e.g. social benefits). Only to a minor extent did these companies adopt telework in order to retain qualified and experienced workers who otherwise would not be able to continue working for the company because of new domestic commitments. However, some of our management interviewees in this sector did also mention the chance to set up their own business as an important reason for taking up telework.

The research and consultancy companies formed another distinct group. Here, an important criterion was the requirement to meet people's needs to regulate their own work. The same holds true for the companies employing journalists and writers remotely and the insurance companies with their mobile insurance agents. The latter also valued the ability to free their workers from the need to be tied to any particular geographical spot.

For the research company, the need to recruit staff with scarce skills was the most important reason for embarking on telework. However, the consultancy company placed the need for reducing high overheads, especially costs for office space in its central location, as its foremost priority.

The translation agency's motivation was different again. This company stated that its foremost reason was to increase company capacity while at the same time incurring minimal fixed costs, either in the form of overheads or in employees' social benefits.

There is a split in the reasons given by the companies along a line separating schemes involving tasks requiring high qualifications from those involving more routine tasks. Managers responsible for the former give the highest ratings to such reasons as improved ability to cope with work peaks, general rationalisation, and reduction of employee turnover. Nevertheless, they are also aware of telework's advantages in allowing work and non-work activities to be combined and enabling flexible hours to be worked.

On the other hand, companies involved in consultancy work or providing programming services mention as their foremost reasons the retention and recruitment of scarce skills, the improved motivation and increased productivity of their staff, and improved ability to cope with varying workloads.

Having looked at management reasons for adopting telework, we now turn to the reasons why the teleworkers themselves have chosen to work in this way. Because, on the whole, the situation is one in which teleworkers have less power than their managers, one would expect that in most cases the only role which workers could play in the decision would be the negative one of refusing to work in this way. Our survey therefore investigated the extent to which teleworkers were involved in decision making about the setting up of the scheme. As we expected, the majority—73 per cent—were not involved at all, but the teleworkers did have some involvement in 16 per cent of cases and had played a major role in 10 per cent. Given that in many cases the teleworkers in our survey were not even in post at the time when their scheme was set up, the fact that in over a quarter of cases there was some degree of worker involvement in the initiative is surprising. This unexpectedly high involvement of staff in the reorganisation of their own work does not seem to be so much a measure of enlightened management practice as an indication that would-be teleworkers themselves have been the initiators of many schemes, possibly in the face of initial management opposition.

One source of information which can throw some light on teleworkers' motivation for taking up remote work is their own immediate work history. Table 9.4 summarises the changes made by each teleworker in the sample when becoming a teleworker. It can be seen that nearly a third of the respondents had moved into a remote work arrangement while remaining with the same employer. Whereas over a quarter had changed neither company nor job to take up telework, some 6 per cent had changed their job in order to continue working for the same organisation as teleworkers. Slightly fewer teleworkers—under 30 per cent—had changed their organisation to take up telework. However, a higher proportion of these had also experienced a change of job—some 18 per cent of all the teleworkers.

The growing maturity of telework as a form of work organisation can be seen from the fact that over 10 per cent of the teleworkers surveyed had changed their employer while remaining in a telework situation. The fact that most of these changed employer without changing their job indicates the development of a job market within telework. As yet, few companies practise telework so that a teleworker wanting to continue in a telework arrangement has little choice. Seen against this background, these movements between employers can be interpreted as a sign of the greater locational independence of teleworkers' organisational choice. A rival employer's location plays a smaller role in the decision to change job than it would for an on-site worker because a move to a further or more awkwardly-suited company need not necessarily bring with it a change of residence or a complicated or lengthy journey to work.

A further source of information about the motivation to switch to telework comes from an examination of how the previous work arrangement came to an end. Our teleworker questionnaire included a question on this subject, and Table 9.5 shows the results. This gives us a picture of a situation in which in a majority of cases the circumstances of the individual worker have created a clear demand for a change in the form of work. In four out of five of these cases, the precipitating factor has been the birth of a child. Since many people are forced to move house to take up a new job, citing moving house as a reason for having to change job suggests that the person concerned is not the

TABLE 9.4   *Teleworkers' immediate work history: changes from previous work arrangement (per cent of teleworkers)*

Change of location:	no	no	no	no	yes	yes	yes	yes
Change of company:	no	no	yes	yes	no	no	yes	yes
Change of job:	no	yes	no	yes	no	yes	no	yes
$n = 119$:	—	26.1	11.8	1.7	26.9	5.9	10.1	17.6

TABLE 9.5   Threats to the continuation of the teleworker's previous
work arrangement (per cent of teleworkers)

Pregnancy/child-birth	36.1
—in conjunction with moving house	6.7
Moving house	5.0
Redundancy	6.7
None of these threats/n.a.	45.4

main earner in the household. However, there is a very substantial minority
(45 per cent) of cases where the decision to become a teleworker appears to
have arisen from other causes.

To arrive at an assessment of what these causes might have been, it is
necessary to turn to other methods. The most obvious would appear to be to
ask a direct question. However, this was regarded as problematic since it is often
extremely difficult for people to reconstruct their motivation retrospectively,
especially when this involves recalling their state of mind some years into the
past. Our sample of teleworkers had mostly been working in this way for a
considerable length of time, with over half having notched up more than five
years' experience, and only 8 per cent having been working remotely for less
than a year.

ADVANTAGES AND DISADVANTAGES OF TELEWORK

Rather than attempt a retrospective reconstruction of original motivation, we
decided to enquire into the advantages and disadvantages of telework as
perceived by the individual teleworkers at the time of the survey. The
assumption can reasonably be made in most cases that the majority of
teleworkers had some inkling of the advantages and disadvantages of the
arrangement before becoming involved in the scheme. Whether or not their
evaluation of these features has remained static is an open question. The
investigation of advantages and disadvantages perceived at present is not only
relevant for an examination of initial motivation but also for an analysis of
the later, operational phase of telework since these perceptions have a direct
bearing on whether, given the choice, teleworkers will continue in or abandon
a remote working arrangement.

In drawing up the section of the questionnaire which dealt with advantages
and disadvantages, we drew on the results of past surveys in this area. A
major source of informaton on the US situation was Olson (Olson, 1987,
1983, 1985a,b; Diebold Group, 1981). She identified a list of five common
motivations for telework: the need for flexibility; the desire for autonomy; the

avoidance of commuting hassles; limited alternative work options; and lifestyle demands. To these, we added a number of other factors, both positive and negative, including some based on responses to open-ended questions in the Huws survey of telework in the UK (Huws, 1984a).

Because people's situations differ—teleworkers are by no means a homogenous group—some advantages and disadvantages only apply as such to a subgroup. For instance, the opportunity to combine work with child care, either for someone with no children or for someone working in a satellite work centre, is neither an advantage nor a disadvantage but simply irrelevant. Similarly, the absence of office-type distractions at home might be welcomed by a homeworker whose work requires long bouts of concentrated effort, but disliked by someone carrying out routine work who craves the company of colleagues.

In our survey, respondents were asked to compare their present telework arrangement with equivalent work at fixed times in an office. For those who considered themselves unable to work under these conditions, perhaps because of child-care commitments, this comparison does not represent motivation related to possible choice. However, the majority did seem to find the comparison realistic, stating that if it were not possible for them to continue as teleworkers, they would take up 'normal' employment rather than no work. So for most respondents the comparison did appear to be realistic in the sense that it represented choices they believed to be open to them. The results demonstrate that the top advantage of telework as practised today is the ability to combine care of children or other dependents with work. This is cited as a very important advantage by nearly six out of ten of the sample. The worst drawback, experienced as a disadvantage by more than four teleworkers out of ten, is the lack of benefits, perks and a pensions scheme. The total picture is extremely complex, so, to illuminate it, we carried out a factor analysis, the results of which appear in Appendix D. This was to help us to establish whether particular types of teleworker could be identified with their own distinctive patterns of motivation, satisfaction and dissatisfaction. From this analysis, not unexpectedly, flexibility and child care emerged as particularly important. For over half of the teleworkers each of these items is a positive advantage.

A very few, mostly male, teleworkers say that the presence of children is a disadvantage of remote work. They find that the demands of caring for children interfere with their working commitments. It is perhaps not surprising that child care and flexibility of working time are evaluated differently by the sexes. Whereas female teleworkers with children seldom rate the advantages as less than 'very important', few males rate the child-care opportunities as more than 'important'. Table 9.6 gives a detailed breakdown of responses to this question by sex.

TABLE 9.6 *Child-care advantages of telework by sex of teleworker (per cent of teleworker sample)*

| | Disadvantage | | | Advantage | | |
	(−−)	(−)	Neutral(0)	(+)	(++)	n.a.
Male	6.7	3.3	10.0	23.3	6.7	50.0
Female		1.2	4.7	5.9	74.1	14.1
Total	1.7	1.7	6.1	10.4	56.5	23.5

It is clear that a typical home-based teleworker who has taken up the arrangement for child-care reasons will give high scores to the family-related items—the ability to combine care of children or other dependents with work, the ability to meet family demands and the amount of time it is possible to spend with the family. The other two items associated with it in our analysis—the ability to combine other activities with work and the ability to work when it suits the teleworker—are characteristic of many flexible work arrangements, and can be enjoyed independently of child-care responsibilities. Nevertheless, the evidence from the survey is that these particular potential advantages of flexible working are generally seen as much more beneficial when child-care responsibilities are present.

Typists and dp professionals were the two occupational groups most likely to rate child care and flexibility as important advantages, not surprisingly, as these groups contained the largest number of women and the highest proportion of households with small children.

Career development, skill development, status with colleagues, promotion prospects and contacts with colleagues were all found to be associated with each other. On balance, telework seems to be a positive environment for skill development because this was cited as an advantage more often than a disadvantage. However, for promotion prospects the opposite is true. Lack of contact with professional colleagues is also generally seen as a disadvantage of telework. It is interesting that this particular communication problem is not identified with social isolation, but is clearly linked to career development.

Also correlated were the development of entrepreneurial skills and self-employment. Over a third of teleworkers do not see opportunities to set up their own business as relevant to them. However, of those who do, most think that telework offers advantages over more conventional working arrangements. Those who are positively inclined to the small business potential of their telework also, not surprisingly, see self-employed status as a positive attribute. For others, however, self-employment is perceived as a disadvantage.

Orientation to the advantages of telework in setting up an independent business is coupled with a tendency to regard contact with colleagues as less important, or at least not a disadvantage of telework, and this applies equally whether this contact is in a social or a professional capacity. There are two possible ways of interpreting this. Either the entrepreneurially minded teleworkers we are dealing with here have genuinely low needs for social contact or they are already having them met satisfactorily, perhaps because the nature of their work involves a higher amount of personal contact than other types of telework.

Though the differing perception of self-employed status among the occupational groups is not statistically significant, the direction conforms to expectations: typists on the whole tend to find the status a disadvantage; while professionals other than those involved in data processing occupations have the most positive view of it. This is broadly consistent with the order on the item referring to developing business skills suitable for a business start-up: here other professionals consistently see more advantage in telework than do either dp professionals or typists.

Pay is an important consideration for most teleworkers. Though a minority think that the pay they are receiving is an advantage of their work situation—and here we have to do with the high-earning networkers of the office equipment manufacturer—over 40 per cent think that they are earning less than they would in an office-based job. However, a good third of the sample are neutral about their pay level suggesting either that they do not care or that they believe they are getting the rate for the job.

Typists are the occupational group who generally perceive telework as bringing them pay advantages over conventional employment. The professionals other than those involved in data processing are ambivalent as a group, whereas most of the data processing professionals feel that their current levels of pay are a disadvantage of telework.

Benefits, perks and pensions are sometimes traded off against pay. However, over 40 per cent of teleworkers in our sample consider their 'benefits, perks and pension scheme' to be inferior to what they could expect in more traditional employment and hence a disadvantage. Of these, nearly half say that they represent a very important disadvantage—a higher proportion than for any other item although, as with pay, there is a minority for whom telework offers a better package of benefits than on-site work. However, there is little evidence that this has led to any great interest in trade union organisation. This may be because a high proportion of the sample are professionals, a group with a relatively low level of organisation, who may feel that it is not relevant to their situation. Of the few who feel that union organisation is an advantage of their situation, most work in electronic service offices rather than at home.

Self-employment is considered by nearly one-third of teleworkers to be an advantage. Of course this is not a relevant factor for teleworkers with employee status, but of those who are self-employed, very few say they find this status as such to be a disadvantage. However, many have decidedly negative attitudes to the employment conditions with which the status is often associated. Nearly half the teleworkers find a lack of office services such as copying facilities a disadvantage of their working arrangement, and quite a number of these consider this to be a very important disadvantage. There appears to be some connection between missing the services an office supplies with missing the people who supply them: 30 per cent of the sample regretted the loss of office social life to a greater or lesser extent.

The next two items are closely connected. They concern the difficulty of separating work and leisure, and the need for self-discipline. The former is experienced particularly strongly in home-based work and is obviously a significant problem, given that some 40 per cent of teleworkers see this as a disadvantage, including some who do not work from home. It should be mentioned here that, although most teleworkers work part-time, there is a sub-group with extremely long working hours, for whom work pressures encroach on leisure rather than the other way round. The latter, self-discipline, is thought by relatively few to be either an advantage or a disadvantage of their work arrangement. This suggests that the problem is not a straightforward one of allocating time for work. Rather, it appears to be connected with difficulty in fending off demands from friends, neighbours and family. This factor is associated with high ratings both for frequency of work interruptions and for ability to combine other activities with work.

Typists as a group see considerable advantages in their ability to mix work and leisure, but the opposite is true of most professionals, who see this as a disadvantage of telework presumably because of their greater need for concentration.

PLACE OF WORK

All but three of the telework schemes in our survey involved workers based either full-time or part-time in their own homes. In some cases this formed part of a flexible work arrangement which included work in other locations: their employers' offices; the offices of clients; or—in the case of sales staff—customers' homes.

Nevertheless, three-quarters of the teleworkers in the sample spent at least half of their working time at home and over a quarter—the typists, word processor operators and translators—worked exclusively at home. If schemes for the disabled are excluded, the proportion of teleworkers working exclusively at home rises to almost 50 per cent.

RECRUITMENT

According to managers, most recruitment of teleworkers was carried out either internally from existing office-based staff or, in the case of low-skilled clerical staff, externally from the local labour market. Wider external recruitment was very rare indeed.

The justification for internal recruitment was the need for proven loyalty to the organisation before an individual could be entrusted with the self-direction required in remote work. In the case of the office equipment manufacturer, the scheme had been set up with the express purpose of cutting down on centrally employed staff, so new recruitment would have been self-defeating.

In no scheme did we find such a complete reliance on telecommunications that location was immaterial when staff were recruited; all schemes continue to rely on some level of direct interpersonal contact. In the cases where recruitment was limited neither to current employees nor to the locality of the parent organisation, either the would-be teleworker was required to move closer to the parent organisation, as in traditional situations, or the recruitment was limited to regions where the parent organisation had, or intended to set up, a local management infrastructure.

An open question to managers about selection criteria yielded the following specifications, after task specific qualifications had been excluded:

- at least four years previous industry experience (software services organisation, computer manufacturer)
- particularly high level of qualification (consultancy, research organisation, business information company)
- self-sufficiency, self-motivation (computer manufacturer, research organisation)
- highly entrepreneurial perspective (office equipment manufacturer)
- flexibility (consultancy)
- reliability (word processing, typing schemes)
- disablement and unemployment (schemes for the disabled)
- ownership of a PC (translation agency)
- technical competence (computer manufacturer)
- ability to handle portable IT equipment (insurance company).

In general, it seems to be the case that managers are reluctant to take on teleworkers for complex tasks without good qualifications and considerable previous experience. One reason for this is the difficulty of providing training in scattered work locations. Also, isolated work clearly requires a measure of self-motivation and self-sufficiency. These qualities are less important in the less skilled jobs, where the emphasis is more on reliability.

Entrepreneurial drive is a more ambiguous advantage. In the case of the office equipment manufacturer it was a requirement for the job because the intention was to launch the individual teleworkers as directors of their own independent businesses. In other schemes, however, managers were wary of employing people with too much independent initiative, suspecting that in a remote and loosely supervised context it might lead to disloyalty.

INVOLVEMENT IN THE INTRODUCTION OF TELEWORK

Where schemes had been set up by existing organisations, this had almost always been with the involvement of top management. The only exception was the business information company where department heads had only been involved in some cases. Managers do not disguise the fact that in the majority of schemes, individuals now teleworking played at least some role in their initiation. As already noted, in a number of cases teleworkers themselves report having had a part, in some cases a major part, to play in the introduction of remote work.

Notable exceptions to this high involvement of teleworkers in the birth of the work arrangements which affect them are the typesetting, word processing and data entry companies. This is another example of the necessity of distinguishing telework schemes by the availability of the skills the teleworkers are using: where there is a ready supply of such skills, the setting up of the scheme is likely to precede the recruitment of staff. Where skills are scarce, the opposite is likely to be the case.

Union participation in the initiation of the telework projects was very rare. Only in one scheme—the computer manufacturer—did managers report union involvement prior to or during the introductory phase.

The pattern which emerges with regard to the subsequent planning of the projects is very similar. Here again the major factors are—according to reporting managers—on the one hand the top management of an organisation and on the other, with the exception as before of low-skill telework schemes, the teleworkers themselves. Trade union influence has been negligible and only in two schemes, both connected with the employment of people with disabilities, have the statutory authorities played an important role in the initiation and subsequent planning of a telework project.

SKILLS AND QUALIFICATIONS

As can be seen from Table 9.7, over 70 per cent of the teleworkers in our sample possess qualifications high enough for university admission and, in many cases, considerably higher, making them much better qualified than the average group of workers. However, this picture might well have been different had lower-skilled jobs, such as typing and data entry, not been underrepresented.

Another way in which the sample differs from the working population as a whole is in the fact that it is the women who are more likely to be highly

TABLE 9.7 Educational qualifications of teleworkers

		Low	Medium	High	Row total
Male	*n*	4	10	17	31
	%	12.9	32.3	54.8	26.7
Female	*n*	5	14	66	85
	%	5.9	16.5	77.6	73.3
AGE					
<30 years	*n*	1	6	11	18
	%	5.6	33.3	61.1	15.5
30–40 years	*n*	4	13	52	69
	%	5.8	18.8	75.4	59.5
40–50 years	*n*	2	6	17	25
	%	8.0	24.0	68.0	21.6
>50 years	*n*			4	4
	%			100.0	3.4
Column total	*n*	7	25	84	116
	%	6.0	21.6	72.4	100.0

qualified, whereas among employed people generally, men have on average a higher level of educational qualifications. This suggests that telework arrangements are attracting a particularly high proportion of well-qualified women.

The relationship between age and qualificational level shows an even distribution. There is no sign of the general decrease in qualification level with increasing age which exists in the population at large. Clearly, a particularly low proportion of older and poorly qualified people take up telework. This fits the general picture of telework being an innovative way of working, most likely to be taken up by younger and better educated people, with education and age playing a mutually reinforcing role. It is worth noting that all the over-50s in the sample had high qualifications.

Table 9.8 shows the distribution of qualifications for all teleworkers in each of the schemes in the sample. As would be expected, the qualification level in a telework scheme is related to the task performed. Where word processing or other simple keyboard work is carried out, more than 80 per cent of the teleworkers have low or medium qualifications. This contrasts with a 5 per cent proportion of low-skilled staff in companies whose remote workers are mainly doing programming. Table 9.9 shows the same sort of correlation between occupation and skill level among teleworkers as would be expected in a comparable group of office-based workers.

TABLE 9.8   *Educational qualifications of all teleworkers employed by organisations in the survey*

Company	Low[a]	Medium[b]	High[c]	Very high[d]
1. Software services co.	—	15	348	500
2. Computer manufacturer	1	2	47	110
3. Consultancy	—	—	—	7
4. Accountancy services	—	3	2	—
5. Scheme for the disabled (programming)	33	39	8	12
6. Printing company	3	3	—	—
7. Typesetting company	15	—	—	—
8. Typing services	30	6	—	—
9. Scheme for the disabled (clerical work)	30	5	3	2
10. Translation agency	—	—	—	10
11. Research company	—	—	—	2
12. Office equipment manufacturer	—	—	2	57
13. Business information company	—	—	—	6
14. Insurance company	127	118	20	25
Total	239	191	430	731

[a] 1 CSE and lower/Hauptschule
[b] 1 GCE 'O'-level/Realschule
[c] GCE 'A'-level/Abitur
[d] 1 BA/BSc degree, higher qualifications/Fachhochschul- und Hochschulabschuss.

TABLE 9.9   *Educational qualifications and task of teleworkers in the sample*

		Dp prof.	Typist	Other professional	Other	Row total
EDUCATION						
Low	n	4	2	1	2	9
	%	44.4	22.2	11.1	22.2	7.6
Medium	n	11	5	7	2	25
	%	44.0	20.0	28.0	8.0	21.0
High	n	62		22	1	85
	%	72.9		25.9	1.2	71.4
Column total	n	77	7	30	5	119
	%	64.7	5.9	25.2	4.2	100.0

OCCUPATION

Table 9.10 shows the occupations of all the teleworkers in the schemes sampled. Most of these occupations clearly fall into the 'output mode' category generally regarded as suitable for decentralisation. However, there is one exception: the group of 116 professional managers. This is an occupation which is generally thought to require frequent face-to-face contact. However, managers make up a surprisingly high 7 per cent of the teleworkers working for our sample companies. This is largely explained by the view, common in the larger schemes, that the most effective management of teleworkers is by people who have first-hand experience of telework themselves and can empathise with the people they are supervising. Thus many of the managers in these schemes work in flexible work arrangements, based sometimes at home, and sometimes in the various other locations where their distributed workforce is to be found. A few of the teleworker-managers are in charge of electronic service offices rather than being home-based, while some, particularly the 'networkers' working for the office equipment manufacturer, are in fact running their own businesses.

Not surprisingly, there are differences in the age and sex structure of teleworkers according to the type of task being performed in telework. In particular, in companies carrying out consultancy, research work or insurance sales, the majority of teleworkers are male and between 39 and 50 years of age. Table 9.11 shows task-related differences by sex and age. As is the case in conventional offices, typing is performed mainly by women. However, in conventional offices the majority of programmers and other data processing professionals are male, yet almost 90 per cent of the teleworking dp professionals

TABLE 9.10   Occupations found in telework

| | Teleworkers | |
Occupation	*n*	%
1. Dp professional	920	57.6
2. Sales	320	20.0
3. Secretary, typist	124	7.8
4. Manager	116	7.3
5. Clerical worker	39	2.4
6. Journalist/technical author	36	2.3
7. Business professional	23	1.4
8. Academic	11	0.7
9. Production and service worker	5	0.3
10. Scientist/engineer	2	0.1
11. Health/medical worker	2	0.1

TABLE 9.11 Sex, age and task of teleworkers

		Dp prof.	Typist	Other professional	Other	Row total
Male	n	10		20	1	31
	%	32.3		64.5	3.2	26.7
Female	n	65	6	10	4	85
	%	76.5	7.1	11.8	4.7	73.3
AGE						
<30 years	n	13	1	3	1	18
	%	72.2	5.6	16.7	5.6	15.5
30–40 years	n	47	3	17	2	69
	%	68.1	4.3	24.6	2.9	59.5
40–50 years	n	15	2	7	1	25
	%	60.0	8.0	28.0	4.0	21.6
>50 years	n	1		3		4
	%	25.0		75.0		3.4
Column total	n	76	6	30	4	116
	%	65.5	5.2	25.9	3.4	100.0

are female. In contrast to this, the overall majority of the other professionals is male.

USE OF INFORMATION TECHNOLOGY

We have already outlined, in the last chapter, the types of hardware and telecommunications systems in use in the companies in our survey. This information is summarised in table form in Appendix E. Here we describe the ways in which information technology is used by teleworkers at their remote work stations.

Personal computers and microcomputers or terminals are the commonest form of hardware used by these teleworkers. However, there is also some use of dedicated word processors and electronic typewriters. Public telecommunications networks requiring user equipment to handle digital information are almost exclusively used by the software and consultancy companies. It is these same companies which, according to their managers, also use terminals to a significant extent in their telework schemes. Though there are some reports of the use of terminals connected to a local processing unit, most are connected to a remote host via some sort of telecommunications link.

The transfer of work is not necessarily by electronic means. In over a third of the schemes, teleworkers collect and deliver work in person. This applies mainly but by no means exclusively to decentralised typing schemes. Where teleworkers are carrying out complex work, it is common to find that completed work is handed over during the course of meetings with managers or clients, which also cover progress reports, briefings and discussions of any problems which may have arisen. However, meetings do not feature in the typing and clerical schemes. Though transfers of work through personal contact do occur, these are merely 'collections' and 'deliveries'—the work tasks are routine and of themselves give rise to no need for discussion. There is no particular structure to the use of handwritten texts sent by ordinary mail; some third of the schemes use this method of work transfer frequently.

Frequent use is made of work transfer on floppy disk by over half the schemes. This method of transfer is mostly found in typing and programming schemes. The diskettes are collected and delivered by ordinary mail, by courier or personally by the teleworkers. According to managers, frequent or heavy use was made of electronic mail in 3 out of 14 schemes and this medium was used to some extent in over a third of the schemes. However, when teleworkers were questioned a somewhat different picture emerged: 84 per cent stated that they made no use at all of electronic mail, while only 1.7 per cent said that they used it more than twice a day. Tables 9.12 and 9.13 show their use of information technology in terms of the proportion of working time spent using the equipment and in terms of the frequency of use of particular forms of communication.

From table 9.12, it can be seen that IT equipment is used by teleworkers both for the performance of their work and for communication with co-workers, managers and clients. Terminals are used by under a third of the teleworkers in the sample, for the majority in conjunction with a modem for connection to an external mainframe. However, there are occasional examples of the use of leased lines and also of connection to a local processing unit.

Microcomputers are available to a majority of the teleworkers, yet a large proportion of these use the machines only quite rarely. Only about 20 per

TABLE 9.12   Teleworkers' use of electronic hard- and software

Equipment	Proportion of working time spent using the equipment				
	None	Very low	$\leq\frac{1}{3}$	$\frac{1}{2}$	$\geq\frac{3}{4}$
Terminal	63.0	6.7	8.4	3.4	18.4
PC	45.4	19.3	15.1	6.7	13.4
Elec. typewriter	95.0	4.2		0.8	
Modem	52.9	21.0	7.6	2.5	15.9
Wp software	54.6	23.5	8.4	8.4	5.0
Videotex	95.8	3.4	0.8		
Other	74.8	6.7	5.0	5.0	8.4

cent of teleworkers spend over half their working time using them. Again, some 20 per cent spend a large proportion of their time connected to other computing equipment via modems, the majority of which are acoustically coupled into the telephone network. Modems are either used with a simple terminal or with a microcomputer used as a stand-alone processor and intelligent terminal. The data link is used by this group as a working connection rather than merely for finite communications such as the transmission and reception of work orders and results.

Despite the widespread availability of electronic typewriters reported by managers, these play a very small role in practice, being used by only 5 per cent of the teleworkers.

Word processing software is used extensively by under 15 per cent of the teleworker sample, though nearly half have such software available and use it at least occasionally. The unclear distinction between editors for programming languages on the one hand and data entry systems with editing facilities on the other makes the interpretation of this proportion difficult. Videotex services are very rarely used.

Communication is a particularly important component of distance working, and for this reason the teleworkers were asked not only about IT-based but also about more traditional communications media. Table 9.13 summarises what they reported, while Table 9.14 gives some additional information on their use of digital means of communication.

It can be assumed that very few teleworkers spend a large proportion of their time communicating—tasks which are suitable for telework are generally output-orientated and do not involve communication as part of the substance

TABLE 9.13   Teleworkers' use of communications media

		Usage per week			Usage per day	
Equipment	No use	<1	1,2	3–6	1,2	>2
Modem	61.3	5.9	5.9	9.2	1.7	16.0
Teletex	98.3	1.7				
Videotex	99.2	0.8				
Electronic mail	84.0	2.5	4.2	2.5	5.0	1.7
Disk	70.6	11.8	7.6	5.0	2.5	2.5
Texts	19.3	10.9	31.9	19.3	5.9	12.6
Tapes	88.2	2.5	1.7	1.7	1.7	4.2
Postal service	29.4	6.7	26.1	21.0	10.9	5.9
Courier	68.9	21.0	4.2	3.4	1.7	0.8
Meetings	25.2	45.4	19.3	7.6	2.5	
Other (telephone)	46.2	2.5	10.1	9.2	7.6	24.4

TABLE 9.14   Teleworkers' use of digital equipment for communication

Number of digital means of communication used	n	%
None	44	37.0
At least one	75	63.0
Total	119	100.0

(digital means include: modem, teletex, videotex, electronic mail, disk)

of the work. Thus for measurement of the importance of the various means of communication it is appropriate to examine the frequency of use of a particular medium. From the information supplied by the teleworkers in this sample it is clear that telework today is heavily supported by non-IT-based means of communication.

Over 70 per cent of teleworkers continue to use postal services, and some 80 per cent communicate by means of handwritten letters or other paper-based documents. The alternative to the postal services for transport of text communications—but also of information on diskette or tape—is a courier service, used by under one-third of teleworkers, and by the majority of these less than once a week. Face-to-face meetings away from the remote work site are normal for three-quarters of the teleworkers, although only 30 per cent have them once a week or more.

Some 40 per cent of teleworkers use modem links for communication, at least occasionally. It will be noted that this·is less than the proportion using modems in the course of their work. This is because many teleworkers do not regard performing data entry tasks on a remote computer or interrogating databases as 'communication' and so do not appear as modem users here. Some one in five stated that they used a modem for 'normal' communication purposes at least once daily, most of these several times daily.

Videotex has negligible value for teleworkers' communication, at least at the present stage of implementation in the two countries studied. The same applies to teletex, though this service would seem technically very suitable for use in many of the tasks carried out by teleworkers. As already noted, the use of electronic mail is more limited than might be expected from managers' statements. Less than 15 per cent of teleworkers use electronic mail at all, and only 7 per cent daily or more.

EMPLOYMENT STATUS

In over half the sample of teleworking schemes, the teleworkers concerned are self-employed. If the two schemes designed to offer employment opportunities to disabled people are excluded the proportion rises to over 60 per cent. Companies' choice of this employment status has to be seen in the context of their reasons for setting up telework schemes (which were discussed earlier and are summarised in Appendix C), in particular, the attractions of telework as a means of reducing existing costs or of increasing capacity without incurring additional fixed costs. These kinds of benefits can generally only be achieved if the workers concerned accept self-employed status.

Self-employed status does offer practical advantages to individuals with skills which are in demand and highly valued, because—unless they are disadvantaged by other factors—they generally have the bargaining power to negotiate contracts which suit their own particular needs. Teleworking on a self-employed basis is sometimes seen very positively by this group as offering an opportunity to set up their own business. This is illustrated by the networking scheme of the office equipment manufacturer in the study.

Conversely, for individuals working in areas characterised by skill oversupply, such as typing and clerical tasks, self-employed status can rarely be seen as an advantage. Table 9.15 sets out the employment status of the teleworkers in the sample by sex and age. As this table shows, self-employment status is not evenly distributed; considerably more women in the sample were self-employed than men. There is no strong age structure to self-employed status. However, the slightly lower proportion of self-employment in the youngest age group makes sense in the light of their shorter employment experience and lower likely ability to cope with independence and insecurity.

Table 9.16 gives a breakdown of employment status by education, task and occupation. This shows that the proportion of an occupational category which is self-employed does not correspond to those occupations where self-employment is most likely to be an advantage—or less of a disadvantage—to the individual. Roughly the same proportion of teleworking typists have this employment status as do data processing and other professionals. However, there is a positive correlation between self-employment and market power in the sense of having high qualifications.

Turning to teleworkers' perception of their contractual status, shown in Table 9.17, we see that those who are self-employed generally regard this as an advantage. Only 8 per cent find it disadvantageous to them. However, this 8 per cent is largely made up of women performing routine keyboarding tasks, nearly all of whom find self-employment a disadvantage. Had this group been better represented in the sample then it is likely that the proportion of unwilling freelances would have been larger.

Although the table suggests that present employment status is no guide to a teleworker's attitude to self-employment, it should be noted that most of those who were not self-employed also saw no option of self-employment and therefore regarded this question as inapplicable.

TABLE 9.15 Self-employment by sex and age of teleworker

		Self-employed	Not self-employed	Row total
Male	n	9	18	27
	%	33.3	66.7	24.3
Female	n	48	36	84
	%	57.1	42.9	75.7
AGE				
<30 years	n	7	11	18
	%	38.9	61.1	16.2
30–40 years	n	36	30	66
	%	54.5	45.5	59.5
40–50 years	n	13	11	24
	%	54.2	45.8	21.6
>50 years	n	2	1	3
	%	66.7	33.3	2.7
Column total	n	57	54	111
	%	51.4	48.6	100.0

TABLE 9.16 Self-employment by education and task of teleworker

		Self-employed	Not self-employed	Row total
EDUCATION				
Low	n	2	7	9
	%	22.2	77.8	7.9
Medium	n	7	16	23
	%	30.4	69.6	20.2
High	n	50	32	82
	%	61.0	39.0	71.9
OCCUPATION				
Dp prof.	n	43	32	75
	%	57.3	42.7	65.8
Typist	n	4	3	7
	%	57.1	42.9	6.1
Professionals	n	12	15	27
	%	44.4	55.6	23.7
Other	n		5	5
	%		100.0	4.4
Column total	n	59	55	114
	%	51.8	48.2	100.0

TABLE 9.17   Advantageousness of self-employment as perceived by teleworkers (by employment status)

		(−−)	(−)	Neutral	(+)	(++)	Row total
Self-employed	n	2	3	21	26	6	58
	%	3.4	5.2	36.2	44.8	10.3	85.3
Not self-employed	n		2	5	3		10
	%		20.0	50.0	30.0		14.7
Column total	n	2	5	26	29	6	68
	%	2.9	7.4	38.2	42.6	8.8	100.0

PAY

Teleworkers' annual income varies considerably. As can be seen from Table 9.18, the majority earn between $10,000 US and $30,000 US per year, but about one-third of teleworkers earn less than $10,000 US per year, and at the other extreme, 15 per cent earn more than $30,000 US. One of the most striking features of the survey's findings on pay is the disparity it reveals between men's and women's pay, with women earning very much less than men. The proportion of low-paid women (under $10,000 US p.a.) is well over 10 times the equivalent proportion of low-paid men, whereas the proportion of men in the highest earning bracket, $30,000 US and more, is over 20 times greater than the proportion of women earning this amount.

Table 9.19 shows the variation in teleworkers' average income according to their age and sex. As can be seen, women earn on average only a third of the pay of their male counterparts. There is an almost negligible rate of increase in average income with age. This would seem to suggest that older teleworkers are underachieving on income, were it not for other income-relevant variations with age. Some of these can be seen in Table 9.20, which shows average earnings according to education and occupation. This breakdown is intriguing: where considerable difference would be expected, it shows none. The relationship between income and educational level is statistically and substantively non-significant; and the variation of income with occupation is confused, with only the typists conforming roughly to expectations.

An analysis based on average income (shown in Table 9.21) show a peak not in the high-education but in the medium-education category, and shows how little data processing professionals are earning as remote workers compared to the pay they could expect in a traditional working situation.

An important key to the confusion in this picture is the considerable variation in working hours among the teleworkers in the sample. Tables 9.22

TABLE 9.18   Earnings in $US p.a. (thousands) by sex and age of teleworker

		=10	21–20	20–30	>=30	Row total
Male	n	1	3	8	15	27
	%	3.7	11.1	29.6	55.6	24.3
Female	n	37	33	12	2	84
	%	44.0	39.3	14.3	2.4	75.7
AGE						
<30 years	n	7	5	4	2	18
	%	38.9	27.8	22.2	11.1	16.2
30–40 years	n	24	20	12	10	66
	%	36.4	30.3	18.2	15.2	59.5
40–50 years	n	7	9	3	4	23
	%	30.4	39.1	13.0	17.4	20.7
>50 years	n		2	1	1	4
	%		50.0	25.0	25.0	3.6
Column total	n	38	36	20	17	111
	%	34.2	32.4	18.0	15.3	100.0

TABLE 9.19   Average earnings in $US p.a. (thousands) by age and sex of teleworker

	$US	n
Male	37,304	27
Female	13,100	84
AGE		
<30 years	20,119	18
30–40 years	18,208	66
40–50 years	19,787	23
>50 years	23,348	4
All teleworkers	19,031	111

and 9.23 show the length of the working week for the various categories of teleworker. Differences between the sexes are clearly at least part of the explanation for the women teleworkers' low income: nearly 90 per cent of the women work less than a 40 hour week on average and an appreciable number are spending less than half that time at work. For the male teleworkers just

the opposite is true: nearly 90 per cent work at least 40 hours per week, many considerably more.

Again, the relationship between educational level and the length of the working week shows that this is at least partly responsible for the lack of a positive relationship between income and qualifications in telework. Those with high qualifications are significantly more likely to be working less than

TABLE 9.20   Earnings in $US p.a. (thousands) by education and occupation of teleworker

		<=10	10–20	20–60	>=30	Row total
EDUCATION						
Low	n	3	2	2	2	9
	%	33.3	22.2	22.2	22.2	7.9
Medium	n	7	6	4	6	23
	%	30.4	26.1	17.4	26.1	20.2
High	n	30	29	14	9	82
	%	36.6	35.4	17.1	11.0	71.9
OCCUPATION						
Dp professional	n	31	29	12	2	74
	%	41.9	39.2	16.2	2.7	64.9
Typist	n	6	1			7
	%	85.7	14.3			6.1
Other professional	n	2	5	6	15	28
	%	7.1	17.9	21.4	53.6	24.6
Other	n	1	2	2		5
	%	20.0	40.0	40.0		4.4
Column total	n	40	37	20	17	114
	%	35.1	32.5	17.5	14.9	100.0

TABLE 9.21   Average earnings in $US p.a. (thousands) by education and occupation of teleworker

		$US	n
Education	Low	20 293	9
	Medium	24 604	23
	High	16 932	82
Occupation	Dp professional	13 510	74
	Typists	6 437	7
	Other professional	35 891	28
	Other	17 436	5
All teleworkers		19 031	111

TABLE 9.22 *Average working week (hours) by sex and age of teleworker*

		<20 hr	20–39 hr	40–49 hr	>49 hr	Row total
Male	n		4	13	14	31
	%		12.9	41.9	45.2	26.7
Female	n	13	61	9	2	85
	%	15.3	71.8	10.6	2.4	73.3
AGE						
<30 years	n	2	5	8	3	18
	%	11.1	27.8	44.4	16.7	15.5
30–40 years	n	12	41	9	7	69
	%	17.4	59.4	13.0	10.1	59.5
40–50 years	n		16	3	6	25
	%		64.0	12.0	24.0	21.6
>50 years	n		3	1		4
	%		75.0	25.0		3.4
Column total	n	14	65	21	16	116
	%	12.1	56.0	18.1	13.8	100.0

TABLE 9.23 *Average working week (hours) by education and occupation of teleworker*

		<20 hr	20–39 hr	40–49 hr	49 hr	Row total
EDUCATION						
Low	n	1	4	3	1	9
	%	11.1	44.4	33.3	11.1	7.6
Medium	n	4	8	6	7	25
	%	16.0	32.0	24.0	28.0	21.0
High	n	10	54	13	8	85
	%	11.8	63.5	15.3	9.4	71.4
OCCUPATION						
Dp professional	n	10	55	12		77
	%	13.0	71.4	15.6		64.7
Typist	n	2	4	1		7
	%	28.6	57.1	14.3		5.9
Professional	n	2	7	5	16	30
	%	6.7	23.3	16.7	53.3	25.2
Other	n	1		4		5
	%	20.0		80.0		4.2
Column total	n	15	66	22	16	119
	%	12.6	55.5	18.5	13.4	100.0

40 hours a week than those with a lower educational level. Part-time work is also very prevalent among dp professionals.

In order to obtain a more accurate picture of teleworkers' rates of pay, gross earnings were corrected for the length of the average working week so as to arrive at an equivalent income for full-time working (arbitrarily taken to be 40 hours per week). The results are shown in table 9.24. As one might expect, this table shows a reduction in the difference between the sexes, but it has by no means disappeared. There are still three times as many women as men in the lower income brackets. Since the length of the working week is unrelated to age, there is still no upward trend in earnings with age, reinforcing the suspicion that the older age groups are suffering income disadvantages through telework.

The difference in hours of work cannot be held entirely responsible for the unusual relationship between education, occupation and earnings either, as can be seen from Table 9.25. From this table, it can be observed that, in the lowest income category, correction for a 40-hour week has brought about considerable movement towards the expected pattern: there is now a lower proportion of the highly qualified in this category. However, the top income category is virtually unchanged and still exhibits a negative relationship between qualification and effective income level. Of course the small number in this category makes sampling error a strong possibility. Nevertheless, this

TABLE 9.24   Income in $US p.a. (thousands) corrected for 40-hr week by age and sex of teleworker

		<=10	10–20	20–30	>=30	Row total
Male	n	1	4	10	12	27
	%	3.7	14.8	37.0	44.4	24.3
Female	n	8	41	30	5	84
	%	9.5	48.8	35.7	6.0	75.7
AGE						
<30 years	n	1	11	3	3	18
	%	5.6	61.1	16.7	16.7	16.2
30–40 years	n	5	24	26	11	66
	%	7.6	36.4	39.4	16.7	59.5
40–50 years	n	2	10	9	2	23
	%	8.7	43.5	39.1	8.7	20.7
>50 years	n		1	1	2	4
	%		25.0	25.0	50.0	3.6
Column total	n	8	46	39	18	111
	%	7.2	41.4	35.1	16.2	100.0

finding does raise some interesting questions. Is it possible, for instance, that telework allows educational underachievers to blossom in ways which would be impossible in a more conventional work environment? Or could it be that the higher qualified teleworkers are somehow losing out on financial rewards?

Data processing professionals working in telework are clearly earning less than the average for their profession. Part of the reason may be that simple proportional correction for part-time working is not realistic; fixed costs and capital amortisation (e.g. for equipment and training) mean that a longer working week is disproportionately more efficient (neglecting the extent to which productivity depends on the length of time spent working, a hotly disputed area).

On the other hand, home-based telework in particular reduces the capital outlay per workers by removing (from most participants' accounting) the cost of office space and furniture from the capital outlay per worker and so reduces the efficiency penalty for part-time working. It seems, nevertheless, that a disproportionate correction for part-time work would not alter the fact of reduced earnings in the group of teleworking data processing professional staff compared to the profession as a whole.

TABLE 9.25 *Income in $US p.a. (thousands) corrected for 40-hr week by education and task of teleworker*

		<=10	10–20	20–30	>=30	Row total
EDUCATION						
Low	n	3	2	1	3	9
	%	33.3	22.2	11.1	33.3	7.9
Medium	n	4	6	7	6	23
	%	17.4	26.1	30.4	26.1	20.2
High	n	3	38	32	9	82
	%	3.7	46.3	39.0	11.0	71.9
OCCUPATION						
Dp	n	4	36	27	7	74
professional	%	5.4	48.6	36.5	9.5	64.9
Typist	n	5	2			7
	%	71.4	28.6			6.1
Other	n		6	11	11	28
professional	%		21.4	39.3	39.3	24.6
Other	n	1	2	2		5
	%	20.0	40.0	40.0		4.4
Column total	n	10	46	40	18	114
	%	8.8	40.4	35.1	15.8	100.0

Without matching the sample of teleworkers to others in traditional working arrangements with the same level of qualifications and experience, it is not possible to specify accurately the income differential between teleworking and traditional working arrangements. Here, however, teleworkers' own assessments of how they stand in relation to on-site workers are of some value. These are summarised in table 9.26 with a breakdown by age and sex.

As can be seen, the majority think that telework is financially disadvantageous. One in five believes the loss in income is serious, exceeding 20 per cent. A third think that they are earning about the same as they would be on-site. This leaves under 10 per cent of teleworkers who reckon that they are earning more than in traditional forms of work.

Once again, age plays an unexpectedly insignificant role, but there are considerable differences between the sexes. Women teleworkers are particularly likely to judge that they are earning less than they could in traditional working arrangements. Over half the men think that the difference is fairly insignificant, i.e less than 5 per cent either way, and more of the men benefit financially through this form of work.

Data processing professionals are most aware of foregoing income because they are working remotely and it is the non-dp professionals, particularly the

TABLE 9.26 Telework earnings compared to expected earnings in traditional employment by education and task of teleworker

		Much less	Less	Similar	More	Much more	Row total
Male	n	5	4	17	2	3	31
	%	16.1	12.9	54.8	6.5	9.7	27.2
Female	n	16	39	23	4	1	83
	%	19.3	47.0	27.7	4.8	1.2	72.8
AGE							
<30 years	n	3	6	5	3		17
	%	17.6	35.3	29.4	17.6		14.8
30–40 years	n	13	29	21	3	3	69
	%	18.8	42.0	30.4	4.3	4.3	60.0
40–50 years	n	5	6	13		1	25
	%	20.0	24.0	52.0		4.0	21.7
>50 years	n	1	2	1			4
	%	25.0	50.0	25.0			3.5
Column total	n	22	43	40	6	4	115
	%	19.1	37.4	34.8	5.2	3.5	100.0

'networkers', who are most likely to see themselves as gaining financially from this form of work arrangement. More surprisingly, some typists also think that they are financially better off as teleworkers.

As can be seen from Table 9.27, which gives a breakdown by education and occupation, perceived underpayment increases with education, and is found at its greatest among the data processing professionals, bearing out our earlier conclusion that this group of teleworker is particularly low paid compared with on-site workers.

TABLE 9.27 *Telework earnings compared to expected earnings in traditional employment by education, occupation and (corrected) annual income of teleworker*

		Much less	Less	Similar	More	Much more	Row total
EDUCATION							
Low	n	1	2	5		1	9
	%	11.1	22.2	55.6		11.1	7.7
Medium	n	1	5	17	2		25
	%	4.0	20.0	68.0	8.0		21.4
High	n	20	36	20	4	3	83
	%	24.1	43.4	24.1	4.8	3.6	70.9
OCCUPATION							
Dp professional	n	18	37	19	2		76
	%	23.7	48.7	25.0	2.6		65.0
Typist	n			5	1	1	7
	%			71.4	14.3	14.3	6.0
Professional	n	4	5	16	2	3	30
	%	13.3	16.7	53.3	6.7	10.0	25.6
Other	n		1	2	1		4
	%		25.0	50.0	25.0		3.4
INCOME							
<=20k	n	1	2	7			10
	%	10.0	20.0	70.0			8.9
20–40k	n	11	23	7	3	1	45
	%	24.4	51.1	15.6	6.7	2.2	40.2
40–60k	n	7	12	16	2	2	39
	%	17.9	30.8	41.0	5.1	5.1	34.8
>=60k	n	2	5	9	1	1	18
	%	11.1	27.8	50.0	5.6	5.6	16.1
Column total	n	21	42	39	6	4	112
	%	18.8	37.5	34.8	5.4	3.6	100.0

Given that this is a group of workers whose skills are in relatively high demand, the question occurs, why do they put up with it? One way of approaching this puzzle is to investigate the importance of high earnings to this group compared with other factors. Some light can be shed on the subject by examining the role which their income plays in their household, shown in Table 9.28.

Overall, under one-third of teleworkers in the teleworker sample are the main earners in their household. A glance at the difference between the sexes reveals a continuing role division between men and women, especially pronounced where the women have young children. 90 per cent of the women teleworkers are not the primary earner in the household. This suggests that earning a high income may not be the foremost priority for most of them.

TABLE 9.28   Teleworkers' earning status: main or secondary earner in the household by sex, education and occupation

		Not 1. earner	Primary earner	Row total
Male	n	3	25	28
	%	10.7	89.3	25.2
Female	n	76	7	83
	%	91.6	8.4	74.8
EDUCATION				
Low	n	4	5	9
	%	44.4	55.6	7.9
Medium	n	13	10	23
	%	56.5	43.5	20.2
High	n	64	18	82
	%	78.0	22.0	71.9
OCCUPATION				
Dp professional	n	60	13	73
	%	82.2	17.8	64.0
Typist	n	6	1	7
	%	85.7	14.3	6.1
Professional	n	11	18	29
	%	37.9	62.1	25.4
Other		4	1	5
	80.0	20.0	4.4
Column total	n	81	33	114
	%	71.1	28.9	100.0

WORKING HOURS

As has been seen, only a minority of teleworkers work a 'standard' 40-hour week. The majority work part-time, but there is considerable flexibility in the timing and length of periods of work. Approximately two-thirds of our sample worked less than 40 hours per week, i.e. less than 8 hours per day in a five-day week. One in five worked half-time or less. At the other end of the scale there was an appreciable proportion of teleworkers working over 10 hours per day on average.

This difference in working hours corresponds to a difference between the sexes giving us a picture in which women typically work part-time while male teleworkers exceed the normal working day, sometimes by large margins. Age is not linked to length of working time. As might be expected, however, there is a link between working hours and the number of children for whom a teleworker is responsible.

Reduced working time is consistently linked with family size over all categories, with the greatest difference between those with and those without any children at all. Whereas over 85 per cent of teleworkers with no children work at least 8 hours per day, this drops to under 40 per cent of those with one child and less than 20 per cent of those with three or more children.

There is a predominance of non-dp professionals, particularly the 'networkers' associated with the office equipment manufacturer, among the teleworkers reporting particularly long hours. Here working days between 12 and 15 hours are the rule, more than five days are worked in a week and this results in average working weeks which often exceed 60 hours. There is a concentration of data processing staff in the 5 to 7 hours per day category, while a particularly high proportion of typists work very short hours in an average day. The variation in working time is, as we have seen, partly due to varying family commitments, but the differing ways teleworkers are linked into the market for the products of their work are also significant.

Telework, as well as making work more independent of place, is also often associated with a reduced rigidity of working time, at least on a short time scale. This time flexibility, where it exists, can be used to shift workloads between days, and within a day to avoid having to perform work at times when there are other demands on the attention or when other interests can be followed. The survey provides us with two kinds of information on the use of time flexibility: the consistency or variation in the length of a working day (measured by comparing average working hours per day with the length of the longest working day over a three-month period); and the proportion of time spent working outside normal working hours. These are shown in Table 9.29 and 9.30.

If we look at the longest day worked over a three-month period, we find that nearly 90 per cent of teleworkers work a full 8-hour day at least

TABLE 9.29   Longest working day (hours) by sex and occupation of teleworker

		<5 hr	5–7 hr	8–10 hr	>10 hr	Row total
Male	n		1	5	25	31
	%		3.2	16.1	80.6	27.0
Female	n	3	6	46	29	84
	%	3.6	7.1	54.8	34.5	73.0
OCCUPATION						
Dp professional	n	1	8	39	29	77
	%	1.3	10.4	50.6	37.7	65.3
Typist	n	2		4	1	7
	%	28.6		57.1	14.3	5.9
Professional	n			6	24	30
	%			20.0	80.0	25.4
Other	n	1		2	1	4
	%	25.0		50.0	25.0	3.4
Column total	n	4	8	51	55	118
	%	3.4	6.8	43.2	46.6	100.0

occasionally. The difference between the sexes parallels the length of the average working day: most women work shorter hours than most male teleworkers. Table 9.30 shows that a quarter of teleworkers do all their work within normal working hours. However, the majority do perform some of their work in the evenings or at weekends. For half, the amount extends up to one-third of their total working time. For one in five, evening and weekend work makes up more than half of total working time while 5 per cent perform more than two-thirds of their work outside normal working hours.

The difference between the sexes is such that male teleworkers are not only more likely to limit their work to normal working hours but are also more likely to extend or shift their work by considerable amounts to evenings and weekends. Women teleworkers mostly do a moderate amount of evening and weekend work.

Table 9.31 shows that a large part of the explanation for the displacement of work outside normal working hours is the need to spend that time caring for children. Whereas nearly two-thirds of teleworkers with no children restrict their work to normal hours, the proportion drops to under 5 per cent in the cases of teleworkers with three or more children. Of those with any family at all, from a quarter to a third do at least half their work outside office hours.

The opportunity to shift work to unusual hours is coupled with job characteristics typical of telework—an output orientated mode and moderate

TABLE 9.30   Proportion of work done outside normal working hours by sex, education and occupation of teleworker

		None	Up to $\frac{1}{3}$	Approx. half	At least $\frac{2}{3}$	Row total
Male	n	11	7	10	3	31
	%	35.5	22.6	32.3	9.7	26.7
Female	n	18	53	12	2	85
	%	21.2	62.4	14.1	2.4	73.3
EDUCATION						
Low	n	7		1	1	9
	%	77.8		11.1	11.1	7.6
Medium	n	7	10	5	3	25
	%	28.0	40.0	20.0	12.0	21.0
High	n	16	51	16	2	85
	%	18.8	60.0	18.8	2.4	71.4
OCCUPATION						
Dp professional	n	18	48	9	2	77
	%	23.4	62.3	11.7	2.6	64.7
Typist	n	3	3	1		7
	%	42.9	42.9	14.3		5.9
Professional	n	4	10	12	4	30
	%	13.3	33.3	40.0	13.3	25.2
Other	n	5				5
	%	100.0				4.2
Column total	n	30	61	22	6	119
	%	25.2	51.3	18.5	5.0	100.0

to long-term deadlines—and much of the use of this opportunity arises from family responsibilities. However, another potential explanation for the high proportion of work done out of normal working hours has little to do with time flexibility as such but arises from the self-evident fact that the longer the working day, the more likely it is that some work will spill over into conventional leisure time.

Comparing different occupations, it seems that the high proportion of dp professionals working outside normal hours can largely be explained by child-care needs, but non-dp professionals are usually working 'unsocial' hours because their working day is simply too long to be fitted into the conventional office day and spills over into evenings or weekends.

Coupled with the flexibility of time allocation within the day is the question of time allocation over days. If work is in the output mode, with long-term

TABLE 9.31 Proportion of work done outside normal working hours by number of children of teleworker

			None	Up to $\frac{1}{3}$	Approx. half	At least $\frac{2}{3}$	Row total
Children	0	n	14	7	1		22
		%	63.6	31.8	4.5		18.5
	1	n	6	10	5	2	23
		%	26.1	43.5	21.7	8.7	19.3
	2	n	9	30	10	1	50
		%	18.0	60.0	20.0	2.0	42.0
	>2	n	1	14	6	3	24
		%	4.2	58.3	25.0	12.5	20.2
Column total		n	30	61	22	6	119
		%	25.2	51.3	18.5	5.0	100.0

TABLE 9.32 Proportion of work done outside normal working hours by average length of working day (hours)

		None	Up to $\frac{1}{3}$	Approx. half	At least $\frac{2}{3}$	Row total
AVERAGE DAY						
<5	n	7	13	3	3	26
	%	26.9	50.0	11.5	11.5	22.0
5–7	n	8	34	7		49
	%	16.3	69.4	14.3		41.5
8–10	n	13	13	4	1	31
	%	41.9	41.9	12.9	3.2	26.3
>10	n	1	1	8	2	12
	%	8.3	8.3	66.7	16.7	10.2
Column total	n	29	61	22	6	118
	%	24.6	51.7	18.6	5.1	100.0

deadlines, then working time can be shifted from one day to another, avoiding days where other pressures predominate, or putting in extra hours to meet important deadlines. Table 9.33 shows that there is considerable variation in the length of time worked. The comparison is drawn by calculating the difference between the longest day worked in the three-month period before the survey and the average working day and expressing this as a percentage

TABLE 9.33 Variability of the working day. Difference between maximum and average day length (%) by sex, education and occupation of teleworker

		<20%	20–49%	50–99%	>=100%	Row total
Male	n	5	14	10	2	31
	%	16.1	45.2	32.3	6.5	27.0
Female	n	6	20	24	34	84
	%	7.1	23.8	28.6	40.5	73.0
EDUCATION						
Low	n	2	6		1	9
	%	22.2	66.7		11.1	7.6
Medium	n	2	10	4	9	25
	%	8.0	40.0	16.0	36.0	21.2
High	n	8	18	32	26	84
	%	9.5	21.4	38.1	31.0	71.2
OCCUPATION						
Dp professional	n	6	20	27	24	77
	%	7.8	26.0	35.1	31.2	65.3
Typist	n	1	1		5	7
	%	14.3	14.3		71.4	5.9
Professionals	n	4	10	9	7	30
	%	13.3	33.3	30.0	23.3	25.4
Other	n	1	3			4
	%	25.0	75.0			3.4
Column total	n	12	34	36	36	118
	%	10.2	28.8	30.5	30.5	100.0

of the length of the average working day. This shows that variability is the norm in telework. Only 10 per cent of teleworkers have fairly constant allocations of working time, as seen in the lowest category, where maximum time worked is less than 20 per cent longer than average.

Women teleworkers have much more variable workloads than men with 40 per cent reporting maximum working times of double the average, or more, whereas the proportion of male teleworkers with this variability is under 10 per cent. Typists have particularly variable workloads: most of them have maximum working days over twice as long as their average working day. This group also finds variability of work a particular problem and feels that working conditions would be greatly improved if it could be levelled out. As we have seen, such an improvement is not likely; this flexibility in adapting to strongly fluctuating workloads is a major advantage of telework to employers, and one which makes telework schemes of this type particularly attractive to them.

Table 9.34 shows a consistent relationship between the variability of working time and the presence of children in a teleworker's household. Clearly, the time flexibility of telework is more advantageous the more children there are to be cared for.

Tables 9.35 and 9.36 show that some two-thirds of the teleworkers in our sample felt that the amount of work with which they were provided was about right. The numbers who thought that they had either too much or too little were fairly evenly balanced. There was some difference between the sexes here: women were much more likely to be satisfied with their current levels of work than men, perhaps a reflection of the fact that, by securing themselves part-time contracts, most had already negotiated a level of work that suited their circumstances. Typists often wanted more work, while most of those who wanted less were non-dp professionals, who, as we have seen, were generally working very long hours.

These ratings of overall satisfaction with the amount of work received do give some indication of the extent to which the teleworker controls his or her workload and hence also the variability of workload, but a much better indication was provided by the answers to a direct question about the extent to which teleworkers can influence the amount of work they do. These answers are summarised in Table 9.36.

Overall, the majority of teleworkers claim to have at least some control over the amount of work they have to do. However, there is a sizeable minority

TABLE 9.34 Variability of the working day. Difference between maximum and average day length (%) by number of children in teleworker's household

			<20%	20–49%	50–99%	>=100%	Row total
Children	None	n	3	12	6		21
		%	14.3	57.1	28.6		17.8
	1	n	2	7	3	11	23
		%	8.7	30.4	13.0	47.8	19.5
	2	n	4	12	18	16	50
		%	8.0	24.0	36.0	32.0	42.4
	>2	n	3	3	9	9	24
		%	12.5	12.5	37.5	37.5	20.3
Column total		n	12	34	36	36	118
		%	10.2	28.8	30.5	30.5	100.0

TABLE 9.35 Preference for more or less paid work by sex and
occupation of teleworker

		Prefer less	Same amount	Prefer more	Row total
Male	n	11	11	7	29
	%	37.9	37.9	24.1	25.7
Female	n	9	65	10	84
	%	10.7	77.4	11.9	74.3
OCCUPATION					
Dp professional	n	7	60	8	75
	%	9.3	80.0	10.7	64.7
Typist	n		5	2	7
	%		71.4	28.6	6.0
Professional	n	14	11	5	30
	%	46.7	36.7	16.7	25.9
Other	n		2	2	4
	%		50.0	50.0	3.4
Column total	n	21	78	17	116
	%	18.1	67.2	14.7	100.0

reporting little or no control over its workload, and for this group any
variability will be driven by the market or employer. Typists report having
little control over the work they have to do, while a majority of non-dp
professionals have considerable if not complete control over their workload.
Compared to the other professionals, many of the dp professionals report
having only 'some' control over their workload and quite a number have little
or no control. Because dp professionals are an occupational group with
considerable market power, this relative lack of control among teleworkers
illustrates how famiy commitments restrict their choices and hence their
control over their working conditions.

SUPERVISION, CONTROL AND PRODUCTIVITY MEASUREMENT

In many telework schemes, especially home-based ones, continuous or process
supervision is impossible or impracticable. Supervision tends to be infrequent
and completely output-orientated supervision is the norm. This is possible
because the majority of work tasks performed in telework schemes are
performed in 'output mode', in which neither continuous work output nor
short-term reactions to customers' or other workers' demands is required.
Supervision of the teleworkers' performance and productivity can therefore

TABLE 9.36   Extent of influence over workload by sex, education and occupation of teleworker

		No influence	Very little	Some	Considerable	Complete control	Row total
Male	n	2	5	13	7	4	31
	%	6.5	16.1	41.9	22.6	12.9	27.0
Female	n	4	11	38	23	8	84
	%	4.8	13.1	45.2	27.4	9.5	73.0
EDUCATION							
Low	n	1	5	2		1	9
	%	11.1	55.6	22.2		11.1	7.6
Medium	n	3	3	10	6	3	25
	%	12.0	12.0	40.0	24.0	12.0	21.2
High	n	2	8	40	26	8	84
	%	2.4	9.5	47.6	31.0	9.5	71.2
OCCUPATION							
Dp professional	n	4	9	39	19	5	76
	%	5.3	11.8	51.3	25.0	6.6	64.4
Typist	n	2	2	1	1	1	7
	%	28.6	28.6	14.3	14.3	14.3	5.9
Professionals	n		3	10	12	5	30
	%		10.0	33.3	40.0	16.7	25.4
Other	n		2	2		1	5
	%		40.0	40.0		20.0	4.2
Column total	n	6	16	52	32	12	118
	%	5.1	13.6	44.1	27.1	10.2	100.0

rely mainly on the evaluation of work results. In many cases, this style of supervision is reinforced by contracts which stipulate that the teleworker is self-employed. Where organisations are loath to rely on such irregular information, work progress is usually monitored against an agreed project schedule.

The telework schemes for the disabled are generally organised in small groups in such a way that normal forms of continuous supervision are possible. In the case of mobile insurance agents, success and productivity are measured statistically by the number of successful sales they achieve.

The length of time worked is not measured in any way by many of the teleworking organisations. This is consistent with the general orientation to supervision by work output. Where time worked is of importance for the measurement of work, time sheets, diary or work progress reports on hours worked and tasks completed are used. In some cases organisations try to increase supervision by telephone contact and regular meetings between teleworkers and project managers. In relatively few cases, 2 out of the 14 organisations in our sample, is information technology used for supervision purposes. These organisations measure working times by the length of connect or log-on times on the teleworker's terminal or computer. This direct method of supervision is rejected by other organisations partly because of resentment by teleworkers and partly because it is considered to be manipulable.

Qualitative criteria do not just supplement purely quantitative measures of productivity, but play a decisive role. Apart from the quality of work results as such, flexibility in adapting to workloads is regarded as a considerable advantage. Flexibility is stressed particularly by the organisations which employ female teleworkers part-time, either for typing and word-processing tasks or for data processing. As already noted, this flexibility can result in very variable workloads for the teleworkers concerned.

The majority of teleworkers consider the methods of supervision to be an advantage of remote work: 42 per cent compare them favourably with the supervision methods used in their last job, while half do not see any difference from their former situation. Only very few think that the present method of supervision is disadvantageous enough to make them consider giving up telework.

It is striking that the lack of close supervision in their present work arrangement is seen as an important advantage by 80 per cent of the typists compared with only 56 per cent of professionals and 36 per cent of dp professionals. This is perhaps more a reflection of the closeness of supervision in a typical office-based typing pool environment than that of the home-based programmer.

SATISFACTION WITH TELEWORK

Without exception the managers we interviewed said that they were satisfied that the telework schemes they were responsible for had been set up and most were also very satisfied with the way the schemes were now functioning. In addition, they were nearly all of the opinion that the teleworkers involved in their schemes were highly satisfied with them, a view which our survey confirms to a large extent, as can be seen from Table 9.37.

The exception here was the translation agency, whose managing director reported that the teleworkers he employs were initially not at all satisfied with remote work and would today still prefer more traditional working arrangements. The teleworkers in this scheme do, however, appreciate that the company is viable only because of the savings made possible by use of home-based telework, so that their satisfaction with their working arrangements represents a pragmatic acceptance of lack of choice.

TABLE 9.37   Satisfaction with telework arrangement before and
after. Numbers of teleworking organisations

	Satisfaction with telework arrangement after (before)				
	(++)	(+)	0/n.a.	(−)	(−−)
● Decision makers in the organisation	11(12)	2(1)	1(1)	—	—
● Employers working as teleworkers	4(3)	9(8)	1(2)	0(1)	—
● Other employees in central unit	0(0)	8(3)	6(9)	0(2)	—
● Unions	0(0)	3(1)	10(13)	1(0)	—

From the managers' perspective, these telework schemes have maintained stable levels of satisfaction among both higher management in the organisations and the teleworkers involved. There are anecdotal reports in the literature of jealousy of teleworkers from office-based staff, resulting in dissatisfaction among non-teleworkers. However, the evidence from managers in our survey is that this problem is readily avoidable. Indeed, though quite a number of organisations found that their office-based employees were disgruntled when the scheme was first begun, in the course of time this dissatisfaction did not spread but, on the contrary, diminished considerably.

The high proportion of neutral reports on satisfaction with union involvement is due to the fact that, in most schemes, unions were not involved.

The teleworkers in the sample were asked to report on their satisfaction with a number of specific aspects of their working lives, including the equipment used, their financial situation, and their leisure time. Table 9.38 presents an overview of their replies. From this table, it is apparent that the overall picture is one of relative contentment. The proportion expressing satisfaction does not drop below 50 per cent for any aspect of work or leisure, and the proportion reporting extreme dissatisfaction never rises above one in twenty. Interestingly, given the large proportion of home-based workers among teleworkers, living conditions are the aspect for which most report very great satisfaction. Dissatisfaction with work tasks themselves, with living conditions and with place of work are extremely rare, as is dissatisfaction with life as a whole.

The major source of fairly widespread but rarely serious dissatisfaction is leisure time. The amount of leisure time available is a source of dissatisfaction to almost one-third of the teleworkers. Other aspects show moderate degrees of discontent: financial situation, relations with friends and neighbours and equipment are a source of dissatisfaction to 10–15 per cent of teleworkers.

TABLE 9.38 Teleworkers' satisfaction with aspects of their working arrangement (per cent of teleworkers)

	Unsatisfied (very)		Neutral	Satisfied (very)	
• Technical equipment used at work	3.4	10.1	16.8	55.5	14.3
• Communication with employer	1.7	9.5	14.7	63.8	10.3
• Work itself	0.8	5.9	3.4	63.6	26.3
• Place of work	0.8	5.9	14.4	57.6	21.2
• Living conditions	0.8	4.2	10.1	48.7	36.1
• Financial situation	5.0	8.4	17.6	57.1	11.8
• Leisure time	5.0	26.1	14.3	47.9	6.7
• Relations with friends etc.	2.5	10.9	16.8	56.3	13.4
• Life as a whole	1.7	3.4	7.6	63.9	23.5

Factor analysis was used to show the structure of satisfaction among the respondents. A detailed breakdown of this is given in Appendix F. A breakdown by sex revealed surprisingly few differences between men and women, the main one being that women teleworkers are more likely to be satisfied with their leisure situation and, in particular, their relations with neighbours and friends than men. The fact that women are more likely to be well integrated into the local community comes as no surprise. What might be seen as surprising is the apparently low level of conflict between work and social obligations. The most likely explanation for this lies in the fact that women are more likely to work part-time than men. In choosing the working hours which they are able to offer, they have already accommodated the demands made on their time by family, friends and neighbours.

To gain an impression of one strong measure of satisfaction, we asked the teleworkers in our survey the direct question: 'If you could not work in the present arrangement but had to work elsewhere, would you give up work?' The answers to this are summarised in Table 9.39. Comparison of the response behaviour of the sexes reveals little difference in the proportion who would give up work, which is low in any case. The difference lies in the 'undecided' category. This shows a higher attachment of women teleworkers to work, independent of their current situation, than would perhaps be expected given the fact that most were secondary earners. For primary earners whose spouses are without an income, stopping work is simply not an option. There are occupational differences in the responses to this question. Typists are particularly unlikely to consider going out to work as a viable option.

TABLE 9.39 Work and non-work options outside telework by sex and occupation of teleworker

Question: 'If you could not work in the present arrangements but had to work elsewhere, would you give up work?'

		Work elsewhere	Give up work	Undecided	Row total
Male	n	24	3	3	30
	%	80.0	10.0	10.0	26.1
Female	n	51	11	23	85
	%	60.0	12.9	27.1	73.9
OCCUPATION					
Dp professional	n	46	11	20	77
	%	59.7	14.3	26.0	65.3
Typist	n	2	3	2	7
	%	28.6	42.9	28.6	5.9
Professional	n	23	2	4	29
	%	79.3	6.9	13.8	24.6
Other	n	4		1	5
	%	80.0		20.0	4.2
Column total	n	75	16	27	118
	%	63.6	13.6	22.9	100.0

CONSTRAINTS ON TELEWORK

As might be expected, managers' perceptions of the constraints on the further development of telework are different from those of teleworkers. From the manager's point of view, four major constraints stand out: organisational difficulties; the need to train employees; lack of the appropriate equipment; and the inadequacy of the telecommunications infrastructure.

The managers' perspective on constraints on telework is presented in Table 9.40. The main distinction observable from this table is between schemes involving highly qualified staff and those involving relatively low-skilled work.

Managers of highly-qualified teleworkers focused on organisational difficult-ies, while managers of typists and other lower-skilled staff gave more extensive lists of constraints. In addition to organisational difficulties, they cited: high expenses, the need to train employees and the expense and inadequacy of the available telecommunications. Many of these companies had invested heavily in hardware to enable them to start or expand their telework schemes.

TABLE 9.40 Constraints on telework: managers' perceptions

Constraining factors	Present position: Importance			Future perspectives: Importance		
	Unimportant	Important	N.A.	Less than now	More than now	N.A.
• Organisational difficulties	1	7	2	2	6	2
• Expenses	4	4	2	1	6	3
• The need to train employees	2	7	1	2	5	3
• Lack of technical equipment such as computers or terminals	4	6	0	6	3	0
• Lack of knowledge of requirements and potential	5	4	1	2	4	3
• Low productivity (not economical)	8	1	1	3	4	3
• Telecommunications infrastructure is too expensive to use	4	5	1	2	6	2
• Lack of clarity as to the costs which will arise for the use of the telecommunications infrastructure	4	4	2	3	4	3
• Insufficient/inadequate telecommunications infrastructure	2	6	2	2	5	3
• Management resistance	8	1	1	7	1	2
• Difficulties in supervision and control	7	2	1	6	0	4
• Union resistance	6	2	2	5	1	4
• Employee resistance	6	2	2	4	1	5
• Company's conservative thinking	6	1	3	5	0	5

$n = 10$

In one case—the software services company—factors which had initially been seen as constraints had been overcome. It had only recently become cost-effective to instal computers in the homes of its teleworkers, and doing so had improved internal communications and increased efficiency.

Technical hitches had been common in setting up telework schemes. Over half the managers admitting to constraints on telework reported difficulties resulting from lack of appropriate equipment, or costly or inadequate telecommunications. More specifically, the most common problems were:

- difficulties in achieving compatibility between different systems used within a scheme
- communication and information transmission and exchange problems between the different organisational units
- software adaptation difficulties
- the low speed of data transmission using current equipment.

However, technical problems were not the only ones. Additional difficulties were caused in some schemes by the high level of investment required to set them up. In this context, over half of the managers also mention communication problems resulting from the wide geographical separation between workers and managers. Where teleworkers are based at home, communication is seen as a major constraint. The distribution of work can also cause problems when it has to be sent by ordinary mail or picked up in person by the teleworkers.

Closely related to the difficulty of ensuring a sufficient flow of information and communication is the social problem of isolation which, according to most observers, is experienced by many homebased workers. The managers in our sample, however, did not on the whole see this as a major problem. Less than a third mentioned isolation. Among this minority was the managing director of the translation agency who had noticed that working from home had led to a decrease in personal contact between the workers.

In other schemes, even when managers did not identify isolation as a problem, considerable efforts had been made to minimise it. The office equipment manufacturer, for instance, went to some lengths to ensure that all its teleworkers, however loosely associated with it, built up a sense of identification with the company. It had also set up an independent association run by and for its teleworkers to help them interchange business leads, services and information; to facilitate the group purchase of services; and to maintain contact with the parent company.

Some managers point out that social interaction with colleagues, not just superiors, is especially important for those without very much job experience. The teleworker sample shows a more complex relationship: both those who have worked as teleworkers for more than five years and those with only a little experience in remote work indicated that the lack of contact with others in similar work was a problem for them.

Virtually all the managers denied that trade unions had had any influence on the setting up, development or implementation of their telework schemes. Nevertheless, more than 50 per cent of them considered the unions and their attitudes to the introduction of new technology to be an important or very important constraint on the wider development of telework. This would suggest that the almost non-existent involvement of trade unions in setting up the schemes in our survey shows only that unions have not been active in promoting telework in the past. On the other hand, we have no information of schemes which have foundered as a result of union opposition.

The results of Empirica's survey of European decision makers, described in greater detail in Chapter 10, suggest that union resistance is not considered to be a significant factor by management as a whole—however, it could be argued that the managers in our survey are rather better informed about telework than average, which would give greater weight to their opinions. Interestingly enough, the three cases where managers did expect their telework schemes to be acceptable to the unions all concerned teleworkers with full employee status: the computer manufacturer, where women with children were employed part-time; the research company, where the flexible work arrangement was for full-time salaried staff; and the schemes for disabled people.

There is much discussion in the literature about the problems of supervision and control of telework, and many managers with no direct experience of telework give this as their main reason for not embarking on telework experiments. However, the reports of the managers of successful schemes in our survey indicate that supervision and control is a relatively minor problem, an important constraint for only about one in five organisations once the schemes are up and running.

To discover the main constraints on teleworkers from their own point of view, we asked both pre-coded and open-ended questions. Table 9.41 sets out their replies, ranked according to the proportion of the teleworker sample who considered a particular aspect to be an important or very important disadvantage of his or her work arrangement.

In response to an open question about which aspects of their working situation they felt it most important to change, teleworkers mentioned the following, ranked in order of the frequency with which they were mentioned:

- better child-care and nursery facilities
- improved communication with employer and colleagues
- more social benefits
- better pay

TABLE 9.41　Constraining factors from the teleworkers' perspective. Disadvantages of telework ranked by the proportion finding each important (%)

• Availability of office services	52.3
• Benefits, perks, pension schemes	48.1
• Extent to which working time and free time mix	45.6
• Level of pay	44.0
• Contacts with others in similar work	42.1
• Clerical support	35.1
• Promotion chances	34.5
• Participation in social gatherings of work colleagues	34.0
• Participation in working meetings	33.9
• Workspace	26.9

NB: Multiple answers were possible, 'not applicable' responses are excluded from percentages

- tax deductions for childminder fees
- a steadier pattern of work
- more opportunities for promotion
- more training for self-employed teleworkers

The demand for child-care facilities shows that, whatever its promoters contend, telework does not of itself provide an adequate solution to the problem of combining work with motherhood.

Most workers, asked a question like this, are likely to say they would like better pay and benefits, so their frequent mention here is no *prima facie* indication that pay level or benefits are of peculiar importance to teleworkers. However, our earlier analysis of income levels showed that many teleworkers are in fact accepting lower levels of pay than they would be offered in traditional working arrangements, so it is likely that the appearance of these demands here is a genuine indication that pay and benefits are a cause for concern. This applies to monetary provisions such as pension schemes, too. Teleworkers are frequently excluded from pension schemes, often because company schemes explicitly exclude part-time workers and the self-employed.

The lack of clear boundaries between work and leisure is perceived by many teleworkers as problematic, particularly when they are home-based and vulnerable to interruptions from family and friends. However, not all the encroachments of leisure on work come from others; the link with problems of self-discipline indicates that some are internally motivated. For many teleworkers, the way in which work impinges on leisure is a greater problem than its reverse. Despite this widespread dissatisfaction with the blurring of distinctions between work and leisure, nobody in the survey had any suggestions to make for changing it. Presumably this is because it was seen as an insoluble problem, intrinsic to telework.

Communication problems, on the other hand, were mentioned frequently, despite the inclusion of a number of electronic services offices and a satellite work centre where respondents were working alongside their colleagues and the problem of a lack of face-to-face contact did not arise.

The lack of social interaction with colleagues and employers and dearth of meetings can be subsumed under the general area of communications. Despite the fact that only some 10 per cent report real dissatisfaction with this aspect of telework, many feel it is a disadvantage and one which their employers could and should put some effort into remedying, by arranging more meetings and more opportunities for social and work-related contact with colleagues.

Whereas managers rarely cite the lack of office support services such as copying machines as a constraint on telework, teleworkers frequently mention this as a major disadvantage. A large number also explicitly ask for such services to be provided. This can probably be explained in part by the fact that equipment such as fax or photocopying machines is seen by teleworkers as relatively straightforward to supply. For employers, however, the picture is somewhat different. Economies of scale are not possible when they are installed in individual homes and it is difficult to justify the expense of providing relatively costly machines which may only be used occasionally—certainly less than they would be in an office where they would be shared between several workers.

FACTORS WHICH FACILITATE TELEWORK

As well as being asked about the constraints on telework, the managers in our survey were also asked for their views on factors which might encourage its future development. Table 9.42 gives their responses. Perhaps not surprisingly, the factors which are seen as most important for the successful running of a telework scheme are much the same as those which are necessary for setting it up. However, some additional positive features have emerged, for instance, there is now some mention of off-peak use of computing power as an important advantage, although this was never mentioned as a reason for introducing telework in the first place. The overall order of importance of items has not changed significantly, though. The two most important are still the ability to cope with peaks of work and the recruitment and retention of scarce skills.

The most surprising result was that eight managers out of ten now rated improved motivation and increased productivity as an important or very important advantage of telework. For several managers, this was obviously a

TABLE 9.42 *Facilitating factors in the operational phase of telework. Present importance and expected changes in importance*

Facilitating factors	Present position: Importance			Future perspectives: Importance		
	Unimportant	Important	N.A.	Less than now	More than now	N.A.
● Reduction in central facilities costs and overhead expenses	6	5	1	1	6	4
● Off-peak utilisation of the computer	8	2	2	3	5	4
● Improved motivation and increased productivity of employees	4	8	0	2	7	3
● Retention and recruiting of scarce skills	4	8	0	3	7	2
● Retention of employee turnover absenteeism generally	6	4	2	3	5	6
● Improved coping with surplus work (work peaks)	3	8	1	1	6	5
● Flexibility in determining conditions laid down in work contract	10	1	1	4	3	5
● Reduced costs for long-term employee welfare	7	4	1	3	4	6
● Rationalisation effort	4	7	1	3	5	4
● Flexibility in location of work	6	5	1	4	3	5
● Skill upgrading of employees	5	5	2	4	4	4
● Possibility for employee to combine work and non-work activities (e.g. child care)	3	7	2	2	4	5
● Reduced commuting efforts and costs for employees	7	4	1	3	4	5

$n = 12$

surprise, a discovery made during the course of the experiment, not one which they had anticipated when they set the scheme up.

There were other significant differences too. After the scheme had been set up, more managers thought that the opportunity for employees to combine work and child care was an important advantage. About the same number also felt that telework's contribution to staff rationalisation had been important, although this had rarely been mentioned as a reason for first introducing it. When it comes to reducing staff turnover, the opposite was the case, with fewer attributing importance to this than when the scheme was conceived. Taking these last two together, one gets the impression that telework offered a potential for shedding staff or reducing total working time which was only recognised (or admitted to) once the schemes were in operation.

Another aspect of telework which is given great importance is the opportunity it provides for flexibility in the location of work. All the managers in the sample predicted that these aspects would assume greater importance in the future.

When looking at the views of individual teleworkers, we found it impracticable—for the methodological reasons described earlier—to adopt the 'before and after' comparison we used with managers. Instead, we focused on what they currently perceived as the advantages of their working situation compared with traditional office-based work. Table 9.43 summarises the results. The five items heading the list are closely interlinked, forming a complex of advantages which we can call 'work flexibility and child care'. Flexibility in the allocation of working time, the ability to combine work with other activities, family and child-care advantages are very important for many teleworkers. These aspects of telework appear to bind them to this form of employment and ensure stability in the operational phase.

Unsurprisingly, more women teleworkers than men are in a situation where these opportunities are important to them. However, most men with young children also think that there are important advantages of telework. Working time flexibility is valued by nearly all teleworkers. It is nevertheless most important for those with child-care commitments. The typists stand out as the occupational group in which there is most agreement that child care is a very important advantage.

A large proportion of teleworkers who are self-employed find the status an advantage. This is linked to a positive attitude to the opportunities to develop their own businesses. It is likely that this reflects an extensive self-selection into telework of individuals preferring autonomy to job security in their working lives. Self-employed status is accordingly felt as an advantage, provided the individuals concerned are in a good market position, i.e. their particular skills are in high demand. For this group, telework even from a home-base can be practical and lucrative. Those who are positively inclined

TABLE 9.43   *Facilitating factors from the teleworkers' perspective.*
Advantages of telework ranked by the proportion finding each
important (%)

● Flexibility in working times	91.2
● Ability to combine child care with work	87.9
● Time for family	75.0
● Ability to meet family demands	71.5
● Ability to combine other activities with work	71.0
● Reduction of commuting time and expenses	69.7
● Reduction of distractions	54.2
● Self-employed status	52.2

NB: Multiple answers were possible; 'not applicable' responses are excluded from percentages

to the small business potential of their telework also not surprisingly see self-employed status as a positive attribute.

This does not hold for teleworkers whose skills are in oversupply in the workforce. This group recognises its insecure market position, tends not to feel at all satisfied with self-employment and prefers the security of being an employee. Evaluation of self-employed status is thus also linked to other perceived advantages and disadvantages of telework in the context of unionisation, pensions and self-employment. Self-employment is seen as neither an advantage nor a disadvantage by those who would prefer better union organisation. The lower qualified groups of teleworkers on the whole tend to find self-employed status a disadvantage, while the non-dp professionals have the most positive view.

Another factor which is generally regarded as an advantage of working away from a central office, especially by keyboard operators, is relative freedom from interruptions. A substantial majority also welcome the fact that there is no need to commute.

All these attitudes, it can be argued, represent factors which will facilitate the future development of telework.

EXPECTATIONS AND FUTURE PLANS

In contrast to the managers in Empirica's general survey of managers, described in Chapter 10, the managers in this survey were generally optimistic about the future development of telework. Well over half the managers of telework schemes in this survey believed that telework would expand considerably in the future, while the remainder thought that it would become more viable than at present. Their reasons related to technology as well as to company strategies. Many managers pointed out that they expected telecommunications and computer technology to become both more sophisticated and cheaper in the future. As a result, they expected telework to gain in importance as part of a strategy for minimising costs, ensuring a high level of flexibility to adapt to changing market conditions and, where appropriate, optimising the quality of services. Others thought that telework would come into its own as a tool for the retention and recruitment of staff with hard-to-find skills. General changes in attitude would, it was thought, also play a role.

Telework was becoming more feasible with the spread of computing skills and there was, according to these managers, increasing organisational acceptance of it. Some company managers considered up to a quarter of office jobs to be suitable for telework . In their opinion, there were no significant constraints preventing companies from decentralising these tasks, and they foresaw a growth of telework in these areas.

Over half the managers expected at least a moderate increase in the number of teleworkers in Europe in the next decade, with a majority expecting this increase to be considerable.

Putting these beliefs into practice, all but three of the organisations in our sample intended to expand their telework schemes, while none planned to contract them. A homogeneous pattern thus emerges with regard to the attitudes managers have towards the major changes they expect to take place in the future affecting telework. They all foresee a corporate environment in which most factors will combine to facilitate the growth of telework, including: the company inventory of IT; its costs and sophistication; decision makers' attitudes and general trends in society such as the spread of computer literacy. With some exceptions among the companies which employ teleworkers for typing and clerical work, it is also generally assumed that employee- or population-related developments (such as the attitudes of employees towards telework, the IT orientation of the population, and the household penetration of IT) will also be conducive to the growth of telework.

According to these managers, a definite constraint on the future spread of telework is trade unions' policy towards the introduction of information technology and, at least in West Germany, their outright opposition to telework. Over three-quarters of the managers surveyed expressed the view that union policy would tend to constrain the future development of telework.

CONCLUSIONS

Overall, our survey revealed a surprisingly complex picture. The participants in the telework schemes have clearly brought a wide range of differing motivations and experiences to them, which have shaped them in diverse and apparently contradictory ways. Generalisations are therefore fraught with danger. While some teleworkers can be said to be underpaid in relation to their office-based colleagues, others earn less. While some work shorter hours, others work longer. While some feel more in control of their lives, others feel more powerless. Similar contrasts could be drawn along almost any dimension of working experience.

Nevertheless, while aware of the risk of oversimplifying, we do feel that it is possible to draw certain general conclusions. Among the wide variety of telework schemes, two dominant types seem to emerge. While they may be superficially similar in some respects, they are radically different in their effects. One way of distinguishing them is by the motivations of the employers who have set them up.

TABLE 9.44   Expectations with regard to major changes affecting telework from a manager's perspective

	Constraining	Ambivalent, No effect etc.	Facilitating
• Company inventory of information and communication equipment	—	4	8
• Household penetration with home and personal computers	2	1	9
• Attitudes of employed people towards telework	—	6	6
• Attitudes of decision makers in companies towards telework	—	3	9
• Office work content and tasks	—	5	7
• Cost reductions and/or increasing sophistication in the area of computer technology	—	2	10
• Cost reductions and/or increasing sophistication in the area of telecommunications infrastructure	—	2	10
• Developments in organisational concepts, including supervision and control	—	5	7
• Training, skills, qualifications of employees/teleworkers	—	2	9
• IT orientation of population	1	4	7
• Unions' position	7	3	1
• General trends in society	—	2	9

The first type of scheme is one which has been set up primarily for the purpose of cutting costs by converting fixed costs into variable ones. Here the strategy is simply to externalise labour. It is a strategy which only works effectively when there is a relative overabundance of labour, so that the employer can to a large extent dictate the conditions of employment. It is therefore largely confined to low-skill areas such as typing, data entry or routine office work and is typically associated with self-employment, payment by results and work which is exclusively home-based. The typical teleworker in this scenario is a women with young children, the secondary earner in her household, motivated by the desire to combine work with child care.

In the second type, the relative bargaining positions of employer and teleworker are very different. The employer's primary motivation is to find or retain scarce skills. Here, teleworkers have a substantial say in determining the terms of their employment, which may, as a result, take a number of contractual forms: a straightforward employment contract; a freelance contract; or a sub-contract to perform certain services made with an independent company directed by the teleworker. The place of work may also be flexible, with teleworkers retaining a desk in the office in addition to working at home or on clients' premises on occasion. Teleworkers in this category are as likely to be male as female and, although some are motivated by the desire to integrate work with their domestic commitments, others are more interested in setting up their own independent businesses. In contrast with the first group, these teleworkers are likely to be relatively high earners. Typical occupations in this category are computer professionals of various types, writers and consultants.

Needless to say, reality is not as strongly polarised as this typology might suggest. There are a number of schemes which share some of the characteristics of both extremes. Numerically the most important of these, at least in our survey, are those in which female computer programmers are employed. In some respects, they fall firmly into our second category. On the other hand, many of these teleworkers are severely restricted in the labour market by their child-care commitments and have therefore accepted types of employment contract and pay levels which place them closer to the first in terms of their job security and their pay levels relative to staff doing the same work on-site. However, most appear to have arrived in this position as a result of a conscious tradeoff. It seems likely that in a high proportion of these cases telework has been chosen, not as a permanent way of life, but as a compromise to see them through a particular phase in their lives.

Although telework schemes remain few and far between, the circumstances which have given rise to them are common, and by no means confined to certain industries. Skill shortages in certain professional areas; skill oversupply among women with routine office skills; a lack of good alternative child-care facilities; a desire on the part of many employers to reduce fixed costs and increase flexibility: all these are likely to remain with us, indeed, in most cases to grow in coming years. At the same time, the technical barriers to telework are diminishing, as equipment prices continue to fall, new and more easily operated communications software becomes available and the telecommunications infrastructure is upgraded. Organisations are changing both in their structure and in their culture. The stage seems set for an expansion of telework.

Our survey shows that a number of different forms of remote work are feasible and that the organisational and technical obstacles feared by many managers can be overcome. The social obstacles are less easily defined but will undoubtedly be critical in determining both the future extent of telework and the specific forms which it takes. There is at present enormous scope for designing new telework schemes tailored to meet the needs of particular organisations and their workforces, or to integrate particular social groups into the labour market. How successful these schemes are will depend not so much on factors intrinsic to telework but on how well they meet these specific needs by matching supply and demand. Clearly a scheme which meets a management need at the cost of unhappiness for the workforce is unlikely to be acceptable in the long term; neither is a scheme which perfectly suits the domestic circumstances of its participants at the cost of high organisational inefficiency. Telework opens up diverse new options in the organisation of work, where it is based, how it is managed, and the terms and conditions of employment. We believe that its most successful applications will be those which increase the range of choice both for organisations and for individuals.

Chapter 10

*THE DEMAND FOR TELEWORK—AN EMPIRICA SURVEY OF
DECISION MAKERS IN EUROPE*

Useful though it is to gain a detailed picture of how telework functions in
individual organisations, we were well aware of the danger of extrapolating
from the experiences of a small selection of organisations to society at large.
To try to get a more complete impression of the likely future development of
telework in Europe, we carried out, in addition to our survey of teleworkers,
two further surveys as part of Empirica's general programme of research on
the subject. The first of these, which looks more broadly at the demand for
telework, is the subject of this chapter; the second, a survey of the employed
population which set out to estimate the supply side, will be examined in
Chapter 11.

Our objective in carrying out the demand-side survey was to determine the
opinions and attitudes of decision makers towards telework and the organisational changes it implies. The 4000 decision makers interviewed comprised
a representative cross-section of the manufacturing and service industries in
both the public and the private sectors in four European countries: West
Germany, France, the United Kingdom and Italy.

One of the assumptions underlying the survey was the belief, backed up by
the literature on the subject, that the potential market for telework will depend
on the interest and willingness of decision makers to make use of the
opportunities it offers for decentralising office services.

METHODOLOGY

In each of the four countries, approximately 1000 managers (928 in Germany,
1000 in France, 1378 in the UK and 702 in Italy) were asked about their
attitudes towards and their willingness to use telework (defined as information
technology-based decentralised forms of work) and their reasons for and
against using it.

The structure of the survey, and detailed methodological information can
be found in Appendix G. The results of the survey were carefully weighted
to ensure that they reflected the typical European company size structure,
with its high proportion of small organisations. Details of the weighting
procedure can also be found in Appendix G.

THE TASKS CONSIDERED MOST SUITABLE FOR TELEWORK

Manager's responses to questions about which tasks they considered most suitable for decentralisation reflected fairly closely the reality revealed by Empirica's own telework survey, described in Chapter 9. Top of the list was 'computer programming tasks', followed by 'typing and word processing' and 'data entry and amendment'. In fourth and fifth place came, respectively, 'qualified administrative work' (such as book-keeping and accounting) and 'clerical work' (such as filing business records). 'Management tasks' came last, with respondents indicating that they saw little potential for the decentralisation of management functions. Interestingly enough, this is the one area where the respondents' opinions departed significantly from the actuality of telework which, as can be seen from the preceding chapter, includes a surprisingly high proportion of remotely-based managers. In Germany, an additional category, 'documentation and evaluation tasks' was mentioned, its place being taken in the other three countries by 'stock control and replacement'.

The high place of computer programming in this list can be largely attributed to the very high interest in decentralising it among Italian managers. The Italian figures are consistently twice if not three times as high as those for other countries in relation to most of these tasks, pushing up the average degree of interest from levels which would otherwise appear to be low or, at best, moderate. At the other extreme are the results from the UK which show a very low interest in telework, rarely rising above 10 per cent.

INTEREST IN TELEWORK

When the results are analysed according to company size, a discernible trend comes to light: the greater the size of a company, the more interest there is in telework. This is the case in every country except Italy, as can be seen from Figure 10.1. There is also a relationship between company size and the range of tasks considered suitable for decentralisation: the larger the company, the greater the variety of tasks considered appropriate for telework.

If we take the input and amendment of data, for instance, we find a marked increase in interest according to company size: for organisations with fewer than 10 employees the average is 12 per cent; for companies with a payroll of 10 to 99 employees it rises to 15.6 per cent, in companies employing 100 to 499 people it leaps to 24 per cent, reaching a full 33 per cent in companies with over 500 employees.

Interest in decentralising typing or word-processing tasks shows a similar, though slightly less dramatic, pattern of progression, with the largest organisations two and a half times as likely as the smallest to be interested.

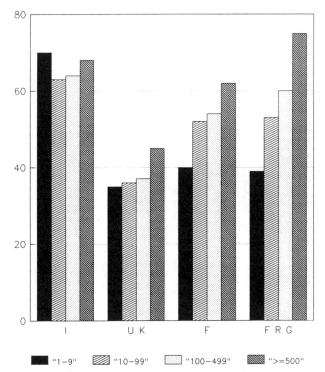

"1-9"   "10-99"   "100-499"   ">=500"

FIGURE 10.1   General interest in telework according to size of company (percentage of decision makers showing interest)

With computer programming the picture is similar, with a threefold increase in the degree of interest according to company size.

The two exceptions to this pattern are qualified administrative work and management tasks (such as invoice control employee records, and cash flow monitoring). There is no consistent pattern to the distribution of interest in qualified administrative work, perhaps because larger companies tend to hive these functions off into separate, self-contained departments.

An analysis by industry reveals considerable differences. It was the banking and insurance sector which displayed the highest interest of all in telework. The functions which managers in these industries were most keen to decentralise were data entry, typing and work processing, with computer programming attracting varying degrees of interest. In Italy, where 64 per cent of managers in this industry expressed an interest in decentralising programming tasks, it was the most popular task of all for telework, while French managers showed an interest at half this level, 32 per cent. However, only 8 per cent of German

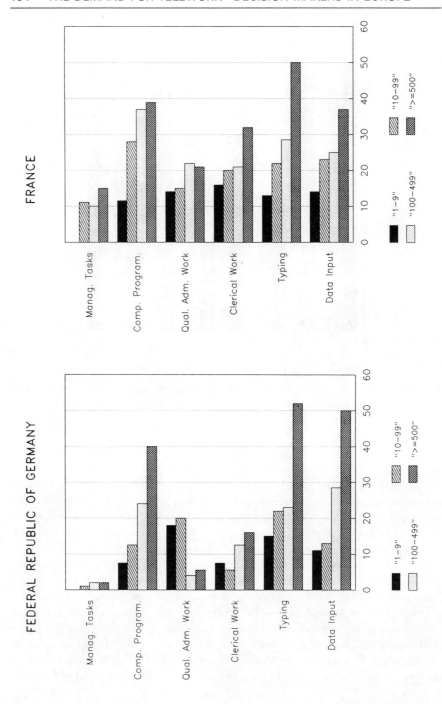

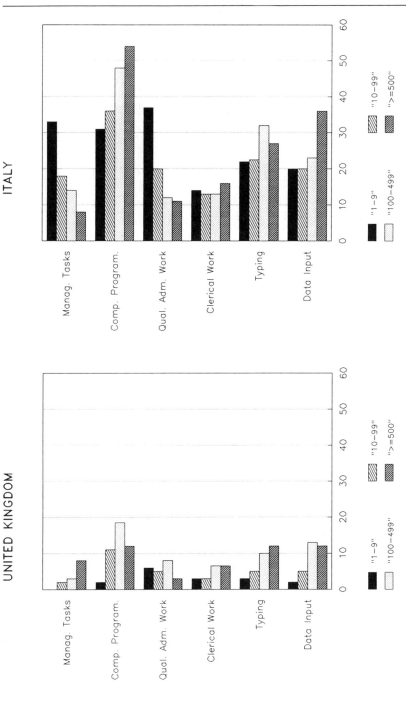

FIGURE 10.2 *Interest in telework by task and company size in West Germany, France, the United Kingdom and Italy (percentage of decision makers showing interest)*

managers in this sector thought that it was suitable to introduce remote working for such tasks, a proportion which fell still lower, to a mere 5 per cent, in the UK.

Second only to the finance sector was retail and wholesale distribution. Here too, interest in telework is highest in Italy, where 52 per cent of managers in this sector think that computer programming is suitable for decentralisation. In Germany and France, however, only 12 per cent share this view. There is also interest in decentralising typing and word processing, qualified administrative work, clerical work and data entry.

In manufacturing industry (for which we used a definition which included the power and construction industries), computer programming was the function most commonly thought suitable for decentralisation. Once again, the Italians were the most enthusiastic proponents of telework, with a level of interest three times as high as that of the French and Germans (45 per cent compared with 15 per cent in France and 17 per cent in Germany).

When we turn to the service industries, the picture changes somewhat. In companies in the private sector the tasks receiving the highest ratings are typing and word processing. Qualified administrative work and data entry exhibit similar degrees of interest. However, the interest in decentralising computer programming differs widely among the four countries surveyed, as can be seen from Figure 10.6.

On average, the public services sector showed less interest in telework than any of the others bar one. French managers showed the most consistency here, like their colleagues in other sectors, rating stock control and replacement as the task category with the greatest potential for decentralisation, with 32 per cent indicating interest. In Italy no less than 46 per cent of managers in this sector thought that computer programming could be decentralised, a higher proportion than in any other sector. In France and Germany there was also moderate interest in telework for programmers in the public services (at 17 and 11 per cent respectively). In the UK, however, only 2 per cent of managers were interested, comparable to the 2.5 per cent national average for this task category.

Businesses with fewer than ten employees and self-employed individuals show a somewhat different pattern of interest in telework from their colleagues in larger organisations. Here, there is interest in both qualified administrative work and typing and word processing. However, the French respondents in this sector followed the pattern of other managers in that country by expressing a strong interest in decentralising stock control with 39 per cent showing interest. Clerical work and data entry received above-average interest in Italy and France, but below average in Germany.

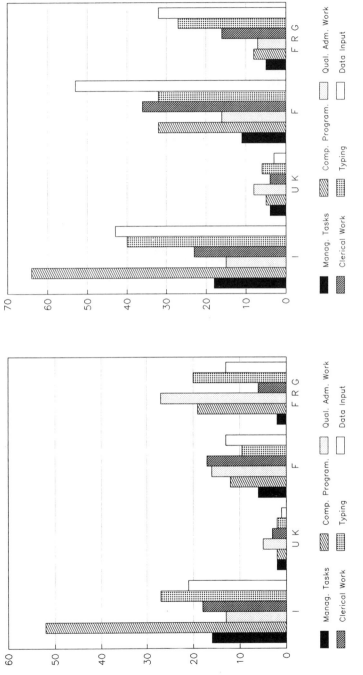

FIGURE 10.3 *Interest in telework in the banking and insurance sectors, by task (percentage of decision makers showing interest)*

FIGURE 10.4 *Interest in telework in the wholesale and retail distribution sectors, by task (percentage of decision makers showing interest)*

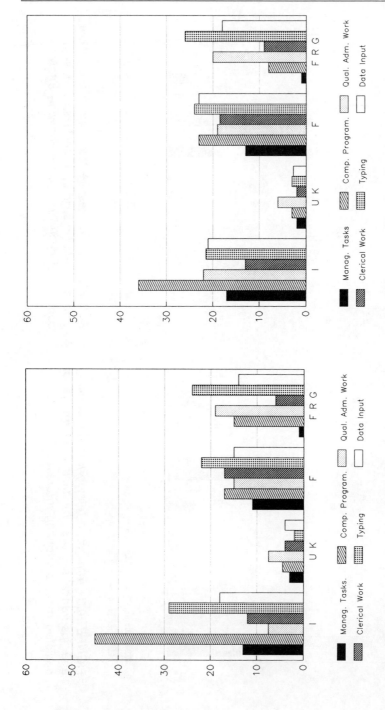

FIGURE 10.5   Interest in telework in the manufacturing sector, by task (percentage of decision makers showing interest)

FIGURE 10.6   Interest in telework in the private services sector, by task (percentage of decision makers showing interest)
Note   Apart from France, this figure excludes companies with less than 10 employees

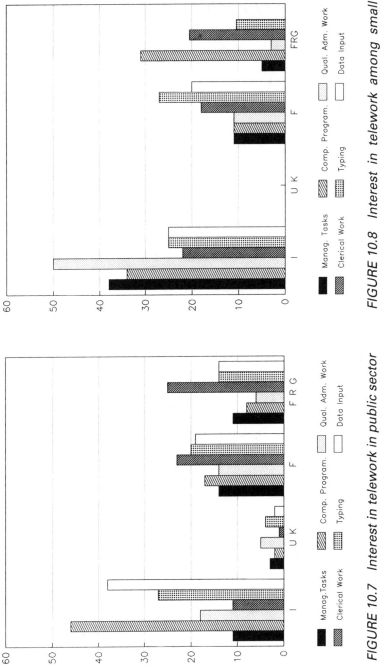

FIGURE 10.7 *Interest in telework in public sector services, by task (percentage of decision makers indicating interest)*

FIGURE 10.8 *Interest in telework among small businesses and the self-employed* (percentage of decision makers showing interest)*
* *Companies with less than 10 employees*

THE DECISION MAKERS IN THE SURVEY

In evaluating the significance of these results, it is useful to have some impression of the characteristics of the decision makers who took part in the survey. We were also interested to discover whether attitudes to telework were affected by such variables as the age, sex or position within the organisation of a respondent. The analysis which follows is based on the data from the French, German and Italian surveys, since sufficiently detailed information for this purpose was unfortunately not available from the United Kingdom.

When considering the general interest in decentralising the tasks listed in the survey according to age groups, a trend comes to light which indicates that the older the decision maker, the less interest he or she has in using decentralised electronic work.

The respondent's position within the organisation turned out to be a relatively insignificant variable both within and between countries. Germany showed the greatest variation, with 41 per cent of owners, 43 per cent of executive directors and 53 per cent of departmental directors indicating some interest in telework. In France, the comparable figures were 44, 37 and 43 per cent respectively, while in Italy there was virtually no difference at all between these categories, which were all around 35 per cent.

An analysis by gender reveals greater variation, but this is not consistent. Most dramatically, in Germany, male managers were nearly twice as likely as their female colleagues (48, compared with 25 per cent) to be interested in telework. Men were also more interested in France, where the difference was less marked (46, compared with 37 per cent). However, in Italy, women were slightly more likely than men to be interested (68, compared wth 66 per cent) in decentralising office work.

This result suggests that it is possible that some of the non-interest in telework revealed by the survey may be an expression of a belief not so much that telework is not feasible but that it is undesirable. In West Germany, as noted in earlier chapters, the trade unions and the women's movement have conducted strong campaigns against electronic homework, arguing that it is against womens' interests. The low rate of interest in telework among female German managers could therefore possibly be due to a greater sympathy for such arguments among women than from their male colleagues. The reasons for lack of interest in telework will be explored further in the next section of this chapter.

REASONS FOR NOT DECENTRALISING OFFICE WORK

In the previous section, we noted a considerable variation between countries and, to some extent, between industries, in managers' willingness to consider telework and in the types of tasks which they regarded as appropriate for such decentralisation. However, when we came to examine the reasons why decision makers thought that telework would not be suitable, we discovered that there was considerably more unanimity amongst the respondents. In this section, therefore, we focus on the most frequent reasons mentioned, and—in order to identify exceptions—on the most infrequently cited reasons for refusing to consider remote work.

In the survey as a whole, two reasons stand out as the most usual explanations for lack of interest: the difficulty of organising telework, and the lack of any apparent need to change from the current situation. This gives us an impression that the typical situation is one where organisational structures and work forms are static, with considerable management inertia. The reason cited least frequently was 'problems with the unions' which seem to worry very few managers, regardless of the industry in which they operate or the size of the organisation, with one exception, which is described below.

Figure 10.11 shows the reasons for not wanting to use decentralised electronic work according to company size. As can be seen, among those who might at some point be interested in introducing telework, it was 'availability of the necessary equipment' which was regarded as posing the greatest obstacle. It is worth noting, however, that anxiety about both 'organisational difficulties' and 'lack of supervision and control' increased with company size. While larger companies saw these as significant disadvantages, smaller companies considered 'high costs' to be a greater drawback.

Also, the attitude characterised by the phrase 'no need to change the current situation', consistently rated as one of the foremost reasons for not favouring telework, moved down from first position to third among companies with over 500 employees.

Another variable we examined in this context was the age of the respondent. As might be expected, we found that there was a significant correlation between the age of a manager and the view that there was no need to change the current situation: the older the respondent, the less likelihood there was of any need for change being perceived. The exception to this rule was Italy, where the proportion of decision makers expressing this view was in the region of 40 per cent across all age groups. In Germany it rose from 57 per cent in the youngest age group to 66 per cent in the highest, while in France the comparable rise was even more dramatic, from 42 to 74 per cent. No data were available for the United Kingdom.

Other reasons are much less closely linked with age. Nevertheless, it is possible to discern a pattern whereby older respondents are less likely to regard organisational difficulties, limited supervision or high costs as major difficulties than their less experienced colleagues.

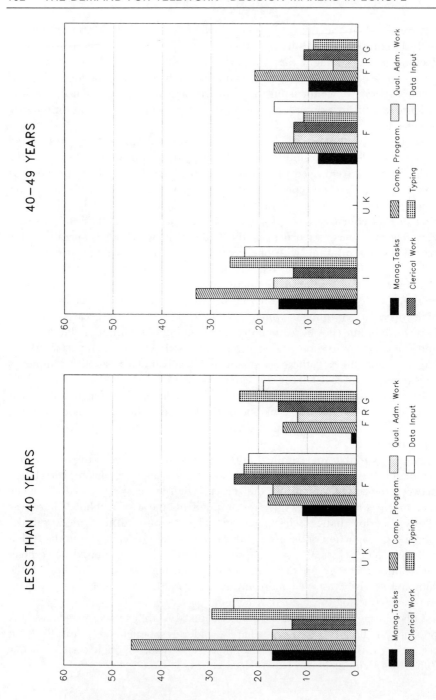

50 YEARS AND OVER

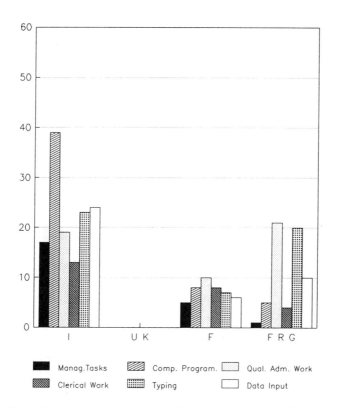

FIGURE 10.9   *Interest in telework by the decision maker's age (percentage of decision makers showing interest)*

When we isolated self-employed professionals and small firms carrying out professional services (a group which is frequently seen as a prime target for telework) from the rest of the sample, we found a picture which was remarkably consistent across national boundaries. The most frequently cited reason for not adopting telework in France, Germany and Italy (there were no data for the UK) was 'no need to change from the current situation'. This was followed by 'high costs'. 'Organisational difficulties' and 'lack of supervision over employees' were also seen as problems, by around a quarter of the sample in Italy and Germany but over half in France. A lack of suitable skills among the workforce and of suitable equipment are next in importance. Only in France does concern about the employees' acceptance of telework appear to take on some significance.

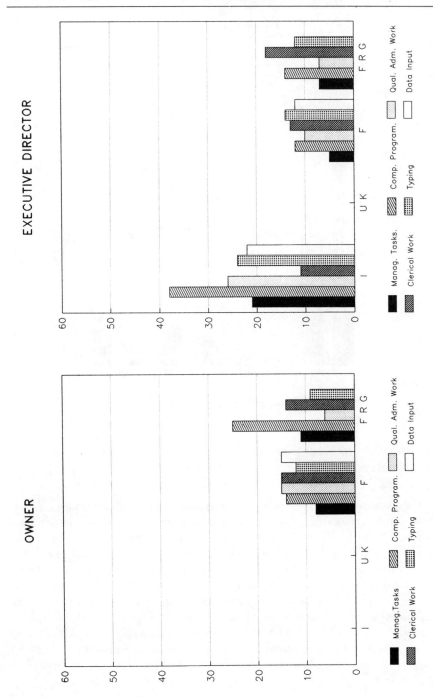

DEPARTMENT DIRECTOR

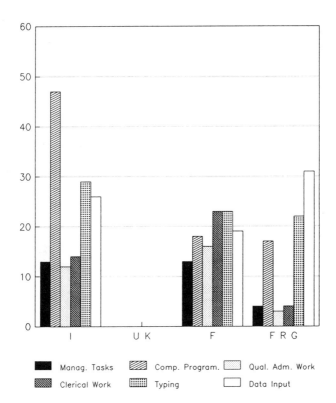

Manag. Tasks   Comp. Program.   Qual. Adm. Work

Clerical Work   Typing   Data Input

FIGURE 10.10 Interest in telework by the decision maker's position (percentage of decision makers showing interest)

Our respondents in the craft trades proved even more resistant to change. 'No need to change the current situation' was cited by no less than 79 per cent of this group in Germany, 72 per cent in France and 62.5 per cent in Italy.

The last group of small firms we studied in detail was in the distribution sector, where there were data only for Italy and Germany. In both countries, apart from the feeling that change is unnecessary, which is, as usual, the dominant reason for rejecting telework, organisational and financial problems are considered the main obstacles to adopting it.

Turning to larger organisations, we find considerably greater variance between countries. In the manufacturing sector, for instance, each country gives a different reason the greatest importance. In Germany, high costs are

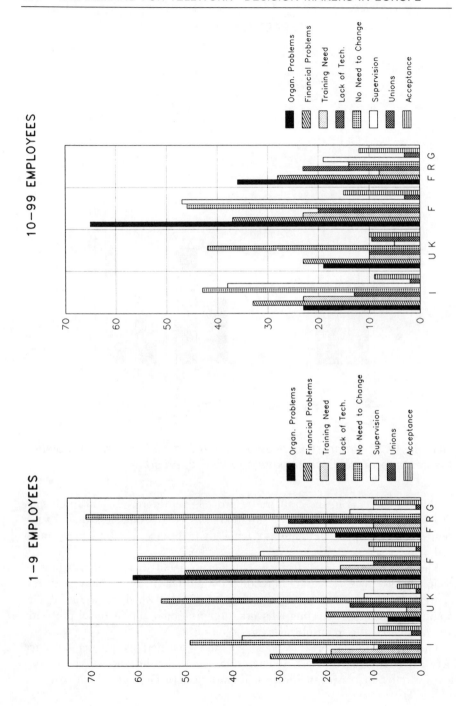

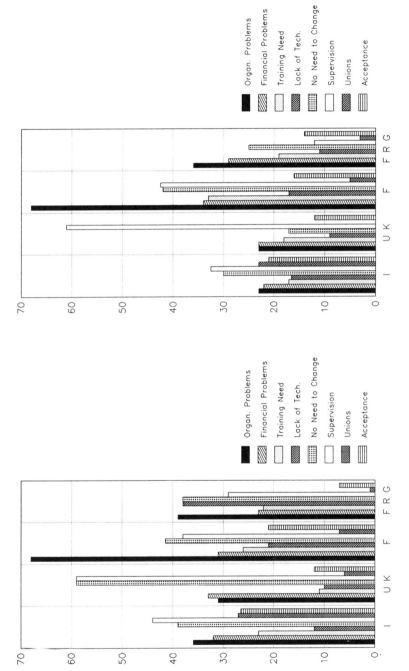

FIGURE 10.11 Reasons given by decision makers for not using telework by company size

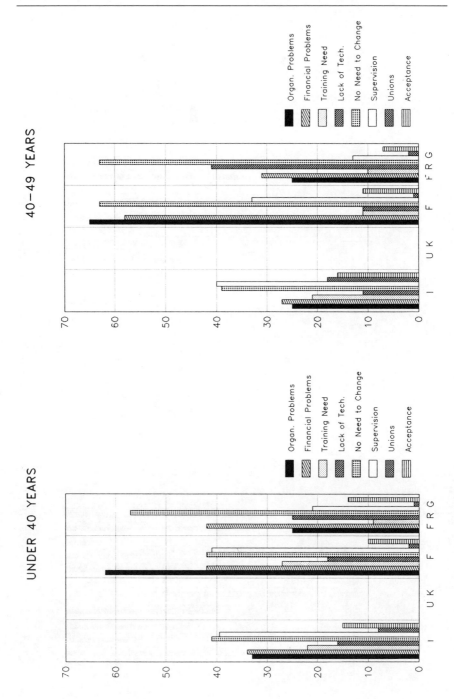

50 YEARS AND OVER

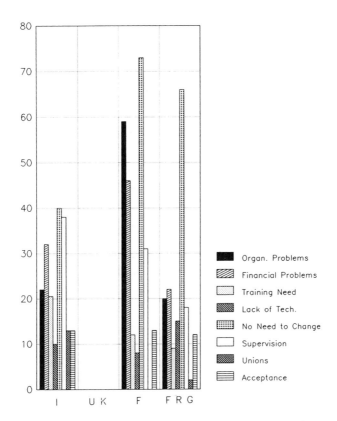

FIGURE 10.12 Reasons given by decision makers for not using decentralised electronic work by age group of decision maker

the main problem; in France, it is lack of union acceptance; in Italy, difficulties in supervising a remote workforce, while in the United Kingdom the belief that things are fine as they are is the main constraint.

In the distribution sector, there is less contrast. The lack of any reason to change, high costs and organisational difficulties all score fairly high, as does the lack of supervisory control, except in Germany.

In banking and insurance, however, we find a different picture. Managers in this industry seem much more prepared for change. The 'no need to change' response has dropped to third place in Germany and fourth in France and Italy. On the other hand, supervisory difficulties have gained in importance. In Germany and Italy there is also some concern about employee acceptance.

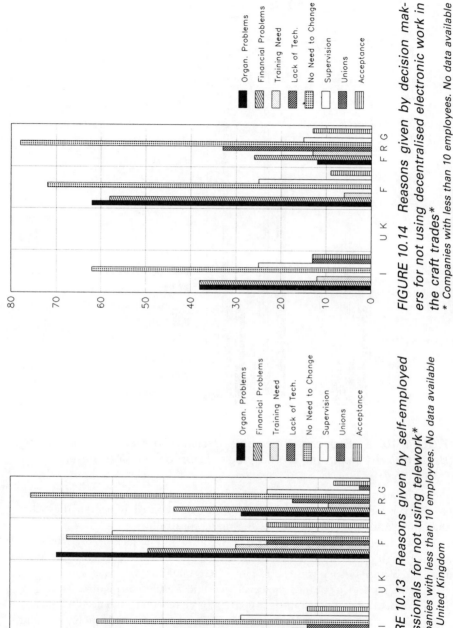

FIGURE 10.13 Reasons given by self-employed professionals for not using telework*
* Companies with less than 10 employees. No data available for the United Kingdom

FIGURE 10.14 Reasons given by decision makers for not using decentralised electronic work in the craft trades*
* Companies with less than 10 employees. No data available from the United Kingdom

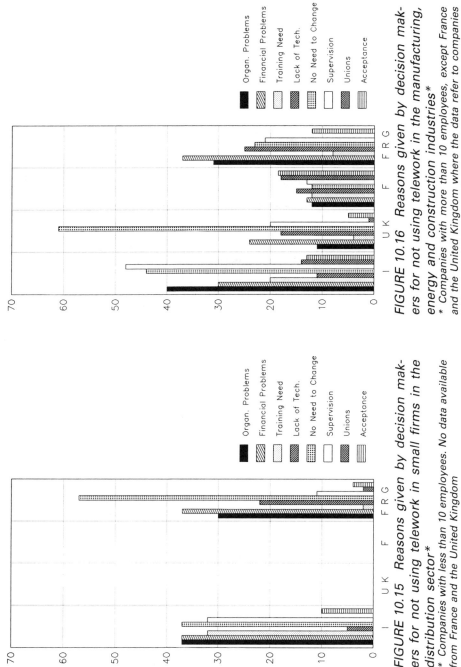

FIGURE 10.16 *Reasons given by decision makers for not using telework in the manufacturing, energy and construction industries**
* *Companies with more than 10 employees, except France and the United Kingdom where the data refer to companies with more than one employee*

FIGURE 10.15 *Reasons given by decision makers for not using telework in small firms in the distribution sector**
* *Companies with less than 10 employees. No data available from France and the United Kingdom*

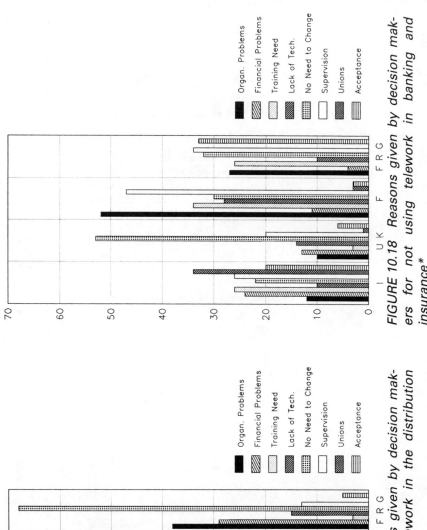

FIGURE 10.17 Reasons given by decision makers for not using telework in the distribution sector*

* Companies with more than 10 employees, except the United Kingdom and France, where the data refer to companies with more than one employee

FIGURE 10.18 Reasons given by decision makers for not using telework in banking and insurance*

* Companies with more than 10 employees, except France and the United Kingdom, where the data refer to companies with more than one employee

In the other services, both public and private, the pattern reverts to a more familiar one: 'no need to change' reappears as the main deterrent to introducing telework, with the exception of France, where organisational difficulties are paramount.

The reasons for lack of interest in telework can be summarised fairly readily. However, in most cases it is the exception which proves more interesting than the rule. Generally speaking, the lack of a need to change the current situation is by far the most common objection to telework, regardless of country, reaching first or second place in virtually all industries. The five exceptions to this rule are therefore significant in themselves, especially since three of them occur in the same industry—banking and insurance—where the main objection to telework is the difficulty of exercising adequate supervisory control of a remote workforce.

The other main impediment is organisational difficulties, which exceed costs in importance. Here, company size is an important factor. The smaller the firm, the less likely organisational difficulties are to figure as a major obstacle, but the greater the importance attached to cost. Conversely, in large organisations, costs diminish in significance as organisational problems multiply.

French decision makers consistently ascribe greater importance to organisational difficulties than their counterparts in other countries. This attitude may, perhaps, derive from the particular organisational structures which have arisen from France's distinctive employment legislation.

By contrast, in Italy and the UK, where the labour market is comparatively deregulated, organisational difficulties assume relatively less importance, falling below high costs in the scale of deterrents to decentralisation. There is also a relationship between company size and supervisory difficulties, which rise in importance along with the scale of the enterprise. This problem is particularly important in the banking and insurance sector, perhaps because, in addition to the large size and hence the complexity of administration of most companies in this sector, there are also major problems of security. Supervisory problems are also of above-average importance in Italy.

In Germany, with the exception of two industries, the availability of equipment is seen as particularly problematic.

CONCLUSIONS

The most striking feature of this survey as a whole is its revelation that telework is still very much a minority interest among European managers, with apathy and more concrete objections to it greatly outnumbering expressions of interest. Interest is highest in Italy and lowest in the UK. However, in some industries the minority which is interested is large enough

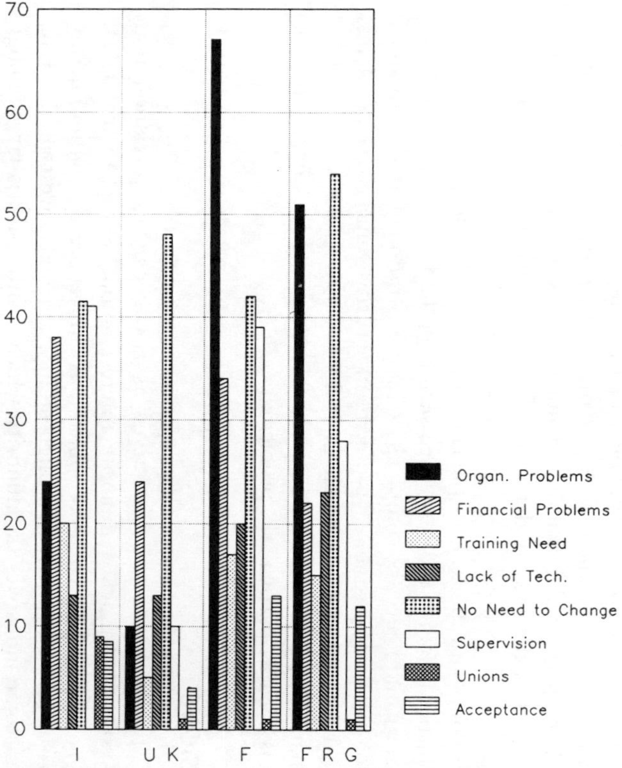

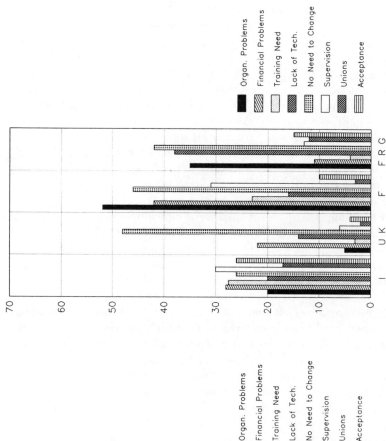

FIGURE 10.19 Reasons given by decision makers for not using telework in other private service industries*
* Companies with more than 10 employees, except France and the United Kingdom, where the data refer to companies with more than one employee

FIGURE 10.20 Reasons given by decision makers for not using telework in the public sector, railway and postal services*
* Companies with more than 10 employees, except France and the United Kingdom, where the data refer to companies with more than one employee

to suggest that telework could reach significant proportions in certain specialised areas.

These conclusions were substantiated by the results of a workshop held by Empirica in Britain in 1986 on *The Potential for Decentralised Electronic Working in the Banking, Insurance and Software Industries*. At this workshop participants generally agreed that telework was highly unlikely to prove attractive to employers in these industries except in a few minor and exceptional cases (Empirica, 1986a).

A US survey carried out in 1984 produced similar findings, leading the researchers to conclude that, 'those with supervisory duties are more resistant to the idea. Because management is not embracing the concept, we might expect that telecommuting will not become widely practised by full-time organisation employees in the near future, even though the technology is already available' (DeSanctis, 1984, p. 138).

We also found that the overwhelmingly dominant reason for this lack of interest was that 'there is no need to change from the current situation'. The conservatism expressed in this attitude is buttressed by a secondary desire to avoid the 'organisational difficulties' which it is widely believed that telework will entail. Despite this overall impression of organisational inertia, markets for telework do, however, appear to exist in some areas. Virtually all sectors include a minority of managers who are interested in putting out such office services as word processing, typing, data entry and, to a lesser extent, computer programming. This demand seems to be greatest in, although it is by no means confined to, the banking and insurance industries. Apart from the fact that these industries involve very large volumes of routine processing of information, this may be explained in part by the fact that they already have a highly dispersed workforce, scattered in local branch offices, or in the case of some insurance companies, a mobile sales force, for whom remote access to the employer's central computer facilities is nothing new. Telework technologies are already in use, and functions previously carried out at head office have, in many cases, already been decentralised. Managers in these industries therefore already have some practical experience to support their views on telework. However, because of the confidential nature of much of the information they are handling and because of the ever-present danger of fraud or theft, these industries also present particularly intractable security problems which mitigate against forms of decentralisation, such as homework, which are difficult to supervise closely.

Another and very different market for telework can be identified, catering to the needs of very small companies or individual freelances, many of whom, it is clear, would welcome the opportunity to sub-contract office services which they lack the time, the expertise or the inclination to perform for themselves. The demand for such qualified administrative tasks as accounting, keeping employee records or invoice control is strongly dependent on company size, with a marked falling off in companies employing over 100 people and a peak in the smallest size category—those with fewer than ten employees. We might speculate that telework of this type has a particularly strong growth potential because of the snowball effect whereby one individual freelance or entrepreneur, say a computer programmer, generates a requirement for others to carry out such tasks as designing stationery, or book-keeping, and these in turn create a need for other specialist office services.

According to our survey, the demand for such services exists not just among self-employed professionals and craftspeople but also in small firms throughout the service industries, including the wholesale and retail sectors, and in communications and news services. However, the demand for more routine office services, such as typing, data entry or word processing, shows an opposite tendency, with an increase with the size of the company. The fact that this demand is expressed across all industries suggests that a mass market for such services may well develop.

A similar trend is discernible with the demand for computer programming, although here the most likely reason is simply that small firms rarely have a need for this service, being mainly reliant—where they use information technology at all—on standard systems using off-the-peg software.

The generally high popularity of computer programming as a candidate for telework must be partly attributable to the fact that the industry has a well-publicised tradition, extending back a quarter of a century in the UK, of using homeworkers. Familiarity with the idea of the home programmer must have paved the way for its acceptance among managers still suspicious of the idea of other types of staff working remotely. This suggests that interest in telework may grow as managers become more familiar with it in different fields and gain direct experience of using information technology for remote communications. Certainly the results of Empirica's supply-side survey, described in the next chapter, indicate that managers already using IT in the office on a more or less regular basis are more likely to be interested in becoming teleworkers themselves than those who lack such first-hand experience.

Discounting, for a moment, the apathy and conservatism which appear to constitute the main obstacles to the growth of telework, the main constraints on its rapid development seem to be in the case of small firms, its high cost and, in the case of larger organisations, the difficulties of supervising a remote workforce. Except in Germany, there appear to be few technical impediments and remarkably few managers seem to think that a lack of acceptance by employees or their trade unions would pose problems. Whether this is because they do not believe that the workforce would object or because they are not in the habit of taking account of such objections is not clear from this survey.

In the next chapter we examine the findings of Empirica's survey of employed people which sheds more light on employees' attitudes to telework. For managers, it is apparent that the main barrier to a rapid development of telework is their own reluctance to depart from existing practices. Such attitudes are likely to change with greater first-hand experience of the technology and familiarity with the organisational possibilities opened up by telework.

Chapter 11

THE SUPPLY OF TELEWORK—AN EMPIRICA SURVEY OF EMPLOYEES IN EUROPE

So far, we have presented the results of our survey of people currently involved in telework schemes, to gain an impression of the actuality of decentralised electronic work in Europe, and of managers, to assess the future demand for telework. The picture is not complete without also looking at the supply side. What are the attitudes of the European workforce to the possibility of working remotely?

To gauge these, we carried out a representative survey of 16,000 households in West Germany, France, the United Kingdom and Italy. The respondents were a random sample of all employed people in these countries in households with telephones. About 4000 people were interviewed in each country and asked about their attitudes towards working with a computer from their homes. Appendix H shows the structure of the survey.

Appendix I gives details of how the data were weighted to take account of different population sizes and to allow for comparisons with other national statistics. Before being asked about their attitudes towards home-based telework, the respondents were given a brief explanation of the technical possibility of linking a remote terminal in their homes to a central computer on the employer's premises. It was decided to restrict the questioning to home-based work because other forms of telework, such as neighbourhood offices or satellite workcentres, were unlikely to be familiar to the general public. Appendix J lists all the socio-economic and demographic variables which were taken into account.

GENERAL RESULTS

One of the surprises of the survey was the variation in response between the different European countries included in the survey. Interest in telework ranged from a low of 8.5 per cent in West Germany to a peak of 23 per cent in the United Kingdom, with France (14 per cent) and Italy (11 per cent) in intermediate positions. Assuming that our sample was representative of the employed population as a whole, this means that an average of 14 per cent of the labour force—nearly 13 million people in the four major European countries—shows an interest in home-based telework.

Comparable survey results from the USA indicate that 7 per cent of the employed US population is interested in working from a home base using a computer connected to the main office (Blumenstein 1985). However, the same survey indicated that a much higher proportion—36 per cent—would welcome the chance to work partly in an office and partly from home, an option which was not presented to the respondents in our survey.

A figure of 13 million people constitutes a very large pool of potential teleworkers, although when it is compared to the size of the total workforce in these four countries, which is nearly 92 million, it is still a minority. A majority of the workforce is still uninterested in telework. As can be seen from Table 11.1, the share of people expressing negative attitudes towards telework varies considerably among the four countries. It is at its highest in Germany where over half the sample (53 per cent) had no interest in becoming electronic homeworkers. It is lowest in Italy where the proportion was 28 per cent.

It is striking that in the United Kingdom, where there was the highest proportion of people interested in telework, there were still twice as many— 44 per cent—who were opposed to it. This apparently greater polarisation of British attitudes to telework is largely a reflection of the much lower proportion of employees in the UK who thought that telework was not possible for them—29.5 per cent—compared with 35 per cent in Germany, 47 per cent in France and 60 per cent In Italy.

Overall, there appears to be little difference between the attitudes of men and women. Although men are on average slightly more likely to be interested in telework, this is not the case everywhere.

EXISTING COMPUTER USERS

People whose jobs already involve using workstations of the type which could be decentralised show distinctly more interest in telework than other workers, though the majority are still in favour of staying in an office. As Table 11.2 shows, interest is still highest in the UK at 33 per cent. The UK has the highest penetration of home computers in Europe. It seems likely that familiarity with the equipment is associated with acceptance of the idea of telework.

By focusing even more tightly on workstation users who also have home computers, we found further confirmation of a correlation between familiarity with new technologies and interest in telework. In almost all cases, home computer users are even more likely than those using a computer at work to be interested in remote work. In the United Kingdom, France and Italy, up to a third of this category showed interest. Figure 11.1 and Table 11.4 give a detailed breakdown, making it possible to analyse the data according to whether the home computers were used for private or for business purposes.

TABLE 11.1 Attitudes of employees towards telework in Europe

	Total employees (in thousands)			Yes (in thousands)			No (in thousands)			Don't know (in thousands)			Not possible (in thousands)		
	Total	Male	Female	Total	Male	Female	Total	Male	Female	Total	Male	Female	Total	Male	Female
Federal Republic of Germany															
In %	100.0	62.0	38.0	8.5	9.1	7.5	53.1	49.6	58.8	3.7	2.9	4.9	34.7	38.4	28.7
Numbers	26 401	16 362	10 039	2 244	1 487	757	14 019	8 116	5 903	971	475	496	9 167	6 284	2 883
France															
In %	100.0	59.2	40.8	14.0	13.4	14.9	35.8	31.2	42.5	3.0	3.0	2.9	47.2	52.3	39.7
Numbers	21 449	12 691	8 758	3 005	1 700	1 304	7 684	3 065	3 719	639	384	255	10 121	6 641	3 479
United Kingdom															
In %	100.0	60.8	39.2	22.6	22.4	22.8	44.3	39.5	51.6	3.5	2.7	4.6	29.5	35.1	20.7
Numbers	23 077	14 023	9 054	5 205	3 141	2 064	10 216	5 541	4 675	797	376	421	6 803	4 924	1 879
Italy															
In %	100.0	67.2	32.8	11.1	11.8	9.8	28.1	24.9	34.6	0.7	0.8	0.7	60.0	62.5	55.0
Numbers	20 889	14 041	6 848	2 329	1 661	668	5 865	3 494	2 371	156	112	45	12 539	8 774	3 765

Source: Survey data

TABLE 11.2   Attitudes of workstation users towards telework (in %)

	Yes	No	Don't know	Not possible
Federal Republic of Germany	16.5	54.8	5.2	22.9
France	28.4	45.0	3.6	23.0
United Kingdom	33.2	44.2	3.8	18.8
Italy	20.9	42.5	0.9	36.1

Source: Survey data

This information provides further evidence that the use of home computers in private homes plays a decisive role in shaping attitudes towards decentralised electronic work. Those who use their home computers only for private purposes are as likely to be interested as those who combine this with some business use. People who use them solely for business purposes show even more enthusiasm for the idea of telework. In general, people already using their home computers for work show the highest interest in telework of all respondents in each country in the survey, varying from 26 per cent in West Germany to 60 per cent in the United Kingdom with France (38 per cent) and Italy (32 per cent) in intermediate positions. With some exceptions, men show more interest than women.

AGE

Turning to an analysis of the responses by age, we find, not entirely surprisingly, that interest in telework is highest among the young, with a decline among the over-40s. As Table 11.5 shows, across the countries studied, the highest interest was found in the 15–19 age group and among 20–29 year olds. The exception to this rule was Germany, where the highest interest was found in the 30–39 age group.

In all age groups, negative attitudes dominate the picture, as can be seen from Table 11.6. Opposition to telework ranged from 28 per cent in Italy to 53 per cent in Germany. This table supplies some evidence of polarisation, with the youngest employees, who also evinced the greatest interest, showing the highest rejection rates, reaching a peak in Germany, where 58 per cent of 15–19 year olds are against the idea of telework. Leaving aside this youngest age group, where—except in France—opposition is at its highest, negative attitudes towards decentralised electronic work increase with age.

The pattern of opposition to telework is broadly similar for men and for women, with the important exception that women show a higher rate of

TABLE 11.3 Attitudes of employees to telework according to the use of home computers (in %)

	Yes			No			Don't know			Not possible		
	Total	Male	Female	Total	Male	Female	Total	Male	Female	Total	Male	Female
Federal Republic of Germany												
Usage for												
● private purposes	9.6	8.4	14.2	42.7	41.9	45.7	2.9	3.7	—	44.8	46.1	40.1
● business purposes	26.3	28.1	*	27.3	22.2	100.0	7.2	7.7	—	39.2	42.0	—
● equally	23.8	25.4	*	34.0	32.9	49.2	3.2	3.4	—	39.0	38.3	50.8
France												
Usage for												
● private purposes	33.7	36.7	27.4	34.0	32.6	36.9	1.1	1.5	—	31.2	29.1	35.7
● business purposes	38.1	35.3	54.4	29.7	27.0	45.6	9.7	11.4	—	22.4	26.3	—
● equally	29.5	28.0	34.3	21.6	22.5	18.9	5.4	7.1	—	43.5	42.4	46.8
United Kingdom												
Usage for												
● private purposes	32.3	34.4	25.9	35.3	32.1	45.1	2.7	2.7	2.9	29.6	30.8	26.1
● business purposes	60.4	60.4	*	21.7	21.7	—	—	—	—	17.9	17.9	—
● equally	52.1	49.5	61.5	22.1	22.4	20.7	—	—	—	25.9	28.1	17.8
Italy												
Usage for												
● private purposes	34.3	37.4	19.4	23.9	18.9	48.0	—	—	—	41.8	43.7	32.6
● business purposes	32.3	35.5	*	24.6	27.1	—	—	—	—	43.1	37.4	100.0
● equally	13.2	14.4	*	49.0	53.4	—	—	—	—	37.8	32.2	100.0

* = Number of cases too small
Source: Survey data

TABLE 11.4 Attitudes of workstation users to telework according to the use of home computers (in %)

	Yes			No			Don't know			Not possible		
	Total	Male	Female	Total	Male	Female	Total	Male	Female	Total	Male	Female
Federal Republic of Germany												
Usage for												
● private purposes	12.0	9.1	33.0	52.0	29.0	50.0	66.7	4.0	4.5	32.0	36.4	—
● business purposes	23.1	25.0	*	38.5		33.3	100.0	—	—	38.5	41.7	—
● equally	29.0	32.1	*		21.4	25.0	66.7	6.5	7.1	35.5	35.7	33.3
France												
Usage for												
● private purposes	46.2	50.0	38.5	41.0	38.5	46.2	—	—	—	12.8	11.5	15.4
● business purposes	*	*	—	—	—	—	50.0	50.0	—	50.0	50.0	—
● equally	43.8	42.9	50.0	18.8	21.4	—	6.3	7.1	—	31.3	28.6	50.0
United Kingdom												
Usage for												
● private purposes	38.0	40.0	31.8	37.0	32.9	50.0	4.3	4.3	4.5	20.7	22.9	13.6
● business purposes	50.0	50.0	*	28.6	28.6	—	—	—	—	21.4	21.4	—
● equally	52.9	46.7	100.0	17.6	20.0	—	—	—	—	29.4	33.3	—
Italy												
Usage for												
● private purposes	50.0	52.4	—	22.7	23.8	—	—	—	—	27.3	23.8	100.0
● business purposes	25.0	25.0	—	50.0	50.0	—	—	—	—	25.0	25.0	—
● equally	14.3	14.3	—	71.4	71.4	—	—	—	—	14.3	14.3	—

* = Number of cases too small
Source: Survey data

TABLE 11.5 Interest of the employed population in telework by age (in %)

Age groups	Federal Republic of Germany			France			United Kingdom			Italy		
	Total	Male	Female	Total	Male	Female	Total	Male	Female	Total	Male	Female
15–19	8.5	10.2	6.3	28.9	34.0	20.6	28.2	28.7	27.6	13.3	17.5	7.4
20–29	11.1	11.8	10.1	19.9	17.4	22.7	28.4	28.7	27.9	13.3	12.4	14.6
30–39	12.3	13.1	11.0	15.2	14.7	15.9	24.6	22.5	28.2	12.5	13.7	10.3
40–49	6.9	7.7	5.4	11.0	10.7	11.5	19.8	19.5	20.3	9.6	11.0	5.9
50–59	3.6	3.4	3.8	5.7	6.4	4.4	16.6	18.1	14.3	8.8	9.5	6.8
≥60	6.9	*	5.0	5.4	7.3	—	*	*	*	4.6	5.8	1.1
Ø	8.5	9.1	7.5	14.0	13.4	14.9	22.6	22.4	22.8	11.1	11.8	9.8

* = Number of cases too small
Source: Survey data

TABLE 11.6 *Rejection rates of telework by age among the employed population (in %)*

Age groups	Federal Republic of Germany			France			United Kingdom			Italy		
	Total	Male	Female	Total	Male	Female	Total	Male	Female	Total	Male	Female
15–19	57.8	54.2	62.4	24.5	11.9	45.3	46.9	41.7	53.2	27.8	27.1	28.7
20–29	49.1	43.3	56.8	35.6	29.8	42.1	40.8	35.4	48.8	28.9	23.6	36.9
30–39	53.6	51.1	58.0	33.8	29.5	40.4	40.0	37.0	45.1	25.8	21.8	32.7
40–49	52.0	47.3	60.5	37.0	36.4	38.0	43.4	37.4	51.7	25.2	22.2	33.2
50–59	55.0	53.8	57.1	39.9	34.3	49.7	51.8	46.4	60.3	32.5	31.3	36.3
≥60	53.7	63.9	59.9	41.5	35.9	52.0	29.0	46.1	36.9	39.0	35.5	56.0
Ø	53.1	49.6	58.8	35.8	31.2	42.5	44.3	39.5	51.6	28.1	24.9	34.6

* = Number of cases too small
Source: Survey data

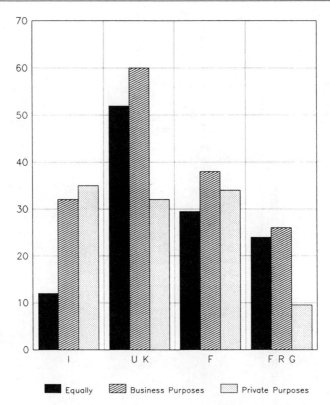

FIGURE 11.1   Interest in telework according to the use of home computers (in %)

rejection. As already noted, people who use computerised workstations in all age groups are both more likely to be interested in telework and more likely to be opposed to it than their counterparts in non-automated jobs. This difference can be explained by the much smaller proportion of workstation users who see their work as unsuitable for decentralisation.

There are several possible ways of interpreting these findings on the relationship between age and interest in telework. The greater than average interest of the youngest age group in telework seems in part to reflect the greater familiarity with information technology in this age group. However, we must also account for the negative attitude to telework which is also to be found among some younger employees. An alternative explanation might be found in the social situations of respondents. If we presume that opposition to telework stems from a reluctance to lose the social advantages of a workplace where it is possible to interact with a range of different workmates, while the

TABLE 11.7 Interest of workstation users in telework by age (in %)

Age groups	Federal Republic of Germany			France			United Kingdom			Italy		
	Total	Male	Female	Total	Male	Female	Total	Male	Female	Total	Male	Female
15–19	10.3	20.0	4.2	50.0	100.0	28.6	34.3	47.1	30.2	23.1	50.0	11.1
20–29	22.2	27.6	18.2	32.4	32.6	32.3	36.7	37.6	35.9	24.8	27.1	23.1
30–39	20.9	24.1	15.6	28.7	28.8	28.7	36.6	36.3	37.2	19.0	25.7	8.7
40–49	10.1	12.2	7.2	22.5	28.3	17.9	27.5	31.8	22.8	21.0	23.1	15.4
50–59	12.2	11.4	13.9	19.0	25.0	9.1	23.1	22.1	24.5	21.0	15.7	21.1
≥60	*	*	*	—	—	—	*	*	*	16.7	*	—
Ø	16.5	20.0	13.5	28.4	29.5	27.5	33.2	34.7	31.5	20.6	23.5	16.0

* = Number of cases too small

Source: Survey data

TABLE 11.8 Workstation users' rejection of telework by age (in %)

Age groups	Federal Republic of Germany			France			United Kingdom			Italy		
	Total	Male	Female	Total	Male	Female	Total	Male	Female	Total	Male	Female
15–19	71.8	60.0	79.2	50.0	—	71.4	50.0	35.3	54.7	69.2	50.0	77.8
20–29	52.0	42.9	58.7	45.8	30.4	53.1	42.9	37.6	47.6	44.2	29.4	54.5
30–39	51.3	46.0	60.0	42.8	38.1	47.3	37.4	33.8	43.6	40.7	32.6	53.0
40–49	61.2	50.3	75.7	40.8	30.2	49.3	48.5	36.4	62.0	39.8	33.6	55.8
50–59	53.9	50.6	61.1	60.3	47.2	81.3	52.9	45.6	62.3	46.1	49.4	31.6
≥60	55.6	57.1	50.0	42.9	20.0	*	22.2	*	—	41.2	*	*
Ø	54.8	47.4	64.3	45.0	35.2	52.4	44.2	36.7	52.6	42.5	35.4	53.5

* = Number of cases too small
Source: Survey data

desire for telework results from a situation where there are social reasons to remain in the home, then we can construct a picture which fits the findings of our survey. According to this view, young single childless people would be anxious to remain in a work situation where social contacts could be maximised. However, their colleagues who were already settled down with children might well prefer to stay at home where they could maximise the time spent with their families. In the 29–40 age group, the latter group would be expected to outnumber the former, producing a drop in opposition to telework. As well as being the years where child-care problems are likely to be at their greatest, these are also critical career-building years, when social considerations may take second place to work-related ones for some people. However, the older age groups would include more people who had established themselves in their careers as well as a higher proportion of households where children were old enough to look after themselves, permitting their parents to rediscover the advantages of the social workplace and therefore producing a revival in the opposition to remote work. Such an explanation, based as it is on fairly universal demographic characteristics, might also explain the relative uniformity of these patterns across national boundaries.

VARIATIONS BY INDUSTRY

In general, attitudes to telework varied remarkably little between workers employed in different industries, regardless of nationality. With one exception, responses did not stray far from the national average in any industry. The single significant exception was the banking and finance sector, interestingly enough the industry in which the highest proportion of managers was also in favour of telework (see Chapter 10). Here, interest was well above average, especially in Britain where 27 per cent of people employed in this sector were interested. Even in Germany, where interest was lowest, 13 per cent of finance workers were positive about telework, compared with a national average of 8 per cent. A search for sex-related differences here produced few surprises. In Italy and Germany, the familiar pattern of men being more interested than women was repeated. In Britain, gender differences were barely discernible, while France produced a small exception by revealing a group of female bank and insurance workers who were keener than their male colleagues to work remotely.

Negative attitudes dominate the picture in all industries, as can be seen from Table 11.9, with a peak of 61 per cent in the finance sector in Germany. This sector also produces exceptionally high rates of opposition elsewhere: 42 per cent in Italy, 48 per cent in France and 52.5 per cent in the UK. Here is another example of a high degree of opposition in a group which also demonstrates an above-average degree of acceptance, which can be attributed,

TABLE 11.9 *Interest in telework in the employed population by industry (in %)*

Industries	Federal Republic of Germany			France			United Kingdom			Italy		
	Total	Male	Female	Total	Male	Female	Total	Male	Female	Total	Male	Female
Public sector	53.7	52.0	56.0	36.3	30.7	41.3	45.0	40.5	49.8	26.0	22.4	32.2
Finance	61.0	58.1	64.5	47.8	43.0	59.9	52.5	44.8	59.0	41.9	37.0	59.2
Distribution	55.5	49.7	60.2	32.9	26.4	40.7	44.6	38.0	51.5	27.6	22.8	35.2
Manufacturing	47.7	45.6	58.6	34.0	30.4	51.8	39.2	37.1	51.7	29.6	27.7	41.2
Ø	53.1	49.6	58.8	35.8	31.2	42.5	44.3	39.5	51.6	28.1	24.9	34.6

Source: Survey data

TABLE 11.10 *Interest in telework in the employed population by job content (in %)*

Job content	Federal Republic of Germany			France			United Kingdom			Italy		
	Total	Male	Female	Total	Male	Female	Total	Male	Female	Total	Male	Female
Dp prof.	41.4	41.9	—	44.0	55.0	13.2	58.4	51.8	73.8	31.4	35.0	—
Scientific	17.6	17.8	16.3	21.3	21.1	23.0	39.5	40.8	24.6	13.2	14.5	—
Manager	10.1	11.0	7.8	8.8	9.4	7.6	21.9	22.4	18.9	12.6	11.6	16.8
Secretaries and typists	12.8	5.8	13.0	27.5	12.5	28.2	30.4	45.1	30.2	19.8	37.9	13.5
Ø	8.5	9.1	7.5	14.0	13.4	14.9	22.6	22.4	22.8	11.1	11.8	9.8

* = Number of cases too small
Source: Survey data

at least in part, to the above-average suitability of the jobs for telework and a corresponding fall in the 'not applicable' category.

VARIATIONS BY JOB CONTENT

It was no great surprise to discover that the people most interested in telework were those whose jobs already involved considerable use of new information and communications technologies, with data processing professionals scoring the highest—31 per cent in Italy; 41 per cent in Germany; 44 per cent in France and 58 per cent in the United Kingdom. Scientific and engineering workers also had an interest in telework which was well above the average as did secretaries, stenographers and typists. With the exception of France, managers were also more likely than average to be interested in telework.

Perhaps the most striking finding to emerge from this part of the survey is the exceptionally high interest in telework among British data processing professionals already using computerised workstations, of whom over 60 per cent were in favour. To a lesser degree, this interest was shared by their counterparts in other countries. Managers using workstations were also much more likely to favour telework than their colleagues who did not work directly with information technology. However, secretaries and typists showed the opposite tendency. Use of a workstation made them less, rather than more likely than average to be interested, as can be seen from Table 11.11.

Secretaries and typists using workstations were also more likely to reject the idea of telework than their less automated colleagues, a pattern which was repeated to a lesser extent among several other occupational groups. Although partly explicable by the very low proportion of workers in this category who consider their jobs impossible to decentralise, this very high rejection rate (ranging from 50 per cent in Italy to 77 per cent in Germany) seems to suggest that, at least among workers carrying out routine keyboard functions, familiarity with the technology does not inevitably lead to interest in telework.

In general, men are more interested in telework than women, and the pattern of opposition to telework mirrors this, with much higher rejection rates among women in almost all cases. Opposition to remote work reaches its peak in two groups of women whose working situations are particularly amenable to decentralisation: German secretaries and typists, and French data processing professionals already using computerised workstations, of whom 79 and 83 per cent respectively are opposed to telework, presumably because they see it as a direct personal threat.

HOUSEHOLD STRUCTURE

Curious to know whether any of these differences in attitude to telework were reflections of different domestic circumstances, we also looked at the household

TABLE 11.11 Interest of workstation users in telework by job content (in %)

Job content	Federal Republic of Germany			France			United Kingdom			Italy		
	Total	Male	Female	Total	Male	Female	Total	Male	Female	Total	Male	Female
Dp prof.	43.2	50.0	*	44.4	58.3	16.7	60.5	60.0	62.5	35.0	42.9	—
Scientific	25.7	25.3	*	22.4	19.7	31.6	47.7	42.6	33.3	21.4	20.0	—
Managers	20.4	23.1	14.3	41.5	33.3	63.6	32.9	35.1	29.4	17.8	18.3	18.2
Secretaries and typists	14.0	—	13.9	27.8	—	28.1	31.1	—	28.7	18.1	40.0	15.0
Ø	16.5	20.0	13.5	28.4	29.5	27.5	33.2	34.7	31.5	20.9	23.5	16.0

* = Number of cases too small
Source: Survey data

TABLE 11.12 Rejection rates of decentralised electronic work according to job content (employed people) (in %)

Job content	Federal Republic of Germany			France			United Kingdom			Italy		
	Total	Male	Female	Total	Male	Female	Total	Male	Female	Total	Male	Female
Dp prof.	25.8	24.8	*	30.0	15.7	70.1	27.3	31.1	18.3	31.3	35.0	—
Scientific	46.5	48.3	27.9	35.6	36.3	30.7	28.4	27.8	35.2	26.9	25.9	36.4
Managers	54.8	52.5	60.6	29.3	27.1	33.6	42.3	42.6	40.4	35.0	35.7	31.7
Secretaries and typists	77.4	—	78.6	56.9	47.1	57.3	57.3	—	58.1	50.2	28.2	58.0
Ø	53.1	49.6	58.8	35.8	31.2	42.5	44.3	39.5	51.6	28.1	24.9	34.6

* = Number of cases too small
Source: Survey data

structure of the respondents, analysing the data according to the total number of people in a household, the number of adults (aged 15 or over) in a household, and the number of employed people in a household.

This produced several interesting findings. Two distinct family types showed the highest interest in telework: those with one or two people, and those with more than four. Three-person households—which can be presumed to consist largely of couples with a single child, were least likely to show interest. The implication is that telework appeals most to the childless and to those with larger families.

Women with two or more children are more likely to be interested in telework than the average. In fact in large households in the UK and France, women were more likely than men to be interested in telework, while in Germany and Italy, the gap between the sexes was considerably narrowed.

The suspicion that many of these people were second earners in their households was confirmed by analysing the data according to the number of employed people in the household. With the exception of Germany, where interest in telework is lowest in all types of household, there is a perceptible tendency for employees in households with two or more working people to show the greatest interest.

The sub-group of workstation users exhibits a similar pattern to the sample as a whole, with interest at its highest in two-person households or those with four or more people, except in Germany. However, women are proportionally less interested than in the employed population as a whole. The only exception to this rule is in the UK, where in households of five or more people, 44 per cent of female workstation users are interested in telework, compared with 35 per cent of men.

OCCUPATIONAL STATUS

Another variable which we thought might be significant in determining attitudes towards telework was occupational status. However, the differences were not great. As Table 11.15 shows, full-timers were slightly more interested in telework than their part-time colleagues, but the difference, although enough to discredit the widely held view that remote work is most attractive to part-timers, was small.

When it came to opposition to telework, however, this difference was more pronounced, with part-time employees showing by far the highest rejection rates. Least likely to reject telework were the self-employed, as can be seen from Table 11.16. The self-employed also stand out as exceptional when workstation users are isolated from the rest of the sample. Although both full-time and part-time employees in this group express average interest, self-employed workstation users' interest is significantly above average, ranging

TABLE 11.13 Interest in telework in the employed population by household structure (in %)

Household structure	Federal Republic of Germany			France			United Kingdom			Italy		
	Total	Male	Female	Total	Male	Female	Total	Male	Female	Total	Male	Female
Total number of persons in household												
1 person	9.0	10.1	8.2	15.3	17.8	11.9	18.8	20.3	16.8	10.2	15.9	3.6
2 persons	8.0	8.3	7.6	14.2	13.4	15.2	23.7	23.5	24.1	11.8	11.5	12.3
3 persons	8.1	8.6	7.1	14.0	13.7	14.5	21.5	21.7	21.1	11.9	12.8	10.2
4 persons	9.8	9.9	9.4	14.9	13.9	16.5	22.6	22.9	22.2	10.4	10.7	9.6
5 and more	8.0	9.4	4.6	11.2	9.7	14.4	23.3	21.5	26.9	11.2	12.4	8.6
Number of persons 15+ in household												
1 person	15.4	21.4	12.0	21.0	16.1	23.8	27.9	42.6	16.9	5.7	—	8.4
2 persons	9.2	9.8	8.1	14.5	13.1	16.5	23.7	22.6	25.5	12.2	12.6	11.2
3 persons	8.2	8.8	6.9	12.5	13.6	11.0	20.5	20.7	20.1	10.0	9.9	10.2
4 persons	7.1	7.2	7.0	13.1	14.1	11.0	22.0	22.0	22.0	10.0	10.0	9.9
5 and more	6.6	7.4	5.2	8.5	4.7	15.3	25.3	26.2	23.6	12.3	15.9	5.4
Number of working people in household												
1 person	9.5	9.8	8.4	12.2	11.8	13.4	21.1	22.1	17.7	9.8	10.4	7.0
2 persons	8.3	8.5	8.0	15.4	14.7	16.1	23.6	22.3	25.2	12.7	13.8	11.2
3 persons	7.6	9.2	5.7	13.4	16.9	8.5	20.3	21.1	19.2	11.2	12.4	9.6
4 persons	5.9	7.3	4.1	10.4	7.2	14.9	24.5	26.2	22.4	9.5	11.8	5.8
Ø	8.5	9.1	7.5	14.0	13.4	11.9	22.6	23.4	22.8	11.1	11.8	9.8

Source: Survey data

TABLE 11.14 *Interest of workstation users in telework by household structure (in %)*

Household structure	Federal Republic of Germany			France			United Kingdom			Italy		
	Total	Male	Female	Total	Male	Female	Total	Male	Female	Total	Male	Female
Total number of persons in household												
1 person	19.4	23.4	17.1	24.2	29.1	18.2	24.5	30.8	17.4	21.4	30.8	13.3
2 persons	18.9	22.3	15.6	33.0	32.9	33.1	39.4	40.2	38.7	21.4	20.9	21.7
3 persons	16.7	20.8	10.8	27.8	31.3	25.4	31.4	33.7	28.9	20.4	25.8	12.7
4 persons	16.6	19.3	11.0	28.1	28.4	27.9	29.6	33.1	25.0	18.9	20.1	16.0
5 and more	12.2	14.3	7.1	23.4	23.3	23.5	38.5	34.8	43.8	23.6	27.2	17.3
Number of persons 15+ in household												
1 person	28.6	66.7	18.2	41.7	33.3	42.9	16.7	50.0	—	12.5	—	14.3
2 persons	19.5	22.1	15.3	30.9	30.7	31.1	36.3	36.1	36.6	21.5	23.7	17.7
3 persons	14.6	19.4	8.9	24.0	34.9	15.8	29.9	29.8	30.1	21.4	28.2	11.4
4 persons	12.0	13.3	10.0	21.1	19.2	22.6	29.9	32.7	28.1	15.8	15.0	17.3
5 and more	4.4	6.9	—	11.1	10.0	12.5	39.0	39.1	38.9	25.9	33.3	18.5
Number of working people in household												
1 person	20.7	22.9	16.1	24.0	24.2	23.8	32.5	33.0	30.6	19.6	22.6	10.8
2 persons	15.7	18.1	13.5	29.9	33.3	28.1	35.1	38.0	32.7	21.6	24.5	18.6
3 persons	10.7	15.6	7.7	38.9	46.7	33.3	29.2	28.4	29.9	21.7	25.0	19.2
4 persons	7.7	12.5	—	25.0	—	40.0	33.8	40.7	30.0	15.4	25.0	—
Ø	16.5	20.0	13.5	28.4	29.5	27.5	32.2	34.7	31.5	20.6	23.5	16.0

Source: Survey data

TABLE 11.15 Interest in telework among the employed population by occupational status (in %)

Occupational status	Federal Republic of Germany			France			United Kingdom			Italy		
	Total	Male	Female	Total	Male	Female	Total	Male	Female	Total	Male	Female
Full-time	8.8	9.4	7.7	15.2	14.7	16.1	23.6	23.5	24.0	11.6	12.1	10.5
Part-time	7.8	9.6	7.7	15.2	18.1	14.5	21.4	20.7	21.5	9.7	14.2	7.1
Self-employed	6.3	6.5	6.0	9.0	9.1	8.7	16.3	15.1	21.5	10.6	11.1	9.1
Total	8.5	9.1	7.5	14.0	13.4	14.9	22.6	22.4	22.8	11.1	11.8	9.8

Source: Survey data

TABLE 11.16 Rejection of telework in the employed population by occupational status (in %)

Occupational status	Federal Republic of Germany			France			United Kingdom			Italy		
	Total	Male	Female	Total	Male	Female	Total	Male	Female	Total	Male	Female
Full-time	52.9	50.2	59.2	37.0	32.8	43.4	43.2	39.8	51.8	28.9	25.4	36.3
Part-time	61.0	44.1	62.0	41.8	34.7	43.6	53.5	56.5	53.3	30.1	34.2	37.3
Self-employed	44.5	44.7	44.0	29.0	26.1	36.2	34.4	34.8	32.8	24.7	22.8	29.5
Total	53.1	49.6	58.8	35.8	31.2	42.5	44.3	39.5	51.6	28.1	24.9	34.6

Source: Survey data

TABLE 11.17 Interest of workstation users in telework by occupational status (in %)

Occupational status	Federal Republic of Germany			France			United Kingdom			Italy		
	Total	Male	Female	Total	Male	Female	Total	Male	Female	Total	Male	Female
Full-time	17.0	20.0	12.2	28.3	28.7	28.0	32.4	34.1	29.9	20.6	22.8	17.5
Part-time	16.8	16.7	16.8	22.0	42.9	20.0	34.1	*	33.3	15.6	30.0	9.1
Self-employed	18.7	19.3	16.7	34.8	32.1	46.2	46.2	40.0	66.7	21.7	25.5	9.1
Total	16.5	20.0	13.5	28.4	29.5	27.5	33.2	34.7	31.5	20.6	23.5	16.0

Source: Survey data

from 19 per cent in Germany to 46 per cent in the United Kingdom. In fact it is three times as high as among the self-employed as a whole, as can be seen from Table 11.17.

Table 11.18 gives a general overview of interest in telework in the employed population. When compared to workstation users by occupational status, it can be seen that interest is significantly higher among workstation users, particularly those who are self-employed.

VARIATIONS BY COMPANY SIZE

The final variable we examined was the size of the employing organisation. With the exception of France, where company size appeared to make no significant difference, the tendency was for interest in telework to increase with the size of the employing organisation. However, as Table 11.19 reveals, there were considerable national variations in the pattern of responses.

SUMMARY

Perhaps the clearest result to emerge from this survey is that, while the majority of the workforce is not interested in telework, a substantial minority

TABLE 11.18 *Interest in telework in the employed population and among workstation users by occupational status (in %)*

Occupational status	Federal Republic of Germany	France	United Kingdom	Italy
Full-time employed				
(a) employed people	8.8	15.2	23.6	11.6
(b) workstation user	17.0	28.3	32.4	20.6
Part-time employed				
(a) employed people	7.8	15.2	21.4	9.7
(b) workstation user	16.8	22.0	34.1	15.6
Self-employed				
(a) employed people	6.3	9.0	16.3	10.6
(b) workstation user	18.7	34.8	46.2	21.7
Total				
(a) employed people	8.5	14.0	22.6	11.1
(b) workstation user	16.5	28.4	33.7	20.9

Source: Survey data

TABLE 11.19 Interest in telework in the employed population by company size (in %)

Company size	Federal Republic of Germany			France			United Kingdom			Italy		
	Total	Male	Female	Total	Male	Female	Total	Male	Female	Total	Male	Female
1	5.9	6.5	5.3	13.2	14.9	10.2	20.7	18.7	26.8	9.2	9.4	8.9
2–4	5.8	4.2	7.3	7.9	8.1	7.6	20.1	15.2	26.5	9.5	10.6	7.5
5–9	7.2	7.8	6.6	17.6	16.3	18.7	22.2	19.1	25.2	10.8	10.1	12.2
10–19	7.2	9.1	4.5	20.7	17.7	24.1	24.7	28.8	19.4	11.8	12.2	11.3
20–49	7.8	6.7	9.8	18.6	18.4	18.9	19.8	19.7	19.8	10.7	14.3	4.2
50–99	10.1	9.1	12.1	16.1	13.6	19.0	22.2	22.5	21.4	13.4	13.8	12.6
100–249	9.7	10.9	7.5	14.3	13.2	16.0	24.5	25.2	23.1	14.1	14.4	13.3
250–499	8.4	10.0	6.3	11.3	10.9	11.9	20.2	20.0	20.3	9.9	10.8	8.4
500–999	8.4	10.1	4.3	14.7	16.8	11.2	27.7	26.3	30.6	13.9	13.2	15.7
≥1000	11.0	10.9	11.2	12.8	11.7	15.3	26.0	26.0	26.0	12.8	11.8	18.5
Ø	8.5	9.1	7.5	14.0	13.4	14.9	22.6	22.4	22.8	11.1	11.8	9.8
1–49	6.9	7.0	6.9	14.2	13.7	14.8	21.3	20.2	22.9	10.3	11.2	8.5
50–999	9.1	10.1	7.4	14.0	13.4	15.0	22.8	23.2	22.3	12.5	13.0	11.5
≥1000	11.0	10.9	11.2	12.8	11.7	15.3	26.0	26.0	26.0	12.8	11.8	18.5

Source: Survey data

does undoubtedly exist for whom it would be a welcome development. In a few industries and occupations this group is large enough to form a majority. Interest in telework is most likely to be found among people who are already familiar with information technology, in occupations which already make use of it, particularly data processing professionals. Potential teleworkers are most likely to be in mid-career with two or more children, in a household with another adult in employment, although they may be childless. They probably work for a large organisation, though there is also a substantial group of individual entrepreneurs interested in remote work.

Chapter 12

FORECASTING FUTURE DEVELOPMENTS

The results of our surveys of employers and employees suggest that there is a minority in each group which is interested in telework and that there is some coincidence between supply and demand in certain occupations (such as computer programming, word processing or typing) and industries (such as the banking and insurance sector). However, at present those who are interested in remote work are heavily outnumbered by those who are not, indicating that the development of telework will be far from straightforward.

Translating the results of such surveys into concrete predictions is notoriously difficult, and the history of telework research is cluttered with the embarrassing relics of attempts to do so which have failed. Nevertheless, the demand for such forecasts from public and politicians is vociferous, and the urge to try again is strong. Before attempting our own assessment, we outline some of the findings of other surveys of attitudes to telework, and estimates of its future spread.

ATTITUDE AND OPINION SURVEYS

In the USA, DeSanctis examined the attitudes of 51 managers and 129 computer programmers to telework. She discovered that programmers were much more favourable to it than their managers, with 81 stating that they would prefer to be teleworkers than to be based in an office (although only 75 believed that their work could be done from home) while 19 managers were in favour of it (of whom only 5 felt that it would in fact be possible). Among the programmers there was a marked preference for a satellite office (68 of the sample) over home-based telework (DeSanctis, 1984).

In a survey of personnel executives in 114 North Carolina firms, Risman and Tomaskovic-Devey found that, although only 7 per cent currently allowed their employees to work from home on a limited basis, 40 per cent said that 'some day they might allow telecommuting'. The main reason for refusing to do so was the fear of losing managerial control (*Telecommuting Review*, 9/1/86).

A somewhat broader survey of the 'Fortune 500' plus 200 other US companies which are members of the Society for Information Management, was carried out in 1985 by Ramsower and Moore at Baylor University. Of 292 respondents, of whom 32.4 per cent presently had some employees telecommuting, 44.5 per cent planned to increase this use, while less than 1 per cent planned to decrease it (*Telecommuting Review*, 6/1/86).

Earlier, a 1973 random survey of Los Angeles residents discovered that about half were willing to work nearer home via telecommunications links, with those who had to commute the furthest distance to work being most in favour (Nilles *et al.*, 1976).

Kraemer quotes a survey by Kollen and Garwood for Bell Canada in which 9619 business travellers were asked whether their trips could be substituted by telecommunications, the results of which indicated that 20 per cent of the reported trips would not have been made if acceptable telecommunications substitutes had been available. Other, smaller surveys found that around 60 per cent of business meetings might be substitutable in this way. However, the proportion of travellers who would have preferred not to make the trip was smaller, ranging from 9 to 51 per cent in various surveys (Kraemer, 1982). It should be emphasised, however, that these attitudes do not necessarily apply to telework, since it was trips made during the course of business, rather than journeys to work, which were at issue.

A 1983 interim report of an ongoing survey of 500 members of the public in Bremen, West Germany, produced more negative results. Many respondents are described as having a 'bad feeling' about the effects of new telecommunications services, expressing particularly strong views that they would reduce face-to-face communications and thus dehumanise private life (Haefner, 1983).

In another survey of employees in West Germany, in 1984, only 10 per cent of women and 15 per cent of men said they felt positive about home-based telework, while approximately 40 per cent rejected it, with the rest giving no indication of their feelings on the subject (Becker, 1984).

That there are national differences in attitudes to telework is borne out by the results of Empirica's survey of European employees, described in the last chapter, which also found a particularly widespread lack of interest, if not antagonism, to telework in Germany (where some 8.5 per cent of people were interested, compared with 11 per cent in Italy, 14 per cent in France and 23 per cent in the UK).

In 1984, the UK National Economic Development Office commissioned a survey of informed opinion on the subject. A majority of respondents took the view that, although technological factors were important in enabling telework to take place, their effects would be modified by economic and social factors. Telework was seen as possible for a larger number of people than would actually like it. There were wide variations between individual responses, but on average it was felt that nearly 25 per cent of the workforce would be based in the home for at least part of the time in 25 years time (Bessant *et al.*, 1986).

A survey by the French research consultancy Futuribles of 240 social science experts in OECD countries found a near-unanimous view that telework will have developed considerably by the year 2005 and that the rise of communications technology will bring about major changes in the distribution of work and housing (Blanc, 1988). In another French survey, by IPSOS and the European Business School, of blue-collar and white-collar workers, managers, middle managers and graduate students, nearly half of each social group agreed that 'telematics and bureaucratics will allow everyone to work from home' and between 37 and 52 per cent thought that it was a desirable option. An even larger proportion, rising to 70 per cent among the graduate students, considered it possible that 'the corporation will not be a place where people meet and spend a large part of their time; it will be an organised community of people working in different places and linked together by computers' (Blanc, 1988).

EXTRAPOLATION FROM EXISTING STATISTICS

Opinion surveys are not, of course, the only methods used by researchers attempting to quantify the future development of telework. Another technique has been to use occupational data derived from the employment statistics in order to arrive at an estimate of the numbers of jobs which it would be practicable to relocate using information technology. Researchers adopting this approach have generally found that the classifications used are too broad to give more than a very rough guide, and sometimes that occupational categories do not take account of the very rapid changes in job design brought about as a result of the widespread introduction of automated office systems. This approach may also—if not modified by other factors—lead to an overly deterministic analysis which ignores the social, economic, legal and political forces which may be acting to constrain the spread of telework.

Nevertheless, such occupational analyses are an important component of any informed forecast, if only because they establish the outer limits of the possible growth of telework. If we assume that they are accurate in their assumptions about what is likely to be technologically possible, then they can at least tell us which jobs can *not* efficiently be relocated to remote sites.

Using 1973 figures and a very broad definition of what constituted information-processing work, Nilles estimated that 48.3 per cent of the total US workforce came into this category, a proportion which he projected would rise to 55 per cent by the year 2000 (Nilles *et al.*, 1976). In this, he was broadly in agreement with Harkness whose technology assessment of telecommunications/transportation interactions at the Stanford Research Institute led him to conclude that 'the only available estimate, which is without strong basis, suggests that roughly half the office workforce is the upper limit' (Kraemer, 1982). However, Nilles did not seriously predict that all these would become teleworkers. In 1981, he was forecasting that there would be 10 million teleworkers in the United States by 1990—less than 10 per cent of the total workforce (Zientara, 1981).

Two years later, Bikson, of the Rand Corporation, was prophesying that 10 per cent of the office-based workforce (around 5 per cent of the total workforce) in the USA might be doing all, or a significant part, of its work from home via a computer (Romero, 1983).

In 1974, Glover carried out an analysis of UK occupational data and arrived at the conclusion that the number of clerical jobs which might be home-based would rise from 5.9 million (21.4 per cent of the workforce) in 1981 to 6.9 million (24.6 per cent of the workforce) in 1991 and 8 million (26.7 per cent of the workforce) in 2001. She followed the methodology of Jones, who carried out a detailed study in the San Francisco Bay area, at Stanford University, and concluded that at 1965 levels 22 per cent of the workforce could be home-based (Glover, 1974).

Kraemer quotes a UK study by the British Telecom Long-range Studies Division which indicates that 41 per cent of all trips to business meetings could, under 'assumed year 2000' conditions, have been replaced by electronic communications. Since this applies to travel to meetings rather than all business travel, and since other surveys have shown that travel to meetings constitutes about 75 per cent of all business travel, he concludes that a saturation level of 25–30 per cent would be reached by the year 2000 (Kraemer, 1982). Although this more or less coincides with Glover's estimate of the saturation level for telework, it should be noted that the topics under discussion are by no means synonymous. 'Remote' business meetings could be conducted as easily from central offices as from homes or neighbourhood centres.

Dover, who studied the substitutability of telecommunications for tranportation in the UK at Aston University, is sceptical that telework or other forms of substitution will in fact develop to anything like this extent, pointing out the high number of journeys to work which are made by foot in the UK and social constraints on the development of homework (Dover, 1982a,b).

In the recent literature on this aspect of telework, most authors have avoided the broad quantitative predictions which were characteristic of the 1970s, adopting a more cautious, qualitative approach. Some have revised earlier estimates downwards, and while all foresee a growth in telework, few forecast more than a modest expansion in the short to medium term (e.g. Gordon, 1988; Olson, 1987; Eder, 1983; Blanc, 1988; Bureau of National Affairs, 1986; US Congress, Office of Technology Assessment, 1985; Nilles, 1985a; Miller, 1985).

ANALYSIS OF EXISTING HOME COMPUTER USE

Another area of research which is pertinent to the quantification of telework is the analysis of the uses to which home computers are put. The reliability of public opinion polls in producing accurate findings in this respect may be limited because of the small proportion of any sample who are home computer owners. Nevertheless, some of the findings of US polls are of interest. In one Gallup poll, 40 per cent of home computer owners surveyed said that they used their computers for 'business or office homework' with a smaller proportion—27 per cent—citing 'business-in-home use'. Another survey, by Yankelovich, Skelly and White, found that 33 per cent of computer owners said that their primary purpose was for business. An IBM survey found that 60 per cent of its computers which sold for $2000 US or more and were not generally considered mass consumer items were being used in the home, and that more than half of these home machines were being used primarily for business-related purposes. A further 11 per cent of the computers were being transported between the home and the office (Pollack, 1983).

Olson's survey of 598 *Datamation* readers found that 64.5 per cent of these data processing professionals sometimes worked at home in addition to their regular office work, 12.4 per cent did it as an occasional substitute and 6.2 per cent worked at home for all of their paid work hours (Olson, 1987).

A study of 282 users of home computers, contacted via computer clubs in Orange County, California, found that 26 per cent stated that their primary use of the computer was for business purposes. The proportion was highest (50 per cent) among the self-employed, who were classified separately. This was followed by engineers and technical staff (26.6 per cent) and professional and managerial staff (25 per cent). Surprisingly, a smaller proportion (22.3 per cent) of programmers and systems analysts used their computers for work. A number of respondents (24 per cent of the total) also said that they used their computers for word processing and the researchers concluded that much of this usage was also for business purposes, arriving at a final estimate of 45 per cent of home computer use being for work-related activities (Vitalari, Venkatesh and Gronhaug, 1985). So far no research appears to have been carried out to extrapolate from these surveys to produce an estimate of the total number of teleworkers.

ESTIMATES OF THE EXTENT OF HOMEWORKING

A final method which has been used to estimate the likely extent of telework has been to measure the prevalence of homeworking, regardless of the extent to which this may involve the use of information technology. Like analyses of the use of home computers, this approach has the disadvantage of ignoring forms of telework which are not based in the home. It also includes large numbers of home-based businesses in industries such as farming, selling or manufacturing which fall well outside most definitions of telework.

In the USA, Joanne H. Pratt Associates carried out a study of the measurement and evaluation of the populations of family-owned and home-based businesses. Written in 1985, their survey quotes Bureau of Census reports that there are approximately 1.5 million home-based business operators and about 0.75 million home-based employees in the USA, contrasting this with a study by AT&T which produced an estimate of 23 million individuals working at home (including people who take work home in addition to work outside the home). Of these, 7 million (including some moonlighters) are in the 'business at home' sector. A Bureau of Census Current Population Survey indicates that over 15 million Americans do some of their work at home (Pratt and Davis, 1985). Kraut, who also analysed the data on place of work from the 1980 US Census, in order to compare it with other data on home-based work, concluded that in that year only 1.6 per cent of the non-farm labour force worked at home (*Telecommuting Review*, 11/1/85).

A market planner for Apple computers is quoted as estimating that there are 13–14 million people working at home in the USA, and that approximately half of the 13 million or so businesses in the country operate from home addresses (Shirley, 1988).

More cautiously, the Yankee Group estimated in 1985 that there were 6 million information-related home businesses in the USA, of which 1 million had computers and less than 300,000 had modems. As part of its 'Home of the Future' research service, it also assessed the number of people involved in corporate telework schemes at 30,000, although a further 100,000 people were believed to be 'telecommuting informally' in the United States.

In 1987, the LINK organisation carried out its second US National Work-at-Home survey. As a result, it concluded that 18 per cent of US households were involved in some home-based work. The number of homeworkers was increasing by 7.5 per cent per year, to a 1987 total of 23.3 million. Of these, 6.9 per cent were self-employed, of whom about half were running their own businesses. Of the homeworkers in the sample 21 per cent described themselves as 'corporate full-time' homeworkers, but on investigation 40 per cent of these turned out to be corporate 'after-hours' homeworkers—in other words, full-time, on-site employees who also did some homework (*Telecommuting Review*, 2/1/88).

In West Germany there is a lack of accurate data on the subject. The last official survey, carried out in 1981, recorded a drop in home-based work from over 200,000 ten years earlier to half that level—0.5 per cent of the workforce. However, all but 7 per cent of this homework consisted of manufacturing work. Such statistics do not provide an accurate source of information about telework (Dostal, 1985).

In the UK, Department of Employment surveys in 1981 revealed 660,000 homeworkers. Of these, however, only 251,000 were working 'at' home, as opposed to 'from' home, of whom 72,000 were engaged in manufacturing work (Hakim, 1984). These estimates have been called into question by Mitter (Mitter, 1986) and by Pugh (Pugh, 1984) who regard them as much too low. After surveying alternative government sources of data on the location of employment for the Low Pay Unit, Bisset and Huws concluded in 1984 that there were 'at least' 300,000 homeworkers in the UK (Bisset and Huws, 1984).

Little research has been carried out in the UK on the proportion of these homeworkers who are proprietors of small businesses, or on the proportion of small businesses which are home-based. Quantitative estimates of the growth of small businesses are also rare, because of problems of definition and because of the existence of a thriving underground economy (Mattera, 1985; Smith and Wied-Nebbeling 1986). However, there has been a dramatic growth in self-employment, with a 32 per cent increase to 2.5 million (some 10 per cent of those in employment) between 1979 and 1984 (Curran, 1986). Excluding craft and manual workers, there was a rise from 1 million in 1981 to 1.68 million in 1984. This has been paralleled both by a growth in the number of small businesses and by a drop in their failure rate. This improvement in the chances of survival for small firms indicates favourable conditions for a continuing increase (Curran, 1986; Ganguly, 1985).

Whatever the differences in exact estimates of the extent of home-based employment or small businesses based in the home in any particular country, there is a clear consensus in the literature that both are flourishing, with further growth indicated.

CONCLUSIONS

These varying approaches to estimating the extent and future potential of telework have produced a wide spectrum of possible interpretations. Extracting from them an authoritative quantitative forecast is no easy matter. However, it is possible to produce some tentative generalisations about what appears to be the most likely scenario.

This is that telework is likely to grow steadily, albeit more slowly than early commentators predicted. Teleworkers who are home-based all the time are likely to be outnumbered by part-time and occasional teleworkers who are otherwise office-based. Although the proportion will be smaller than at present, a majority of the workforce will not be engaged in telework, but will continue to make the daily journey to work by traditional means.

However, this does not mean to say that their working lives will be unaffected by information technology's capacity for facilitating remote communications. We believe that the traditional concept of the workplace as a fixed geographical space will become increasingly outmoded, and will be replaced by more abstract notions of the working context as a set of relationships, a network, an intellectual space, which we call the 'elusive office'. As the means of communication and information generation become less space-dependent (because of the existence of cheap and efficient telecommunications networks) and portable (because of the existence of small, cheap, light, robust terminals and of intelligent interfaces), where the worker is physically based becomes less and less important. Instead of being confined to a particular workplace, be it a central office or a home, the information-processsing worker becomes mobile, capable of being productive and of being managed from virtually any location. With a cell-phone, a portable fax machine and a battery-operated lap-top computer, work which is currently thought of as desk-bound can be carried out while travelling, on a customer's premises, on a beach or—as at least one of the authors of this book can testify—in a children's playground, with only minimal loss of productivity through distractions.

This development, by inserting an element of mobile work into a wide range of jobs, is likely to erode the sharp distinctions currently made between 'telework' and 'non-telework'. The boundaries are also becoming blurred between 'employment' and 'self-employment', because of de-regulation and the growth of new types of temporary, on-call, agency and casual employment contract (Bureau of National Affairs, 1986; Institute of Personnel Management, 1986; Atkinson and Meager, 1986; European Foundation for the Improvement of Living and Working Conditions, 1986). Together with a growth of sub-contracting, both to individual freelances and to independent small businesses, this produces an even more variegated picture, in which the difficulties of analysis outlined in our opening chapter are accentuated, and quantitative forecasts of the future extent of telework become increasingly problematic.

Perhaps more important than mathematically exact prediction, however, is an impression of what these changes are likely to mean, economically and socially, how they may impinge on our legal and political structures and shape the settlements we live in. Some of these more general predictions made by the prophets of telework are discussed in our next, and final, chapter.

Chapter 13

TELEWORK AND SOCIAL AND ECONOMIC CHANGE

Many of the predictions made in the literature on telework about its overall social and economic impacts are strongly coloured by the authors' views about what are, or are not, desirable outcomes, leading to sharply contrasting views about what the effects might be. Commentators attempting to gain an overall impression frequently present future prospects in terms of alternative scenarios. Thus, Hirschheim in his review of the research on office automation presents the evidence separately, under the headings 'the optimist position' and 'the pessimist position' (Hirschheim, 1985). Hedberg and Mehlmann put forward two contrasting scenarios which they identify as resulting from 'the collective approach' and 'the individual approach'—of which the former is positive and the latter negative in social terms (Hedberg and Mehlmann, 1981). Monod and Metayer also foresee two alternative possibilities, which they describe as *'utopie rassurante'* (reassuring utopia) and *'exploitation sauvage'* (savage exploitation) (Monod and Metayer, 1982).

Into the former, optimistic, camp can be placed such writers as Toffler (Toffler, 1981, 1985), Williams (Williams, 1983), Nilles (1976, 1982, 1985[a], 1985[b]), Gordon (Gordon, 1984, 1985a, 1985b, 1988; Gordon and Kelly, 1986), Shirley (Shirley, 1982, 1985, 1987), Postgate (Postgate, 1984) and Aldrich (Aldrich, 1982).

Among the pessimists we find Renfro (Renfro, 1985), Gregory (Gregory, 1983, 1985), Mumme (Mumme, 1983), Siegel and Markoff (Siegel and Markoff, 1985), Chamot and Zalusky (Chamot and Zalusky, 1985), Mehlmann (Mehlmann, 1985), Robins and Hepworth (Robins and Hepworth, 1988) and others.

Without wishing to contribute further to this polarisation of views, our aim in this chapter is to summarise some of the main issues raised in these debates in order to identify the factors most likely to affect the future development of telework and the societal issues most likely to arise as a result.

ENERGY CONSUMPTION, TRANSPORTATION AND THE TELECOMMUNICATIONS INFRASTRUCTURE

The need to explore ways of saving energy gave the investigation of telework its first impetus during the energy crisis of the early 1970s. It is not surprising therefore that the tradeoff between telecommunications and transportation figures large in the literature on the subject.

Nilles concluded that a 1 per cent replacement of urban commuting by telecommuting would result in a net reduction in petrol consumption of 5.36 million barrels per annum in the USA (Nilles *et al.*, 1976). Harkness, slightly more conservatively, estimated that if 50 per cent of all US office employees worked in neighbourhood centres six out of every seven working days, then the savings from reduced commuting would be about 240,000 barrels daily (the equivalent annual figure for 1 per cent of the workforce would be approximately 3.5 million barrels). Using Federal Energy Administration guidelines, he calculated that such a saving would justify a $37 billion investment for energy conservation, using 1976 prices. He also estimated that roughly $30 billion in otherwise necessary freeway expansions might be saved if all office employment growth expected in the 50 largest US cities by the year 2000 (12 million employees) adopted telework rather than commuting by freeway (Harkness, 1977).

Such projections have been criticised as too simplistic by other commentators. It has, for instance, been pointed out that they are 'based on extrapolations from current data . . . on a general assumption that widespread acceptance of some variation of remote work will occur. The limitation of such studies is that they do not examine the process by which that acceptance will occur nor even the likelihood that it will' (Diebold Group, 1981).

Kraemer and King also note another weakness of most studies and technology assessments of telecommunications substitution: that they ignore the costs and the diffusion time requirements of installing the kind of telecommunications infrastructure which would be necessary for widespread substitution to become feasible. The necessary infrastructure for transportation is, of course, already in place even though this may require upgrading in some cases (Kraemer and King, 1982).

Studies of transportation/telecommunications substitution generally take account of the energy consumed in the remote communications process. However, not all take account of other energy uses, such as the energy required to heat and light the remote worksite. In the case of homework, this may involve relatively inefficient uses of energy, where a large space is kept warm and lit for the use of a single worker without the economies of scale which are possible when a number of workers share the same office space.

If widespread substitution of telecommunications for transportation were to take place, one of its likely consequences might be to produce a much more widely dispersed workforce, with a shift of individual workers to remote rural areas, as many researchers have predicted, Nilles and Harkness among them (Toffler, 1981; Medhurst, 1984; Williams, 1982; Nilles *et al.*, 1976, Harkness, 1977). In such a situation, although fewer journeys would take place, those which were undertaken would most likely be considerably longer, thus consuming a considerable portion of the energy saved by the reduction in daily commuting (Pye, Tyler and Cartwright, 1974). The development of such remote rural communities might also lead to a growth in other forms of transportation, for instance those entailed in the delivery of non-information-based goods and services to these communities, or increases in long-distance travel for social purposes.

Many of the technologies proposed for telework, such as broad-band cable networks, would be extremely expensive to deliver to isolated rural homes. A shift in the workforce from urban and suburban to rural areas might also lead to a substitution of travel by private car for travel by more energy-efficient mass transit systems.

All these factors would detract from the cost advantages of telecommuting over commuting. Nevertheless, there appears to be a consensus among researchers that the widespread introduction of telework would result in a net saving of energy. However, it is not so clear that this would be on a sufficiently large scale to justify major investment.

Research in the UK suggests that the proportion of total car travel which is likely to be eliminated by telecommuting is not great. Of all journeys, 22 per cent are to and from work, of which 50 per cent are by car (Dover, 1982a). Even if we take the high estimate of 10 per cent of the workforce becoming teleworkers, this leaves only 1 per cent of all journeys available for elimination in a way which involves significant energy saving. By the time the additional energy consumption involved as a result of telework is offset against this, what is left may not be very great.

PLANNING AND LAND-USE

If telework is to develop on a significant scale, then it is likely to bring with it a number of changes which have implications for planners. One of these concerns a change in use of existing building stocks. It is likely that most telework will take place in buildings currently designated for residential purposes. UK research suggests that only about 1 per cent of the housing stock is replaced each year, which, over a fifteen-year period, leaves 80–90 per cent of needs being accommodated in existing housing (Saxon, 1984). While some homeworkers may be able to create the extra space required for telework by building on an extension (Postgate, 1984) or adapting a spare room (Gordon and Kelly, 1986), stress may be felt in high-density developments of apartments or where dwellings are overcrowded (Saxon, 1984). Purpose-built housing for teleworkers, like the Scottish project described by Shirley (Shirley, 1988) is likely to be the exception for many years to come. It is generally suggested that conversion of existing premises is the most appropriate way of accommodating telework, although a few people are of the opinion that wholesale demolition and redevelopment of inadequate inner-city housing would be more appropriate (Revill, 1984).

For neighbourhood work centres, a greater variety of possible buildings is available. Among other possibilities, it has been suggested that they could be housed in converted schools, suburban shopping malls, disused factories or warehouses (Gordon and Kelly, 1986; Nilles, 1985b; Toffler, 1981). An alternative to the neighbourhood office for the teleworker who, from inclination or necessity, does not wish to work at home is the 'workspace' or 'loft' concept, whereby managed buildings—often with office services laid on—are broken down into small work units which can be rented individually (Saxon, 1984).

Adapting the existing building stock to allow telework to take place in secure, congenial, uninterrupted and ergonomically appropriate conditions will present new challenges to architects. However, planners will also be involved, since in many cases zoning regulations will need to be altered to allow these changes in use to take place.

These changes will produce knock-on effects which also have planning implications. For instance, traffic flows may alter, with fewer journeys in and out of city centres, but more between outlying areas. A need may spring up for new office service industries, such as stationery supply, computer services, fax or photocopying services, in areas which were previously residential, agricultural or industrial.

Some commentators anticipate more radical changes, with major population shifts from urban to rural areas. The social, economic and environmental effects of such developments would be far-reaching. Land values would be likely to decline in the cities and rise elsewhere; there would be a need for new housing stock in rural areas; the infrastructure would have to be upgraded to allow for the delivery of basic services and transportation to the new rural populations; areas of nature conservation and natural beauty might be threatened as might the tourist industries in some areas (Toffler, 1981, 1985; Medhurst, 1984; Williams, 1983; Nilles et al., 1976).

What would be the fate of the inner cities in the meanwhile is the subject of some disagreement. One possibility is that they could become 'garden cities', 'annular concentrations around theatres, clubs and recreational buildings, set in spacious grounds'; on the other hand they could become pockets of extreme deprivation, cut off from the affluence of the dispersed centres of wealth (Medhurst, 1984).

Robins and Hepworth argue that telework must be understood in the context of the 'information city', in which 'concrete, physical geography is transcended' and 'electronic network geography is mapped on *abstract space*'. Their proposition is that 'the new electronic networks are the basis of new circuits of production, distribution and consumption' which will result in a home-centring, not just of work activities, but also of such activities as shopping, banking, education and entertainment. This in turn makes it possible to 'multiplex production and consumption (work time and "free" time)' which will bring 'significant developments in the assignation and partitioning of urban space and new terms of access'. One result they foresee is that 'land and property values seem set to migrate from the high streets of city centres to new drive-in complexes situated by suburban ring-roads and motorway intersections'. They paint a bleak view of the centre of the information city:

> its landmarks are likely to be financial complexes and electronic skyscraper-fortresses, cordoned off from depleted and decaying inner city residential areas. The more affluent private estates and apartments are, similarly, tending to be sealed off from the surrounding community by elaborate surveillance and security systems. In this cybernetic city genuine public space is devalued and 'redefined as a planning problem to be eliminated or privatised' (Davies, 1985, p.113). This is the space of flows that supersedes the space of places; in this space the flow of people gives way to the flow of information and finance. (Robins and Hepworth, 1988, pp. 160–5, their italics, parentheses and inverted commas)

Aside from any socially divisive effects of such developments, they predict that they will also bring political problems for planners:

> A further problem for local government is its diminishing tax base. Less public space, more derelict land, scaled down business districts, and the migration of business to out-of-city and rural sites, all add up to less revenues through rates. Against these countervailing forces it becomes increasingly difficult for local and urban authorities to implement policies aimed at an allocation of land use according to social goals and priorities. (Robins and Hepworth, 1988).

There is an immense difference between this downbeat image of the 'information city' with its social polarities and erosion of public and community life, and Toffler's optimistic vision of the 'telecommunity' with its 'warmer, more bonded families and a closer, more finely-grained community life' which will lead to 'a lively proliferation of neighbourhood restaurants, theatres, pubs and clubs, a revitalisation of church and voluntary group activity—all or mostly on a face-to-face basis' (Toffler, 1981, pp.382–3). His is a vision of decentralisation where urban concentrations of high-rise offices or large-scale factories are replaced by dispersed rural settlements with small-scale units of production.

Because of the inertia inherent in existing systems, and people's tendency to resist changes which they are not sure will benefit them, a more likely scenario is that neither of these extremes is realised. Even the most optimistic forecasts predict that only a minority of the workforce will become teleworkers, leaving a majority which continues to travel to work. And teleworkers will never be able to segregate themselves geographically from other types of workers since, even if they do not share their households with them, they will continue to have needs for goods and services which cannot be delivered electronically, for instance for food, clothing, consumer durables, personal services, entertainment, child care, education, health services and so on.

While there may be shifts in the relative attractions of different areas and changes in the demand for particular types of housing, it is likely that most people will continue to live where housing and services already exist. As far as housing needs are concerned, then, the most important change brought about by telework will therefore not be one of new demand, but of the changing use of existing premises. The new activities will take place within the shells of the old.

REGIONAL DEVELOPMENT

The same forces which could bring about a decentralisation of work into rural areas could also be used consciously as instruments for the economic regeneration of depressed regions. The literature reveals few examples of attempts to do this. In one Swedish experiment a remote work centre was set up in the far north of the country in a region of high unemployment to provide back-office functions for a centrally based organisation. However, the jobs created proved to be low-level and routine, and when there was a fall in demand it was these workers who were laid off (Mehlmann, 1987; Elling, 1985).

Holti and Stern describe an attempt to set up a scheme in the South West of England to enable local small businesses to telecommunicate with Central London. This failed because it was not legally possible for the telecommunications provider to charge them at the local call rate for long-distance use of a land line (Holti and Stern, 1985).

It is likely that the system of applying distance-related (rather than traffic volume-related) charges to telecommunications usage will continue to provide a disincentive to the setting up of such schemes in Europe.

Other constraints are likely to result from the lack of suitable skills in remote areas and the lack of appropriate support services, many of which require a critical mass of customers to be viable. It is unlikely that telework will lead to regional development without active intervention by national or local government to make up such deficiencies and provide pump-priming resources.

On a larger scale, telecommunications networks can be used to transfer work from one country to another. To date, offshore information processing has consisted mainly of routine, low-skill tasks, such as data entry, with little potential for creating permanent jobs or permitting the long-term development of local skills or economies (Posthuma, 1987; Huws, 1985; Office of Technology Assessment, 1985).

> The major motive to go off-shore relates to labour costs: data or text entry costs are 75–90% below European or US American standards in the Caribbean and Asiatic regions. Governments in these regions are quite aware of the fact that this market is temporary and will decrease in size with increased automation. They expect, however, that off-shore activities in their countries, if coupled with appropriate training and skills-upgrading policies, will allow their labour force to adapt to the pace of technical change and thus open up new opportunities in the future. (Steinle, 1988a, p.13)

Whether or not these expectations will be met remains to be seen. On the face of it, as with regional development, it seems unlikely that telework will result in the regeneration of local economies without political intervention to deflect the simple effects of market forces.

LEGAL, TAXATION AND WORKER PROTECTION ISSUES

The social effect of telework which is most feared by its opponents is that it will lead to an atomisation of the workforce, bringing with it exploitative practices and a loss of worker protection. These in turn, it is suggested, will lead to many other social problems which are attendant on poverty and insecurity (Siegel and Markoff, 1985; Mumme, 1983; Chamot and Zalusky, 1985; Gregory, 1983, 1985).

Many other commentators, not necessarily critical of telework *per se*, consider that it may lead to the development of a dual workforce, with a widening gap between professional, managerial and other workers with scarce or easily marketed skills and those with only routine skills to offer who are increasingly likely to be paid on piece-rates and employed on a casual basis (Donnison, 1984; Monod, 1983; Kawakami, 1983).

A major concern is that decentralised workers will not be able to organise effectively into trade unions, which will lead to an erosion of collective bargaining (Mumme, 1983; Chamot and Zalusky, 1985; Gregory, 1983, 1985; Peles, 1985; Empirica, 1986a). Associated with this, is the fear that it will result in low pay (Else, 1982; *New Scientist*, 1984; *Technology*, 1984; Bisset and Huws, 1984), particularly for women workers (Lie, 1985; Vedel, 1984, 1985; Goldmann and Richter, 1986).

A general growth in self-employment, accompanied by a shrinkage in the proportion of the workforce covered by employers' contributions to social security, health insurance and pension schemes will also result in a transfer to the taxpayer of welfare costs currently paid for by direct contributions (Kubicek 1988). This also leads to a decrease in the proportion of a country's total income tax revenue which is deducted at source, and therefore immediately available, and an increase in the proportion which must be recovered retroactively by means which are more labour-intensive for inland revenue staff.

It is also possible that a growth in telework may lead to an expansion of the underground economy (Hirschheim, 1985; Mattera, 1985; Smith and Wied-Nebbeling, 1986) leading to an overall loss of tax revenue.

When the effects of this decrease in revenue from direct taxation, and increase in the cost of collecting such revenue are combined with the larger numbers of workers who must be covered by welfare schemes funded by the taxpayer (because of the declining proportion covered by self-financing social security, sickness insurance or pension schemes), then governments will be left with a choice: to increase the level of indirect taxation or to accept a much lower level of social provision.

Many of these effects could be mitigated by the introduction of legislation ensuring a minimum level of worker protection, by means of measures to ensure minimum rates of pay and employee status to remote workers (US Congress, Office of Technology Assessment, 1985; Bureau of National Affairs, 1986; Huws, 1984a).

FAMILY AND COMMUNITY STRUCTURE

A recurrent theme in the literature on telework is its ability to unite families and strengthen community ties. Some commentators explicitly present telework as an antidote to the rising divorce rate, the growth in numbers of single-parent families and the increasing need for state provision for care of the sick and elderly (Aldrich, 1982; Housing Associations Charitable Trust, 1984).

Others, such as Toffler, see it as encouraging the growth of a variety of different forms of family and communal living. He quotes one report by a team of psychiatrists which discovered no less than 86 different family types in a single poor black neighbourhood of Chicago, and asserts that such diversity will increase as a result of telework, which will allow people to choose a 'personalised' family pattern (Toffler, 1981). There is considerable evidence to support Toffler's view that family structures are changing and the traditional nuclear family becoming a rarity. However, there is none to link this phenomenon with telework. As noted in Chapter 9, in the Empirica survey of teleworkers, 92 per cent turned out to live in households with two adults and dependent children, while in another UK survey of teleworkers it was discovered that 95 per cent were mothers of young children who were secondary earners in their households (Huws, 1984a)—the classic nuclear model which, according to Toffler, now constitutes a small minority in the working population at large.

Telework is sometimes seen as improving family life by encouraging the development of husband-and-wife telework teams (Turoff and Hiltz, 1983; Mason, Jennings and Evans, 1984) and enabling fathers to see more of their children (Applegarth, 1985; Judkins, West and Drew, 1985). This would suggest that it has an egalitarian effect within the family, encouraging partners to participate jointly in economic activity, child care and housework.

However, others believe that telework has the opposite effect, confirming women's primary responsibilities as carers and their secondary place in the workforce (Vedel and Gunnarsson, 1985; Goldmann and Richter, 1986).

It is also widely believed that telework will contribute to a strengthening of the sense of community, particularly in suburbs and commuter towns which currently serve a 'dormitory' function for commuters. It will no longer, according to this view, be necessary for people to move house when they change their employer, which will encourage them to 'put down roots' and make a commitment to community development (Toffler, 1981; Galitz, 1984; Aldrich, 1982).

The underlying assumption behind such statements—which is plausible but by no means proven—is that most people want stability and will stay put if given a choice. Otherwise, it could equally convincingly be argued that the removal of the need to be tied to geographical proximity to the employer might lead to greater mobility—perhaps even to a revival of nomadic lifestyles among some groups. The few studies which have investigated telework in relation to community involvement have not produced any evidence that there is an increase in neighbourhood social activity as a result of telework (Craipeau and Marot, 1984; Diebold Group, 1981). On the contrary, the Diebold Group found that the most 'successful' teleworkers, in that they complained least of isolation and found it easiest to concentrate, were of a solitary personality type with low needs for social interaction and little involvement in local affairs (Diebold Group, 1981).

It is in fact difficult to sustain a case that telework can cause changes in the structure of either families or communities. Rather it should perhaps be seen as a form of work which is facilitated by some structures and domestic situations but not others. Into the former category might come professional couples employed in similar or related fields who wish to work together, or nuclear familes in which the wife wishes to stay at home with the children and continue working part-time while the husband continues to go out to work. Into the latter we could include single people or those in claustrophobic extended families from which they need regular escape.

Looked at in this light, telework could be seen to play a role in exacerbating some tendencies which already exist in society. Just as, in Gordon's phrase, it can 'make a good marriage better and a bad one worse' (Gordon and Kelly, 1986) so it might also cement an already close community and fracture one in which social tensions are already present.

EDUCATION AND TRAINING

If telework is to develop on any scale, there will be implications for education and training policies. As Holti and Stern note, the new 'bundles of skills' involved in telework have yet to be institutionalised, and there are currently a number of different approaches to teaching the skills involved in using information technology (Holti and Stern, 1984).

Hebenstreit emphasises that most of the population will in the future require what he calls the 'skills for the "wired" society'—the ability confidently to use interactive dialogue systems for such purposes as searching databases, sending and receiving electronic mail etc.—which should be made part of all general education and training courses (Hebenstreit, 1983).

Like other workers, teleworkers will also require job-specific training to enable them to carry out their own work effectively and qualify for promotion (Gordon and Kelly, 1986). However, there will also be a need for other skills which are currently rarely taught: in such matters as organising one's time effectively, developing safe working practices, legal rights and obligations, avoiding becoming socially isolated, the management of remote workers, negotiating skills and the skills involved in setting up and running a successful small business. How such training should be developed and who should be responsible for providing it are matters for discussion.

More broadly, there will be a need for general education to develop an understanding of the potential of information technology for transforming working practices and enabling jobs to be redesigned and relocated. The object would be to encourage among workers, managers, educators, planners and politicians the widest possible awareness of the options available. Such an awareness is the best guarantee that the negative features of telework will be minimised and the positive potential of information technology for improving the quality of working life and increasing individual choice will be realised.

CONCLUSIONS

Perhaps the most important conclusion we have drawn from our study of telework is that the future will not be simply determined by information technology and its potential for transforming the nature and location of information-processing work. The technology is a tool with many possible applications. However, the only applications which will be actually developed are those which are perceived to be of some immediate use. And these applications will, in turn, only be taken up and implemented by individuals and organisations which can see how they will facilitate the achievement of their own current aims. The determining factor is therefore not the technology itself, but the aims and objectives of those social actors with the power and resources to purchase and use it for their own particular ends.

Thus telework is likely to be adopted by, and only by, those managers who see it as a solution to their problems of finding scarce skills, of cutting costs, or responding to the changing requirements of volatile markets or some other concrete difficulty; it is likely to be accepted by, and only by, those workers who see it as a solution to their child-care problem, their need to stagger working hours around non-work commitments, their desire to set up as an independent entrepreneur or the lack of any other employment option. Although it can provide new options, and make it possible to combine goals which previously seemed mutually exclusive, the technology is merely a tool. Its role is simply to facilitate the implementation of decisions which have been made for essentially non-technical reasons.

All these individual decisions are, of course, influenced by the social and economic context. The imperative to cut costs, for instance, is less strong during periods when the economy is buoyant and expanding than in periods of recession, heightened competition and uncertain markets. An individual parent's child-care problems are related to the level of public social provision. Even the time and stress involved in commuting to work are affected by external factors such as the availability of public transport, the cost of fuel and so on.

Forecasting the future, then, becomes not so much a question of predicting the future capabilities of information technology, although this will determine the outer limits of the range of options available for reorganising work; rather, it is a matter of assessing economic, social and political trends. To do so, there seem to us to be two sets of questions to be asked: Firstly, what will be the priorities for employers? In what sort of industrial and economic climate will they be operating? What restraints are they likely to encounter? And what solutions are likely to present themselves to these problems? Secondly, what will be the priorities for workers? What choices are likely to be available to them? And how, ultimately, do they want to live?

These are huge questions which we do not claim to be especially qualified to answer in their entirety. For what it is worth, however, we end this book with a brief account of what we see in our own crystal ball.

First, we predict that priorities for managers will remain much as they are at present: to consolidate and expand; to maximise productivity and efficiency; to respond quickly to market changes; to stay one jump ahead of the competition. However, we believe that pressures to meet these aims quickly will intensify. Throughout the world, competitive pressures on companies are likely to increase, an intensification which will be particularly pronounced in Europe with the creation of a single European market in 1992.

One current response to these pressures, which is likely to develop further, is the automation of many production and distribution functions. In many industries, as well as boosting productivity, this also generates a flow of information to management which makes it possible to monitor both supply and demand on a daily or even hourly basis. This poses the problem of responding quickly and flexibly to this demand, leading to a growth in short-run, 'just-in-time' production methods and a requirement for flexible manning. As a result, there is likely to be an increase in the use of casual, temporary and on-call staff, and fluctuations in working hours. Such a market-led approach to production also implies new styles of marketing. We predict that marketing staff will increasingly be required to be in frequent interactive communication with central computers while having to travel physically over larger and larger geographical areas, because of the expansion of markets. These sales staff will effectively become mobile teleworkers.

We also think that the current growth in sub-contracting—the disaggregation of very large organisations into smaller, more streamlined units—is likely to continue. It appears to have several advantages in a fast-changing and competitive business environment: it enables both costs and risk to be externalised, and—except where there are skill shortages—it makes it possible to respond much more quickly to market changes. There will also be a growth in other organisational forms, such as franchising, which involve the spreading of financial risk without the loss of central control over many aspects of an organisation's activity. In fact we think that organisations will increasingly cease to be defined in terms of the numbers of people they have on the payroll and the types of activity being carried out under their direct control, but in terms of the activities which they control indirectly, through a network of contracts with smaller suppliers, with central control over such functions as product image, distribution or sales. Information plays a crucial role in such control, and information technology will be the means of exercising it, spreading out like a great web to attach all the parts of this large, apparently loosely structured, organisation tightly to the centre. As the chains of sub-contractors fragment into smaller and smaller, and more and more widely dispersed units, but the web, though stretched, remains unbroken, more and more functions will be carried out by people whom we might describe as teleworkers. The office—the site where information is generated, processed and exchanged—has ceased to have any fixed geographical boundaries. It exists only as a network—the 'elusive office' has arrived.

If present deregulatory trends continue, the legal obstacles to such developments, in the form of restrictions on certain types of employment practice, are likely to diminish, although companies may well find themselves facing new forms of legal limitation in other areas, such as environmental controls. The latter may further encourage the break-up of very large industrial units and their geographical dispersal.

Turning our attention to the workforce, we again see no fundamental changes in individual goals. Most people will continue to want a financially secure future for themselves and their children, the chance to use their skills creatively, to win the respect of friends and colleagues, to live in a pleasant environment, with sufficient leisure to enjoy it and the company of their loved ones. As at present, they will also be well aware that not all these goals can be met equally well at once and there are complex tradeoffs to be made: more income through overtime means less time with the children; the job with the best pension may be the least satisfying to perform; the work which is the most rewarding socially may involve living in an area which is expensive, overcrowded and polluted.

While the need to make such tradeoffs will not disappear, we foresee major changes in the menus of options facing individual workers when they make such choices, and in the relative value of each option. Some of these changes result from the increasing pace of change. The concept of a 'skill for life' we believe will become increasingly untenable. Everyone will have to be prepared to acquire new skills throughout the course of their working lives and be prepared to accept that their old ones may have become redundant or require adaptation. Such skill changes will also mean occupational changes for many, and—with the structural changes affecting many organisations and industries— often too a change of employer, even, in many cases, a change in employment status.

The loss of the expectation of a job for life is, of course, accompanied by a loss of security. It becomes increasingly difficult to think of the employer as someone who can be taken for granted, leaned on for a minimal level of support. Instead workers must increasingly think of ways they can provide security for themselves and their dependents by other means. Reinforced by the privatisation of many formerly state-provided benefits and services, this is leading to a phenomenal growth in the numbers of people seeking to own their own homes, to subscribe to private pension, health and life insurance schemes, to invest in stocks and shares, and to develop new skills privately. We expect this trend to continue. The individual worker's fear of becoming dependent on a large organisation which is no longer seen as a trustworthy source of lifetime employment may also, in some cases, contribute to a labour supply-side 'pull' towards setting up independent enterprises.

This 'pull' is, however, more than matched by the demand-side 'push' from employers wishing to shed responsibility for a large and inflexible permanent workforce in favour of a flexible and variegated pool of small suppliers who can be drawn on as and when their particular skills are required. For many workers, a permanent full-time job will cease to be an available option: the choice will increasingly be between an ever-widening range of different casual, temporary or part-time employment options which may be carried out on a self-employed, agency or employee basis. However the opportunities for entrepreneurship will expand, many of them created by the gaps created when large organisations or state services are restructured.

Individual entrepreneurs, freelance workers or piece-rate workers have an enormous incentive to increase their own productivity, since they are not paid for time which is not productive. The impetus then comes from them to find ways to upgrade their output or efficiency. Many of these may involve the use of information technology in telework modes, to produce and process information or to communicate it to the client from a fixed or mobile remote site.

However, there will continue to be many functions which need to be carried out face-to-face by human beings who live near each other or can easily travel to a shared workplace: caring for children, the sick, the disabled and the elderly; the delivery of goods and non-information-based services; the construction and upkeep of buildings, roads and other parts of the designed environment; the physical manufacture of most goods; the repair of machines. However simple it becomes to communicate remotely, we cannot imagine a future in which the majority of people are not in regular social contact with each other in the course of carrying out their daily work.

Appendix A

EMPIRICA TELEWORK SURVEY

Manager-Questionnaire

Homework and other Decentralised Forms of Work (Telework)

Please answer all questions to the best of your ability. If you wish, use the back of a page to explain or expand your answer to an item. If you do not know an answer to a question, or the information requested is not available, please note this fact in the space provided.

Telework schemes and Teleworkers

In the questionnaire we refer to telework and to teleworkers, and it is necessary to reach understanding in what is meant by this.

In many cases, a company will have begun to delegate work to small organisations—whose employees and management we refer to as teleworkers under some circumstances—or to individuals working outside the time and space confines of the parent organisation—again, these are teleworkers. A 'telework scheme' in the first case is the small organisation or company itself, in the second case it is the scheme within the parent company. There are many cases in between these, and if you cannot fit your work arrangements easily, please do the best you can and describe the problem—preferably in sufficient detail to enable us to make our own judgement.

1.1   Name (of the person
       completing questionnaire): _____

1.2   Job title: _____

1.3   Organisation/Company: _____

1.4   Location (address):   _____

1.5   Total number of employees in
       organisation: _____

1.6   Number of teleworkers in
       organisation: _____

2.   Short description of the telework scheme

2.1   Date of project inauguration   _____

2.2   Project promotor   _____

2.3   Was the telework scheme designed for a particular group of people (e.g. disabled)?

_____

3.   Project Background

3.1   How did the idea of the scheme come about?

_____

3.2   Who was involved in the initiation and/or subsequent planning of the project?

	involved in initiation	involved in subsequent planning	not involved
3.2.1 Top management	( )	( )	( )
3.2.2 Statutory authorities	( )	( )	( )
3.2.3 Trade unions	( )	( )	( )
3.2.4 Department heads	( )	( )	( )
3.2.5 Employee(s) now teleworking	( )	( )	( )
3.2.6 Others			
_____	( )	( )	( )

3.3   How were teleworkers selected initially? Please list selection criteria in order of importance:

_____

How have selection criteria changed? Since when?

_____

3.4   Is recruitment restricted to employees or regionally?

( )   own employees only
( )   local recruitment
( )   national recruitment

4.   Technical Equipment and Communication Media

4.1   Please list the communication media used in communicating with teleworkers, for the transmission of work results etc.

	Major communication media			
	no usage	some usage	frequent usage	heavy dependence
Public switched telephone network	( )	( )	( )	( )
Public switched data network	( )	( )	( )	( )
Circuit switched data network	( )	( )	( )	( )
Teletex	( )	( )	( )	( )
Videotex	( )	( )	( )	( )
Electronic mail system	( )	( )	( )	( )
Data storage on floppy disc	( )	( )	( )	( )
Handwritten texts via ordinary mail	( )	( )	( )	( )
Tapes/Cassettes via ordinary mail	( )	( )	( )	( )
Dictation via telephone	( )	( )	( )	( )
Handwritten text via courir	( )	( )	( )	( )
Tapes/Cassettes via courir	( )	( )	( )	( )
Collected/delivered by employee	( )	( )	( )	( )
Meeting	( )	( )	( )	( )
Others (e.g. Telecopier) _____	( )	( )	( )	( )

No use of PIT Services   ( )

4.2   If you do not use a PTT service as a communication media, are there plans to do so in the future?

( )   yes
( )   no

Please give the reasons: _____

4.3   Use of hardware in

	decentralised unit(s)		central unit(s)	
	no. of workstations	no. of persons	no. of workstations	no. of persons
4.3.1 General purpose computer				
4.3.2 Small business system				
4.3.3 Micro/Personal computer				
4.3.4 Terminals				
4.3.5 Electronic typewriters				
4.3.6 Word processing systems				
4.3.7 Others				

5.   The Structure of the Project

5.1   Organisational structure of the telework project

	number of persons
5.1.1 Satellite work centre (e.g. branch office)	_____
5.1.2 Neighbourhood work centre (supported by different companies)	_____
5.1.3 Flexible work arrangement (partial work at home)	_____
5.1.4 Work at home	_____
5.1.5 Electronic service office (independent firm offering services)	_____
5.1.6 Others (e.g. 'mobile' work of insurance agents) _____	_____

5.2   Legal status of decentralised office(s)

5.2.1 Branch office (of the own company)	( )
5.2.2 Limited company	( )
5.2.3 Non-profit organisation	( )
5.2.4 Self-employed person	( )
5.2.5 Other _____	( )

5.3   Contractual arrangements with and payment of teleworker(s)

	number of persons			number of persons
5.3.1 piece-rate payment	_____	5.3.4 employees		_____
5.3.2 hourly payment	_____	5.3.5 self-employed		_____
5.3.3 salaried staff	_____	5.3.6 Other		

5.4   Nature of work/office tasks

	number of teleworkers
5.4.1 Input and amendment of data	_____
5.4.2 Typing or word processing	_____
5.4.3 Filing of business records such as correspondence, invoices etc.	_____
5.4.4 Book-keeping and accounts records	_____
5.4.5 Stock control and replacement	_____

5.4.6	Computer programming	_____
5.4.7	Management tasks such as: invoice control, employee records, cash flow monitoring	_____
5.4.8	Evaluation and documentation	_____
5.4.9	Others	_____

5.5   Occupation of the teleworkers

number of
teleworkers

5.5.1	DP professionals	_____
5.5.2	Scientific/engineering	_____
5.5.3	Academic	_____
5.5.4	Health/medical	_____
5.5.5	Business professionals	_____
5.5.6	Managers	_____
5.5.7	Sales workers	_____
5.5.8	Secretarial, stenographic & typists	_____
5.5.9	Commercial, clerical & administrative	_____
5.5.10	Production & service workers	_____

5.6   Please give age groups, sex and working hours of teleworkers.

Age groups	Sex		Full-time	Part-time	Other
	M	F			
Under 20					
20–30					
30–40					
40–50					
50–60					
over 60					
Total					

Please indicate the number of teleworkers

5.7   Educational and vocational background of teleworkers.

number of
teleworkers

Highest academic attainment	
none/lower than CSE	_____
1 CSE	_____
1 GCE 'O'-level..	_____
1 GCE 'A'-level..	_____
1 BA/BSc degree or equivalent.	
higher qualifications...	_____

5.8   Contractants/Employees according to industries/branches and work context of the tasks. Please enter number of employees.

Office task Industry	typing or wordprocessing	input of amendment of data	bookkeeping and accounting records	computer programming	evaluation and documentation	filing of business records	stock control and replacement	management tasks
— self-employed craftsmen	( )	( )	( )	( )	( )	( )	( )	( )
— self-employed professionals	( )	( )	( )	( )	( )	( )	( )	( )
— manufacturing, energy, building and construction	( )	( )	( )	( )	( )	( )	( )	( )
— public sector, railroad, postal system	( )	( )	( )	( )	( )	( )	( )	( )
— private services, transport, telecommunication	( )	( )	( )	( )	( )	( )	( )	( )
— wholesale and retail	( )	( )	( )	( )	( )	( )	( )	( )
— banking, insurance	( )	( )	( )	( )	( )	( )	( )	( )
— own company = employer[1]	( )	( )	( )	( )	( )	( )	( )	( )
— other	( )	( )	( )	( )	( )	( )	( )	( )

[1] please tick industry/branch

6.   Productivity, Supervision, Control

6.1   How is the productivity of the teleworkers measured?

6.2   What quantitative criteria are taken into account?

6.3   Do you take other, qualitative criteria into account as well?

( ) Flexibility
( ) Quality of work
( ) Others, please specify _____

6.4   Is the length of time worked monitored? If so, how?

6.5   Are any other supervision methods employed?

6.6   In what areas were cost savings made?

6.7   In what areas have productivity increases occurred?

_____

7.   Satisfaction and Problems

7.1   In your opinion, are the following groups generally satisfied with the telework arrangement initiated in your company?

	very satisfied	satisfied	not satisfied	very dissatisfied
— decision makers in the organisation	( )	( )	( )	( )
— Employees working as teleworkers (in general, in your opinion)	( )	( )	( )	( )
— Other employees in central unit	( )	( )	( )	( )
— Unions	( )	( )	( )	( )

7.2   Have attitudes changed since the project was started, as far as you know?

If so, how satisfied were the various groups at the start of the project in your opinion?

	very satisfied	satisfied	not satisfied	very dissatisfied
— decision makers in the organisation	( )	( )	( )	( )
— Employees working as teleworkers (in general, in your opinion)	( )	( )	( )	( )
— Other employees in central unit	( )	( )	( )	( )
— Unions	( )	( )	( )	( )

7.3   What problems have occurred so far and in which area did they appear?

( ) technical   _____
( ) organisational   _____
( ) economical   _____
( ) social   _____
( ) others   _____

8.   Facilitating and Constraining Factors and Future Plans

8.1   What were your original reasons for setting up the telework scheme?

	unimportant	less important	important	very important
— Reduction in central facilities costs and overhead expenses	( )	( )	( )	( )
— Off-peak utilisation of the computer	( )	( )	( )	( )
— Improved motivation and increased productivity of employees	( )	( )	( )	( )
— Retention and recruiting of scarce skills	( )	( )	( )	( )
— Reduction of employee turnover absenteeism generally	( )	( )	( )	( )

— Improved coping with surplus work (work peaks)	( )	( )	( )	( )
— Flexibility in determining conditions laid down in work contract	( )	( )	( )	( )
— Reduced costs for long-term employee welfare	( )	( )	( )	( )
— Rationalisation effort	( )	( )	( )	( )
— Flexibility in location of work	( )	( )	( )	( )
— Flexibility in working hours	( )	( )	( )	( )
— Skill upgrading of employees	( )	( )	( )	( )
— Possibility for employee to combine work and non-work activities (e.g. child care)	( )	( )	( )	( )
— Reduced commuting efforts and costs for employees	( )	( )	( )	( )
— Other _____	( )	( )	( )	( )

8.2   What were the major factors facilitating and constraining the telework project in the phases of its life cycle; and what do you expect them to be in the future? Please give some comments, too.

	Present Position importance				Future Perspectives importance	
Facilitating factors	un-important	less important	important	very important	less than now	more than now
— Reduction in central facilities costs and overhead expenses	( )	( )	( )	( )	( )	( )
— Off-peak utilisation of the computer	( )	( )	( )	( )	( )	( )
— Improved motivation and increased productivity of employees	( )	( )	( )	( )	( )	( )
— Retention and recruiting of scarce skills	( )	( )	( )	( )	( )	( )
— Reduction of employee turnover absenteeism generally	( )	( )	( )	( )	( )	( )
— Improved coping with surplus work (work peaks)	( )	( )	( )	( )	( )	( )
— Flexibility in determining conditions laid down in work contract	( )	( )	( )	( )	( )	( )
— Reduced costs for long-term employee welfare	( )	( )	( )	( )	( )	( )
— Rationalisation effort	( )	( )	( )	( )	( )	( )
— Flexibility in location of work	( )	( )	( )	( )	( )	( )
— Flexibility in working hours	( )	( )	( )	( )	( )	( )
— Skill upgrading of employees	( )	( )	( )	( )	( )	( )
— Possibility for employee to combine work and non-work activities (e.g. child care)	( )	( )	( )	( )	( )	( )
— Reduced commuting efforts and costs for employees	( )	( )	( )	( )	( )	( )
— Other _____	( )	( )	( )	( )	( )	( )

Comments: _____

Constraining Factors	Present Position importance				Future Perspectives importance	
	un-important	less important	important	very important	less than now	more than now
— organisational difficulties	( )	( )	( )	( )	( )	( )
— expenses	( )	( )	( )	( )	( )	( )
— the need to train employees	( )	( )	( )	( )	( )	( )
— lack of technical equipment such as computers or terminals	( )	( )	( )	( )	( )	( )
— lack of knowledge of requirements and potential	( )	( )	( )	( )	( )	( )
— low productivity (not economical)	( )	( )	( )	( )	( )	( )
— telecommunications infrastructure is too expensive to use	( )	( )	( )	( )	( )	( )
— lack of clarity as to the costs which will arise for the use of the telecommunications infrastructure	( )	( )	( )	( )	( )	( )
— insufficient/inadequate telecommunications infrastructure	( )	( )	( )	( )	( )	( )
— management resistance	( )	( )	( )	( )	( )	( )
— difficulties in supervision and control	( )	( )	( )	( )	( )	( )
— union resistance	( )	( )	( )	( )	( )	( )
— employee resistance	( )	( )	( )	( )	( )	( )
— company's conservative thinking	( )	( )	( )	( )	( )	( )
— none	( )	( )	( )	( )	( )	( )
— others _____	( )	( )	( )	( )	( )	( )

Comments: _____

8.3   Do you think telework projects will become more or less viable in future than at present?

( ) much less viable
( ) less viable
( ) more viable
( ) much more viable

Reasons, please: _____

8.4   In which branches, occupations, company sizes and in which organisational form (e.g. homework, satellite centres etc.) do you see the largest potential for telework projects? Please give some comments, too. For each industry, work task and company size, please give the organisational form you consider has the *most* potential (tick one box per line).

Branches	Satellite work centres	Neigh-bourhood work centres	Flexible work arrange-ments	Work at home	Elec-tronic Service Offices	Others (e.g. 'mobile' workers)
1. Self-employed craftsmen	( )	( )	( )	( )	( )	( )
2. Self-employed professionals	( )	( )	( )	( )	( )	( )
3. Manufacturing, Energy, Building and Construction	( )	( )	( )	( )	( )	( )
4. Public Sector, Railroad, Postal System	( )	( )	( )	( )	( )	
5. Health Care	( )	( )	( )	( )	( )	( )
6. Private Services, Transport, Telecommunication	( )	( )	( )	( )	( )	( )
7. Wholesale and Retail	( )	( )	( )	( )	( )	( )
8. Banking, Insurance	( )	( )	( )	( )	( )	( )
9. others _____	( )	( )	( )	( )	( )	( )

Occupations (work content)

	Satellite work centres	Neigh-bourhood work centres	Flexible work arrange-ments	Work at home	Elec-tronic Service Offices	Others (e.g. 'mobile' workers)
1. input or amendment of data	( )	( )	( )	( )	( )	( )
2. typing or word processing	( )	( )	( )	( )	( )	( )
3. filing of business records such as correspondence, invoices, etc.	( )	( )	( )	( )	( )	( )
4. bookkeeping and accounts records	( )	( )	( )	( )	( )	( )
5. stock control and replacement	( )	( )	( )	( )	( )	( )
6. computer programming	( )	( )	( )	( )	( )	( )
7. management tasks such as invoice control, employee records, cash flow monitoring	( )	( )	( )	( )	( )	( )
8. evaluation and documentation	( )	( )	( )	( )	( )	( )
9. others _____	( )	( )	( )	( )	( )	( )

Company size	Satellite work centres	Neigh-bourhood work centres	Flexible work arrange-ments	Work at home	Elec-tronic Service Offices	Others (e.g. 'mobile' workers)
1. 1– 9 employees	( )	( )	( )	( )	( )	( )
2. 10– 49 employees	( )	( )	( )	( )	( )	( )
3. 50– 99 employees	( )	( )	( )	( )	( )	( )
4. 100–499 employees	( )	( )	( )	( )	( )	( )
5. 500–999 employees	( )	( )	( )	( )	( )	( )
6. >=1000 employees	( )	( )	( )	( )	( )	( )

Comments: _____

8.5   Which branch of industry, which work task and which company size have the *most* potential for telework? (Please enter numbers according to the lists above)

	Industry	Work task	Company size
— Satellite Work Centres	( )	( )	( )
— Neighbourhood Work Centres	( )	( )	( )
— Flexible Work Arrangements	( )	( )	( )
— Work at Home	( )	( )	( )
— Electronic Service Offices	( )	( )	( )
— Others (e.g. 'mobile' workers)	( )	( )	( )

8.6   What major changes affecting telework do you expect to take place in the future? Please indicate for each area whether you think a change will take place and whether the effect will facilitate or constrain future implementations of telework—the alternatives are that no change is expected, or the changes are not expected to have either a net positive or negative effect (or are ambivalent).

	no changes expected	constraining effect	ambivalent effect	facilitating effect
Company inventory of information and communication equipment				
Comments: _____	( )	( )	( )	( )
Household penetration with home and personal computers				
Comments: _____	( )	( )	( )	( )
Attitudes of employed people towards telework				
Comments: _____	( )	( )	( )	( )
Attitudes of decision makers in companies towards telework				
Comments: _____	( )	( )	( )	( )
Office work content and tasks				
Comments: _____	( )	( )	( )	( )
Cost reductions and/or increasing sophistication in the area of computer technology				
Comments: _____	( )	( )	( )	( )
Cost reductions and/or increasing sophistication in the area of telecommunications infrastructure				
Comments: _____	( )	( )	( )	( )
Developments in organisational concepts, including supervision and control				
Comments: _____	( )	( )	( )	( )

Conservative thinking in companies

Comments: _____   ( )   ( )   ( )   ( )

Training, skills, qualification of
employees/teleworkers

Comments: _____   ( )   ( )   ( )   ( )

IT orientation of population

Comments: _____   ( )   ( )   ( )   ( )

Unions' position

Comments: _____   ( )   ( )   ( )   ( )

General trends in society

Which
ones? _____   ( )   ( )   ( )   ( )

8.7   What are your organisation's future plans regarding its telework activities?

( )   continue as at present
( )   expand
( )   reduce
( )   discontinue

Please give the reasons!

_____

8.8   In the next decade, do you foresee a significant increase in the number of teleworkers in European
industry?

( )   yes, considerable increase
( )   yes, moderate increase
( )   no increase

How to return the questionnaire

Please check that you have answered all the questions.
Please send the completed questionnaire to our freepost address in the envelope provided.

Empirica
Kaiserstr. 29-31
5300 Bonn 1
(0228) 21 00 70/79

Many thanks!

Should you have any questions, do not hesitate to contact us.

Yours sincerely
Empirica

Werner B. Korte   Simon Robinson

Teleworker-Questionnaire

Homework and other decentralised forms of work

Empirica, a research institute in Bonn, West Germany, is investigating the new forms of work which are arising in our society, partly as a result of new technology. Our study, which we invite you to participate in, covers new developments in several countries, including Britain.

New forms of work—work at home and in smaller units, work with new technology—have both advantages and disadvantages to those involved. Our international study will result in recommendations to the Commission of the European Communities how to best avoid the disadvantages and yet profit from the potential advantages in technological applications.

Filling out the questionnaire:

For our (and your) convenience we have provided categories for the answers to many questions. You need only to tick the category which applies to you.

Because this questionnaire has to apply to people working at a wide variety of jobs, it is inevitable that some sets of categories will not be appropriate for everyone.

If the categories provided do not cover what you would like to reply to a question, please PICK THE MOST APPROPRIATE ANSWER you can and describe the problem you have.

Please use the reverse of the questionnaire for comments and more detailed answers if you wish.

Please answer all the questions.

This questionnaire will normally have been sent to you via another organisation, perhaps via the organisation you work for.

If you wish, you may return the completed questionnaire through that organisation. You may also send it to our freepost address in the envelope provided.

All your replies will be treated in the strictest confidence.

1. Do you work at home? Please give the proportion of your working time you spend working at home, if any, by ticking the appropriate statement in the brackets:

    I spend . .

    none... (   ) of my working time at home
    very little .... (   ) of my working time at home
    around one quarter....................................... (   ) of my working time at home
    around one half... (   ) of my working time at home
    around three quarters................................. (   ) of my working time at home
    all or nearly all... (   ) of my working time at home

2. Please indicate whether each of the following statements applies to your work arrangement:

	applicable	not applicable
I only work at home...	( )	( )
I work some or all of the time in an office...	( )	( )
I work in a 'neighbourhood work centre', that is, the people who work in the same office as I do belong to different organisations than I, or are self-employed..	( )	( )

3. How long have you been working in this arrangement?

less than 1 year .... ( )
1 to 2 years .... ( )
3 to 4 years .... ( )
5 years and more .... ( )

4. Were you involved in the initiative to set up the work arrangement within the company (or the company itself)?

no .... ( )
yes, to some extent .... ( )
yes, I took a major part .... ( )

5. What is your occupation?

_____

6. Please describe the kind of work you do, if this is not entirely obvious from the occupation you have given:

_____

7. What was your work situation before taking up the present arrangement?

Previous work situation	applicable	not applicable
worked in a different job (please specify: _____)	( )	( )
worked for a different organisation	( )	( )
worked at a different location..	( )	( )
There was no opportunity for me to continue in the previous work arrangement because of		
— moving house..	( )	( )
— threat of, or actual redundancy	( )	( )
— pregnancy/birth	( )	( )

8. Going back to that time, did you then have any interest in working full-time or part-time at home?

Full-time	Part-time
no .... ( )	no .... ( )
yes...................................... ( )	yes...................................... ( )

9. How many people working for your (old) organisation worked in the same building as you did (or very close by)?

Number working in the same building or nearby

none... ( )
less than 10..................................... ( )
10 to 99... ( )
100 to 999....................................... ( )
1000 and more............................... ( )
not applicable................................. ( )

10.　　How many people there had similar jobs to your own?

Number with similar job:

none (or none nearby) .... (　)
1 or 2 .... (　)
3 to 5 .... (　)
6 to 10 .... (　)
10 to 49 .... (　)
50 or more .... (　)
not applicable .... (　)

11.　　What technical equipment and services do you now use in your work and how much of your working time is spent using them?

Proportion of working time spent
using the equipment etc:

	not used	very low (under 5%)	around a third	around half	three-quarters or more
— Microcomputer/PC	(　)	(　)	(　)	(　)	(　)
— Electronic typewriter	(　)	(　)	(　)	(　)	(　)
— Working connection to another computer via:					
— modem	(　)	(　)	(　)	(　)	(　)
— accoustic coppler	(　)	(　)	(　)	(　)	(　)
— Word processing software	(　)	(　)	(　)	(　)	(　)
— Videotex (Prestel)	(　)	(　)	(　)	(　)	(　)
— other hardware or systems					
_____	(　)	(　)	(　)	(　)	(　)

12.　　What means of communication do you use in your work and how often do you use them on average?

How often the means of communication is used:

	not used	less than once per week	once or twice a week	daily to three times a week	once or twice daily	several times daily
— Connection to another computer via:						
— modem	(　)	(　)	(　)	(　)	(　)	(　)
— accoustic coupler(　)	(　)	(　)	(　)	(　)	(　)	(　)
— Teletex (NOT Ceefax etc.)	(　)	(　)	(　)	(　)	(　)	(　)
— Videotex (Prestel)	(　)	(　)	(　)	(　)	(　)	(　)
— Electronic mail system (e.g. Telecom Gold)	(　)	(　)	(　)	(　)	(　)	(　)
— Floppy disk for data transfer(　)	(　)	(　)	(　)	(　)	(　)	(　)
— Handwritten letters of other texts	(　)	(　)	(　)	(　)	(　)	(　)
— Dictation on tape/cassette(　)	(　)	(　)	(　)	(　)	(　)	(　)

— Postal service .... ( )   ( )   ( )   ( )   ( )   ( )
— Courier .... ( )   ( )   ( )   ( )   ( )   ( )
— Meetings away from
   workplace .... ( )   ( )   ( )   ( )   ( )   ( )
— other communication
   methods
   _____ .... ( )   ( )   ( )   ( )   ( )   ( )

13.   Do you use equipment for your work which you yourself purchased or rent?

no expenses for equipment   ( )
equipment paid for...................................... ( ) _____(cost)
equipment rental.. ( ) _____(cost per month)

14.   Please indicate whether each of the following applies to you:

	applicable	not applicable
self-employed..	( )	( )
work entirely for one organisation...	( )	( )
work for more than one organisation or client..	( )	( )
employee with fixed working hours..	( )	( )
payment continues (retainer fee) if no work available............................	( )	( )
core working time of 4 hours or more..	( )	( )
have to be available at particular times daily..	( )	( )
times worked entirely at own discretion...	( )	( )
piece-rate payment...	( )	( )
payment by the hour..	( )	( )

15.   Is the organisation you work for able to employ you in a similar job in their (more central) office or at another work site?

I could work elsewhere for my employer at a similar job if
I choose to,
certainly .... ( )
probably.. ( )
doubtful... ( )
very unlikely or impossible...................................... ( )

16.   If you were to work there in a similar job do you think chances of promotion would be better or worse?

Chances of promotion compared to present work arrangements:

much better................................... ( )
better... ( )
about the same............................. ( )
worse.. ( )
much worse.................................... ( )
not applicable................................ ( )

The next few questions refer to working time.

17.   How long do you usually actually work for, and does the length of time you work vary much? Please give the length of your working day and week (on average, recently), and the longest time you have worked in a day or week in the last 3 months:

Average working week   _____   hours per week

Longest working week in the last 3 months   _____   hours per week

Average working day .... _____ hours per day

Longest working day in the last 3 months .... _____ hours per day

18.   Do these answers give a good picture of your working time?

_____

19.   Do you usually do much of your work outside normal hours, that is evenings, nights or weekends?

Amount of work outside normal working hours, usually:

very little or none.......................... ( )
a third or less................................ ( )
about a half.................................... ( )
two thirds and more .... ( )
nearly all .... ( )

20.   How long have you been without work in the last 12 months (apart from holidays you had planned)?

not at all, paid work always available ... ( )

The longest period without work
in the last 12 months was:

a week at the most...................................... ( )
1 to 3 weeks .... ( )
1 to 5 months... ( )
6 months or more... ( )

21.   Do you generally have enough paid work to do or too little?

At the rates of pay you accept at present
would you generally prefer

much less work.............................. ( )
less work... ( )
about the same.............................. ( )
more work .... ( )
much more work?.......................... ( )

Please give reasons for your preference:

_____

22.   Can you influence the amount of work you are given to do?

Influence on the amount of work to be done:

no influence at all.. ( )
very little influence... ( )
some influence.. ( )
considerable influence.. ( )
complete control of workload.................................... ( )

23.   If you could not work in the present arrangements but had to work elsewhere, would you give up work?

I would work elsewhere if I could.. ( )
I would give up work... ( )
I am undecided... ( )

24. What are the major advantages and disadvantages of your present working arrangement?

Please compare your present arrangements with working
— roughly the same length of time
— at fixed times, in normal working hours
— as an employee, doing similar work
— at a central location,
and regardless of whether this is a realistic option for you.

Some statements will not apply to your work arrangement or you may not agree with the statement. Tick the 'not true/not applicable' column.

EXAMPLE "travel and commuting time and expenses".

If in your present work arrangement you have no commuting to do, then this is an ADVANTAGE of your present work arrangement and you tick either under the heading "important advantage" or under the heading "very important advantage", depending how important you find the difference in commuting.

If the difference in commuting time and cost is unimportant to you, tick under the "neutral" heading.

Are the following disadvantages or advantages of your PRESENT work arrangement?

DISADVANTAGE . . . . NEUTRAL . . . . ADVANTAGE

	not applicable	very importand disadvantage	important disadvantage	(or no difference)	important advantage	very important advantage
1 travel and commuting time and expense	( )	( )	( )	( )	( )	( )
2 how closely I am supervised	( )	( )	( )	( )	( )	( )
3 how often my work is interrupted by others	( )	( )	( )	( )	( )	( )
4 the ability to combine care of children or other dependents with my work	( )	( )	( )	( )	( )	( )
5 the ability to combine other activities with my work	( )	( )	( )	( )	( )	( )
6 the ability to work when it suits me	( )	( )	( )	( )	( )	( )
7 how well I can meet the demands the family make on me	( )	( )	( )	( )	( )	( )
8 the amount of time I can spend with the family	( )	( )	( )	( )	( )	( )
9 the extent to which working time and free time get mixed up	( )	( )	( )	( )	( )	( )
10 the amount of space I have to do my work in	( )	( )	( )	( )	( )	( )
11 Clerical support	( )	( )	( )	( )	( )	( )
12 availability of other office services, e.g. copying facilities	( )	( )	( )	( )	( )	( )
13 the amount of self-discipline working requires	( )	( )	( )	( )	( )	( )
14 development of my working skills generally	( )	( )	( )	( )	( )	( )
15 development of skills of use in setting up one's own business	( )	( )	( )	( )	( )	( )
16 the status I have in the eyes of other members of the organisation	( )	( )	( )	( )	( )	( )
17 promotion chances	( )	( )	( )	( )	( )	( )
18 level of pay	( )	( )	( )	( )	( )	( )
19 benefits, perks, pension scheme.	( )	( )	( )	( )	( )	( )
20 self-employed status	( )	( )	( )	( )	( )	( )
21 union organisation	( )	( )	( )	( )	( )	( )
22 participation in social gatherings of work colleagues	( )	( )	( )	( )	( )	( )
23 participation in working meetings	( )	( )	( )	( )	( )	( )
24 contacts with others in similar work	( )	( )	( )	( )	( )	( )
25 other_____ ...	( )	( )	( )	( )	( )	( )

Please check that there is one box ticked per line in the above question

25.   Which of the above are the most important reasons for you to continue with your present work arrangement? Please give the statement number according to the list in the last question.

The most important ADVANTAGE is _____

(statement number)

26.   Which of the above are the most important in making you consider not continuing with your present work arrangement?

Most important DISADVANTAGE is _____

(statement number)

27.   What do you usually earn in an average week, month or year?

Average earnings   _____   (   ) weekly
                        _____   (   ) monthly
                        _____   (   ) yearly

28.   Do you think this is more or less than you could expect to earn if you were doing the same work elsewhere?

much less.........................(20% and less).................. (   )
less.....................................(5% to 19% less).............. (   )
about the same... (   )
more.................................(5% to 19% more).......... (   )
much more.......................(20% and more)............... (   )

29.   General statistics

Age.....................................   _____
Male...................................   (   )
Female..............................   (   )

30.   Educational qualifications

CSE's.. (   )
GCE 'O'-levels................................. (   )
GCE 'A'-level.................................... (   )
degree... (   )

other _____   (   )

31.   Vocational qualifications

_____

32.   Do you have a disability affecting the kind of work you can do?

no disability... (   )
sensory disability
(e.g. impaired vision, hearing)................................. (   )
mental disability... (   )
physical disability... (   )
other_____   (   )

33. Marital status

single............................... ( )
married............................. ( )
divorced........................... ( )
widowed........................... ( )

34. How many persons are there in your household, including yourself?

Number in household (at least one!) _____

35. Do others in your household have an income? If so, how many?

no other earners... ( )
husband/wife .... ( )
others... ( )

36. Are you the main earner in your household?

no........................ ( )
yes .... ( )

37. Do you have children? If so, please state how many and the age of the youngest child:

( ) have no children
( ) have children→   number of chilren: _____
youngest child's age: _____

38. Are you responsible for the care of children? If so, what alternative child care facilities could you use?

( ) not responsible for child care
( ) no alternative child care facilities (e.g. childminder) possible
( ) child care available. Please give cost per hr .... _____
.... and problems other than cost _____

39. Do you feel satisfied with your work and your life generally?

How satisfied are you with	very dis- satisfied	dis- satisfied	neutral	satisfied	very satisfied
— the technical equipment used in your work..	( )	( )	( )	( )	( )
— the communication with your employer..	( )	( )	( )	( )	( )
— the work itself	( )	( )	( )	( )	( )
— your place of work............................	( )	( )	( )	( )	( )
— your living conditions........................	( )	( )	( )	( )	( )
— your financial situation	( )	( )	( )	( )	( )
— your leisure time	( )	( )	( )	( )	( )
— your relations with friends and neighbours..	( )	( )	( )	( )	( )
— and, looking at your situation as a whole, how satisfied are you with your life as a whole?...........................	( )	( )	( )	( )	( )

40.   What aspects of your working arrangements would you most like to see changed? Please make any comments you have on what government, employers, trades unions or other organisations might do to improve the situation.

How to return the questionnaire

Please check you have answered all the questions.

Please send the completed questionnaire to our freepost address in the envelope provided.

Empirica
Kaiserstr. 29-31
5300 Bonn 1
Tel: (0228) 21 00 70/79

Many thanks!

Should you have any questions, please do not hesitate to contact us.

Yours sincerely
Empirica

Werner B. Korte   Simon Robinson

Appendix B

DEMOGRAPHIC CHARACTERISTICS OF ALL TELEWORKERS IN THE SAMPLE OF TELEWORKING ORGANISATIONS

	<30 M[1]	<30 F[2]	30-40 M	30-40 F	40-50 M	40-50 F	50-60 M	50-60 F	>60 M	>60 F	Total M	Total F	Full-time	Part-time
1. Software services company	3	184	17	486	10	147	9	6	3	2	42	825	120	747
2. Computer manufacturer	1	3	7	101	2	40	2	4	—	—	12	148	22	138
3. Consultancy	3	2	2	—	—	—	—	—	—	—	5	2	7	—
4. Accountancy services	—	2	—	3	—	—	—	—	—	—	—	5	—	5
5. Scheme for the disabled (programming)	34	13	24	10	8	1	2	—	—	—	68	24	79	12
6. Printing company	—	2	—	2	—	2	—	—	—	—	—	6	3	3
7. Typesetting company	—	5	—	6	—	4	—	—	—	—	—	15	—	15
8. Typing services	4	4	3	15	1	8	—	1	—	—	8	28	25	36
9. Scheme for the disabled (clerical work)	N.D.		N.D.		N.D.		N.D.		N.D.		N.D.		25	—
10. Translation agency	2	2	4	2	—	—	—	—	—	—	6	4	2	8
11. Research company	—	—	2	—	—	—	—	—	—	—	2	—	2	—
12. Office equipment manufacturer	2	—	16	3	17	3	17	—	1	—	53	6	N.A. fee-paid	N.A. basis
13. Business information company	1	—	4	1	—	—	—	—	—	—	—	—	6	—
14. Insurance company	90	—	117	5	58	—	17	—	3	—	285	5	290	—
Total	138	215	192	632	96	205	47	11	7	2	475	1064	546	964

[1] M = Male teleworkers
[2] F = Female teleworkers

Appendix C

MAJOR REASONS FOR TELEWORK INCEPTION ON A CASE-BY-CASE BASIS

Objective/purpose: company reorganisation/decentralisation

Company	Reasons for using telework
1. Office Equipment Manufacturer	• To meet the needs of people to regulate their own work • To reduce the high costs of central London office space and other overheads
2. Computer Manufacturer	• To keep scarce skills of individuals unable to continue working in a conventional office
3. Consultancy	• To meet the needs of own workforce and one big client • To keep scarce skills of individuals unable to continue working in a conventional office
4. Accountancy Services	• To minimise/reduce costs/expenses, e.g. of overheads, social benefits, by giving workers unable to work in a conventional office (domestic commitments) the status of self-employed and employing them in their homes
5. Printing Company	• To minimise/reduce costs/expenses, e.g. of overheads, social benefits, by giving workers unable to work in a conventional office (domestic commitments) the status of self-employed and employing them in their homes
6. Typesetting Company	• To minimise/reduce costs/expenses, e.g. of overheads, social benefits, by giving workers unable to work in a conventional office (domestic commitments), the status of self-employed and employing them in their homes
7. Research Company	• Recruitment of urgently required and otherwise not available skills • To meet the needs of the staff
8. Insurance Company	• To meet the needs of the customers

Objective/purpose: creation of electronic telework-service activities (new business creation)

Company	Reasons for utilising telework
1. Translation Agency	• To set up one's own business at minimal expense • To improve/increase the capacity of the company at minimal cost by employing self-employed workers in their homes
2. Typing Services	• To set up one's own business by employing unemployed women seeking employment in their homes because of domestic commitments on a piece-rate payment basis resulting in • Minimal expenses for salary and overheads
3. Business Information Company	• So that a large company could set up a new business and business information service, employing adequately high-skilled workers working from their homes on a self-employed basis
4. Software Services Company	• To set up a business using the scarce skills of individuals unable to work in a conventional office (domestic commitments) at lower costs, by ·employing them on a freelance basis in their homes
5. Scheme for the Disabled (Programming)	• To create employment opportunities for disabled people (by setting up a teleworking company), in an area of high or reasonably high demand from industries
6. Scheme for the Disabled (Clerical Work)	• To create employment opportunities for disabled people by setting up a teleworking company in an area of high or reasonably high demand from industries

Appendix D

TELEWORKERS' PERCEPTION OF ADVANTAGES AND
DISADVANTAGES OF TELEWORKING

Arrangement by sex, educational level and age (Pearson correlations)

		r	p
1.	Travel and commuting time and expense	.0655	.260
2.	Closeness of supervision	.0081	.467
3.	How often work is interrupted by others	.0894	.187
4.	Ability to combine care of children or other dependents with work	.5748	.000
5.	Ability to combine other activities with work	.3211	.001
6.	Ability to work when it suits	,2680	.004
7.	Ability to meet the demands of the family	.3735	.000
8.	Amount of time able to spend with the family	.3724	.000
9.	Extent to which working time and free time get mixed up	−.1651	.050
10.	Amount of space available to work in	−.1764	.039
11.	Clerical support	.0202	.425
12.	Availability of other office services, e.g. copying facilities	−.3091	.001
13.	Amount of self-discipline	−.3149	.000
14.	Development of working skills generally	−.1986	.019
15.	Development of skills of use in setting up one's own business	−.1054	.191
16.	Status in the eyes of the other members of the organisation	−.1167	.125
17.	Promotion chances	−.0464	.318
18.	Level of pay	−.2465	.004
19.	Benefits, perks, pension schemes	−.3131	.001
20.	Self-employed status	−.0304	.404
21.	Union organisation	−.1267	.165
22.	Participation in social gatherings of work colleagues	−.0658	.258
23.	Participation in working meetings	−.2468	.005
24.	Contacts with others in similar work	.0008	.497

Arrangement by occupational category

Item	Occupation	Advantage (mean)	η	p
1. Travel and commuting time and expense	dp prof. typist professionals other	3.7714 4.0000 4.1818 2.7500	 .2711	 .0571
	NB: 1.0 = very important disadvantage 5.0 = very important advantage			
2. Closeness of supervision	dp prof. typist professionals other	3.3836 4.4000 3.8000 3.0000	 .3752	 .0013
3. How often work is interrupted by others	dp prof. typist professionals other	3.2533 4.5000 4.0000 2.5000	 .4597	 .0000
4. Ability to combine care of children or other dependents with work	dp prof. typist professionals other	4.7541 5.0000 4.0909 2.5000	 .4815	 .0000
5. Ability to combine other activities with work	dp prof. typist professionals other	4.1194 4.6667 3.8000 3.0000	 .2881	 .0391
6. Ability to work when convenient	dp prof. typist professionals other	4.4783 4.6667 4.2593 3.0000	 .2499	 .0931
7. Ability to meet the demands of the family	dp prof. typist professionals other	4.3385 5.0000 4.0000 3.0000	 .3569	 .0049
8. Amount of time able to spend with the family	dp prof. typist professionals other	4.3538 4.3333 3.8400 3.5000	 .2863	 .0411

(continued on p. 248)

Arrangement by occupational category (*cont.*)

Item		Occupation	Advantage (mean)	η	p
9.	Extent to which working time and free time get mixed up	dp prof. typist professionals other	2.6471 4.6667 3.0000 3.0000	.4102	.0004
10.	Amount of space available to work in	dp prof. typist professionals other	2.8219 3.5000 3.1818 3.0000	.2140	.1943
11.	Clerical support	dp prof. typist professionals other	2.7463 4.0000 2.4762 3.6667	.3558	.0066
12.	Availability of other office services, e.g. copying facilities	dp prof. typist professionals other	2.4933 2.8000 2.5926 3.7500	.2357	.1048
13.	Amount of self-discipline	dp prof. typist professionals other	2.8800 3.4286 3.2500 3.0000	.2514	.0654
14.	Development of working skills generally	dp prof. typist professionals other	2.9863 3.2857 3.6071 3.2500	.2739	.0374
15.	Development of skills of use in setting up one's own business	dp prof. typist professionals other	3.1707 3.3333 3.7826 3.3333	.3499	.0283
16.	Status in the eyes of the other members of the organisation	dp prof. typist professionals other	2.9701 3.5000 3.0400 3.2500	.1898	.3064
17.	Promotion chances	dp prof. typist professionals other	2.6842 2.8571 2.6522 2.7500	.0570	.9510

Arrangement by occupational category (*cont.*)

Item	Occupation	Advantage (mean)	η	p
18. Level of pay	dp prof. typist professionals other	2.4286 3.5714 3.1071 2.7500	.3913	.0003
19. Benefits, perks, pension schemes	dp prof. typist professionals other	2.3857 2.5000 2.6296 3.3333	.1670	.4077
20. Self-employed status	dp prof. typist professionals other	3.5000 2.8333 3.7857 3.000	.2973	.1087
21. Union organisation	dp prof. typist professionals other	2.8421 2.5000 2.8125 2.3333	.1695	.6294
22. Participation in social gatherings of work colleagues	dp prof. typist professionals other	2.8219 3.0000 2.4091 2.6667	.2256	.1580
23. Participation in working meetings	dp prof. typist professionals other	2.7067 3.0000 2.9615 2.6667	.1543	.4677
24. Contacts with others in similar work	dp prof. typist professionals other	2.7973 3.0000 2.5833 2.7500	.1196	.6844

Factor loadings are tabulated on pp. 250–1.

Factor loadings × 1000

	F1	F2	F3	F4	F5	F6	F7
1. Travel and commuting time and expense	16	−04	18	66*	24	−13	−13
2. Closeness of supervision	17	−14	48*	28	−04	−03	14
3. How often work is interrupted by others	03	−12	−11	61*	−11	−30	32
4. Ability to combine care of children or other dependents with work	81**	−16	03	−11	−19	20	−11
5. Ability to combine other activities with work	65*	22	−01	−19	−11	−21	36
6. Ability to work when it is convenient	82**	24	11	−06	−11	−01	01
7. Ability to meet the demands the family make	80**	−14	−07	21	16	−01	−08
8. Amount of time able to spend with the family							
9. Extent to which working time and free time get mixed up	24	07	−03	23	−09	36	54
10. Amount of space available to work in	−25	17	07	73**	−18	16	−02
11. Clerical support	12	−07	04	02	−07	88**	13

12. Availability of other office services, e.g. copying facilities	−14	05	−04	14	04	84**	12
13. Amount of self-discipline	−10	−01	10	02	24	21	75**
14. Development of working skills generally	−09	72**	13	−09	14	−08	30
15. Development of skills of use in setting up one's own business	−11	28	86**	03	−1	−00	10
16. Status in the eyes of the other members of the organisation	−09	72**	14	06	07	18	−11
17. Promotion chances	10	86**	09	−01	06	−04	−0
18. Level of pay	−01	24	−01	50	09	34	1
19. Benefits, perks, pension schemes	−11	15	04	−03	69	23	0
20. Self-employed status	15	07	70	03	4	−01	−17
21. Union organisation	−10	−02	−08	−04	90**	−13	11
22. Participation in social gatherings of work colleagues	13	20	−35	13	27	50*	−25
23. Participation in working meetings							
24. Contacts with others in similar work	074	58	−39	15	07	02	06

* Low loading

** High loading

Appendix E

TYPES OF IT AND TELECOMMUNICATIONS NETWORKS USED IN TELEWORK SCHEMES

Company	SBS A[1]	SBS B[2]	MC/PC A	MC/PC B	Terminals A	Terminals B	Electronic typewriters A	Electronic typewriters B	WP-systems A	WP-systems B	Others A	Others B	Telecommunications networks and services used
1. Software services comp.			178	178			80	80	7	21			EMS[3], PSTK[4]
2. Computer manufacturer			60	60	7	7	2	2	32	32			EMS, PSTK, PSDK[5] Public Data Network for Fixed Connections
3. Consultancy			1										PSTK
4. Accountancy services					5	5							PSTK, Public Data Network for Fixed Connect.
5. Scheme for the disabled (programming)			7	7	40	73			4	3			
6. Printing company			3	3	3	3							
7. Typesetting company			19	19									
8. Typing services							15	15	15				PSTK
9. Scheme for the disabled (clerical work)	2	40	2										
10. Translation agency			2	2									Teletex, Telefax

No.	Company													Networks
11.	Research company	2						2						
12.	Office equipment manufacturer	2	40	53	53			84	84	2	60	2	73	2	2	2^{6}	EMS, PSTK, Telefax
13.	Business information company			6	6					9	9				EMS, PSTK
14.	Insurance company			9	9	290	290	84	84					2	2	PSTK, PSDK
	Total	2	40	339	338	335	388	84	84	60	73	2	2	2	

[1] A = no. of workstations
[2] B = no. of teleworkers
[3] EMS = Electronic Mail System
[4] PSTK = Packet-Switched Telephone Network
[5] PSDK = Packet-Switched Data Network
[6] Xerox Star Workstation

Appendix F

RESULTS OF A FACTOR ANALYSIS ON THE RESPONDENT'S STRUCTURE OF SATISFACTION WITH TELEWORKING

Teleworkers' satisfaction with aspects of their working arrangement: factor structure

	F1	F2	F3
● Technical equipment used at work	.07478	.08493	.84221
● Communication with employer	.24563	.22545	.73080
● Work itself	.69404	.03039	.40738
● Place of work	.71949	−.04851	.19377
● Living conditions	.74948	.49295	−.09840
● Financial situation	.52192	.54067	.21388
● Leisure time	.02070	.79461	.23729
● Relations with friends	.14504	.80986	.05985
● Life as a whole	.67305	.49413	.04302

F1 to F3 are factor loadings on 3 factors

Teleworkers' satisfaction with aspects of their working arrangement by sex and education of teleworker (Pearson correlations)

	Sex	Education
● Technical equipment used at work	−.1815	−.0845
● Communication with employer	−.0111	.0493
● Work itself	.0367	.0907
● Place of work	−.0546	−.1241
● Living conditions	.0905	.0275
● Financial situation	−.0601	.1027
● Leisure time	.1046	.0451
● Relations with friends	.1860	−.0167
● Life as a whole	.0429	.1025

Appendix G

*SAMPLING AND WEIGHTING PROCEDURE FOR THE EMPIRICA
SURVEY OF DECISION MAKERS*

The decision maker survey sampling procedure employs a disproportional
random method.

Data are weighted back to the estimated universe on a matrix with 'Industry
Type' and 'Establishment Size' controls. The details are as follows:

Federal Republic of Germany:
   —weighted base: 953,121 establishments
   —representative for the following industries and company sizes:

   Industry:
   • self-employed professionals (1–9 employees)
   • craft professionals (1–9 employees)
   • wholesale and retail (1–9 employees)
   • all establishments with more than 10 employees in the private
     industry and the public sector:

       —manufacturing industry
       —wholesale and retail trade
       —banking and insurance
       —service industry, communication and news agencies
       —public sector, railway and postal services

   Company Size: 1–9 employees
          10–99 employees
         100–499 employees
         over 500 employees

France:
   —weighted base: 1,169,598 establishments
   —representative for the following industries and company sizes:

   Industry:
   • self-employed professionals
   • craft professionals

- all establishments in the private and the public sector:
  —manufacturing industry
  —wholesale and retail trade
  —banking and insurance
  —service industry, communication and news agencies
  —public sector, railway and postal services

Company Size: 1–9 employees
                    10–99 employees
                    100–499 employees
                    over 500 employees

United Kingdom:
—weighted base: 1,221,930 establishments
—representative for all industries and company sizes with one and more employees except farming, forestry and fishing, and from the public sector, police and fire stations

Industry:
—manufacturing industry
—wholesale and retail trade
—banking and insurance
—service industry, communication and news agencies
—public sector, railway and postal services

Company Size: 1–9 employees
                    10–99 employees
                    100–499 employees
                    over 500 employees

Italy:
—weighted base: 2,590,957 establishments (i.e. all economic operators in Italy possessing at least one telephone line)
—representative for the following industries and company sizes:

Industry:
- self-employed professionals (1–9 employees)
- craft professionals (1–9 employees)
- wholesale and retail (1–9 employees)
- all establishments with more than 10 employees in the private industry and the public sector:
  —manufacturing industry

—wholesale and retail trade
—banking and insurance
—service industry, communication and news agencies
—public sector, railway and postal services

Company Size: 1–9 employees
10–99 employees
100–499   employees
over–500 employees

Appendix H

STRUCTURE OF THE EMPLOYED PEOPLE SURVEY

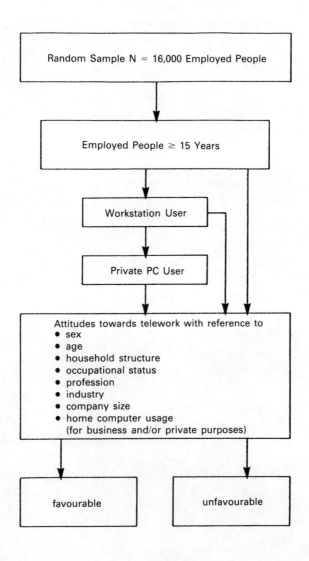

Appendix I

All data were weighted to allow for a comparison with current secondary data. The weighted base is as follows:

Federal Republic of Germany: 26.401 million employees
France: 21.449 million employees
United Kingdom: 23.077 million employees
Italy: 20.890 million employees

Before being asked about their opinions and attitudes towards home-based telework, the employees received a brief explanation of the technical possibilities of connecting decentrally located computers, in this case in their homes, to a central computer in the employees' companies. It was decided that no distinctions would be made between this and various other organisational forms of telework, as these other forms (e.g. neighbourhood centres, satellite centres, etc.) are still unknown to the general public.

Appendix J

SOCIO-ECONOMIC AND DEMOGRAPHIC FACTORS CONSIDERED IN THE ANALYSIS OF THE SURVEY OF EMPLOYED PEOPLE

Population potentially concerned with telework according to:

Sex:	male/female
Age:	15–19, 20–29, 30–39, 40–49, 50–59, $\geq$60 years
Household structure:	1, 2, 3, 4, 5 and more persons
Occupational status:	full-time
	part-time
	self-employed
Profession:	dp-professionals
	scientific, engineering
	business and other professionals
	management
	secretaries, stenographers, typists
	commercial, clerical and administration
	production and service workers
	academic
	health/medical
	sales
Industry:	public sector
	finance
	distribution
	manufacturing
Company size:	1 employee
	2–4
	5–9
	10–19
	20–49
	50–99
	100–249
	250–499
	500–999
	$\geq$1000
Home computer usage:	for private purposes
	for business purposes
	equally
Workstation usage:	
Company size:	1–9 employees
	10–99 employees
	100–499 employees
	$\geq$500

Position of decision maker: ● owner
                                        ● executive director
                                        ● head of department

Age of decision maker: −39 years
                                 40–49 years
                                 $\geq$50 years

Sex of decision maker: male/female

References

Aldrich, M. (1982), *Videotex: Key to the Wired City*, Quiller Press

Aldrich, M. (1984), 'Home: the command base', in *Planning for Homework, Conference Proceedings*, Housing Associations Charitable Trust

Applegarth, J. (1985), 'The other side: what's good about the home office?' in *The Information Technology Revolution*, edited by Forester, T., Basil Blackwell

Ashok, H., Hall, J. and Huws, U. (1986), *Home Sweet Work Station, Homeworking and the Employment Needs of People with Severe Disabilities*, Greater London Council Equal Opportunities Group

Atkinson, J. and Meager, N. (1986), 'New forms of work organisation', in *IMS Report No 121*, Institute of Manpower Studies

Baer, W. S. (1985), 'Information technologies in the home', in *Information Technologies and Social Transformation*, edited by Guile, B. R., National Academy Press

Batt, R. (1982), 'Fairchild giving "telecommuting" a try in Phoenix', *Computerworld*, 26 April

Beck, J. (1984), 'Cottage industries: "80s Issue"', *Chicago Tribune*, 9 January

Becker, H. (1984), 'Bürger in der modernen Informationsgesellschaft. Einstellungen zur Technik und zum Datenschutz', in *Hessische Landesregierung: Informationsgesellschaft oder Überwachungsstaat*, Wiesbaden

Bessant, J., Guy, K., Miles, I. and Rush, H. (1986), *IT Futures Surveyed*, National Economic Development Office

Bisset, L. and Huws, U. (1984), *Sweated Labour: Homeworking in Britain Today*, Low Pay Unit

Bjorn-Andersen, N. (1983), 'The changing roles of secretaries and clerks', in *New Office Technology: Human and Organisational Aspects*, edited by Otway, H. J. and Peltu, M., Frances Pinter for Commission of the European Communities

Blanc, G. (1988), 'Autonomy, telework and emerging cultural values', in *Telework: Present Situation and Future Development of a New Form of Work*, edited by Korte, W. B., Steinle, W. J. and Robinson, S., North-Holland

Brandt, S. (1983), 'Working-at-home: how to cope with spatial design possibilities caused by the new communication media', in *Office Technology and People*, Elsevier Science Publishers

Brooks, R. (1982), 'Mums get market taped', *Sunday Times*, 12 September

Brusco, S. (1981), 'Labour market structure, company policies and technological progress', in *Relations Between Technology, Capital and Labour*, edited by Diettrich, O., Morley, J., EEC

Bureau of National Affairs (1986), *The Changing Workplace: New Directions in Staffing and Scheduling*, Bureau of National Affairs

Business Week (1982), 'The Instant Off-shore Office', March 15

Chalude, M. (1984), 'Appendix: Telecommuting' in *Office Automation and Work for Women'*, EEC Directorate of Employment, Social Affairs and Education, April

Chamot, D. and Zalusky, J. L. (1985), 'Use and misuse of workstations in the home', in *Office Workstations in the Home*, edited by National Academy of Sciences, National Academy Press

Checkland, P. (1986), *Systems Thinking, Systems Practice*, Wiley,

Christensen, K. (1987), 'Impacts of computer-mediated home-based work on women and their families', in *Office Technology and People (1987)*, Elsevier Science Publishers

Clavaud, R. (1981), 'La Révolution sociale du travail à domicile', *Le Monde Dimanche*, 9 August

Clavaud, R. (1982), 'Le Teletravail', *Telesoft*, December/January

Clinton, L. H. (1983), 'The new cottage industry', *Working Mother*, June

Craipeau, S. and Marot, J.-C. (1984), *Telework: The Impact on Living and Working Conditions*, European Foundation for the Improvement of Living and Working Conditions

Cronberg, T. (1982), 'A word processor in her living room? The impact of information technology on the way of life and work of women', in *Information Technology: Impact on the Way of Life, Conference Papers*, edited by Bannon, L., Barry, U. and Holst, O., National Board for Science and Technology, Ireland

Curran, J. (1986), *Bolton Fifteen Years on: A Review and Analysis of Small Business Research in Britain*, Small Business Research Trust

Davies, R. (1984), 'Homeworkers can be employees after a continuous period of work', *Financial Times*, 9 May

DeSanctis, G. (1983), 'A telecommuting primer', in *Datamation*, October

DeSanctis, G. (1984), 'Attitudes towards telecommuting: implications for work-at-home programs', *Information and Management*, **7**, North-Holland

Deutscher Gewerkschaftsbund (1986), *Telearbeit, Elektronische Einsiedelei oder neue Form der Persönlichen Entfaltung?* Hamburg

Diebold Group (1981), *Office Work in the Home: Scenarios and Prospects for the 80s*, Diebold Group, New York

Donnison, D. (1984), 'The home-centred British', in *Planning for Homework, Conference Proceedings*, edited by Housing Associations Charitable Trust, 2 May

Dostal, W. (1985), 'Anmerkungen zur Arbeitsmarktrelevanz dezentraler Information-stätigkeiten', in *Mitteilungen zur Arbeitsmarkt und Berufsorschung*

Dover, M. (1982a), *Technological Change and Spatial Organisation, Some Potential Impacts in Britain*, Technology Policy Unit, University of Aston in Birmingham, August

Dover, M. (1982b), 'Signposts of change: the potential impact of new technology on travel patterns', in *Information Technology: Impact on the Way of Life, Conference Papers*, edited by Bannon, L., Barry, U. and Holst, O., National Board of Science and Technology, Ireland

Drew, J. (1986), 'How to help your company by working elsewhere', *Accountancy Age*, April

Eder, P. F. (1983), 'Telecommuters: the stay-at-home work force of the future', *The Futurist*, June

Edwards, P. and Edwards S. (1985), *Working from Home, Everything you need to know about living and working under the same roof*, Houghton Mifflin

Elisburg, D. (1985), 'Legalities', in *Office Workstations in the Home*, edited by National Academy of Sciences, National Academy Press

Elling, M. (1985), 'Remote work/telecommuting: a means of enhancing the way of life, or just another method of making business more brisk?', *Economic and Industrial Democracy*, **6**

Else, L. (1982), 'Working at home: women's blackspot', *Computing*, 7 October

Empirica (1985), *Results of a Survey in the Major European Countries*, FAST Distance Working Project, Working Paper No. 1, March

Empirica (1986a), *The Potential for Decentralised Electronic Working in the Banking, Insurance and Software Industries*, Empirica

Empirica (1986b), *Policy Instruments to Facilitate the Creation of Small and Medium-Sized Companies*, Commission of the European Communities

Empirica, ADR and Tavistock (1986), *Rapport des Réunions Nationales et du Séminaire Européens sur le travail à distance en milieux urbains et rureaux Européens*, FAST, paper n. 117 Commission of the European Communities

English, C. W. (1984), 'Computers open way to work at home', *US News and World Report*, 18 June

European Foundation for the Improvement of Living and Working Conditions (1984), *Telework: Impact on Living and Working Conditions*, European Foundation for the Improvement of Living and Working Conditions

European Foundation for the Improvement of Living and Working Conditions (1986), *New Forms of Work and Activity*, European Foundation for the Improvement of Living and Working Conditions, Dublin

Evans, A. and Attew, T. (1986), 'Alternatives to full time permanent staff', in *Flexible Patterns of Work*, edited by Curson, C., Institute of Personnel Management

Ewing, K. D. 1982), 'Homeworking: a framework for reform', *Industrial Law Journal*, June,

Foegen, J. H. (1987), 'The menace of high-tech employment', *The Futurist*, September-October

Forester, (1988), 'The myth of the electronic cottage', *Futures*, June

Franklin, D. (1986), *F. International (Case Study)*, Harvard Business School

GLC Industry and Employment Branch (1983), *Community Data Workshops: An Alternative Form of Office Work*, Internal Report, 21 July, Greater London Council.

Galitz, W. O. (1984), *The Office Environment: Automation's Impact on Tomorrow's Workplace*, Administrative Management Society Foundation, Pennsylvania

Ganguly, P. (1985), *UK Small Business Statistics and International Comparisons*, edited by Bannock, G., The Small Business Research Trust

Geisler, G. (1985), 'Blue Cross/Blue Shield of South Carolina', in *Office Workstations in the Home*, edited by National Academy of Sciences, National Academy Press

Glover, J. (1974), *Long Range Social Forecasts: Working from Home*, British Telecom Long Range Studies Division

Goldmann, M. and Richter, G. (1986), *Telehomework by Women*, Sozialforschungsstelle, Landesinstitut, Dortmund

Goldmann, M. and Richter, G. (1987), 'Business interests in flexibility and the origin of home-based teleworkplaces for women: empirical examples from the printing industry', in *Neue Informations und Kommunikationstechniken*, edited by Gehrmann, F., Campus-Verlag

Goldmann, M. and Richter, G. (1988), *Teleheimarbeit von Frauen. Betriebliche Flexibilisierungsstrategien und das Interesse von Frauen an der Vereinbarkeit von Beruf und Familie*, edited by Landesregierung Nordrhein-Westfalen: Dokumente und Berichte 7 der Parlamentarischen Staatssekretärin für die Gleichstellung von Frau und Mann

Gordon, G. E. (1984), 'The office away from the office', *Computerworld*, 17 September

Gordon, G. E. (1985a), 'Microcomputers spur interest in telecommuting', *Computerworld*, 29 April

Gordon, G. E. (1985b), 'Telecommuting: management challenge', *Data Processing Management*, August–September

Gordon, G. E. (1988), 'The dilemmas of telework: technology vs. tradition', in *Telework: Present Situation and Future Development of a New Form of Work Organisation*, edited by Korte, W. B., Steinle, W. J. and Robinson, S., North-Holland

Gordon, G. E. and Kelly, M. M. (1986), *Telecommuting: How to Make it Work for You and Your Company*, Prentice-Hall

Gordon, G. (1985), 'Research roundup: four studies probe work at home from different angles', *Telecommuting Review*, 11 January

Greater London Council Industry and Employment Branch (1985), 'Homeworking', in *London Industrial Strategy*, Greater London Council

Gregory, J. (1983), 'The next move: organising women in the office', in *The Technological Woman: Interfacing with Tomorrow*, edited by Zimmerman, J., Praeger

Gregory, J. (1985), 'Clerical workers and new office technologies', in *Office Workstations in the Home*, edited by National Academy of Sciences, National Academy Press

Groom, B. (1984a), 'Loneliness of the long-distance programmer', *Financial Times*, 28 April

Groom, B. (1984b), 'The networker moves on a step', *Financial Times*, 16 April

Gutek, B. A, (1983), 'Women's work in the office of the future', in *The Technological Woman: Interfacing with Tomorrow*, edited by Zimmerman, J., Praeger

Haefner, Klaus (1983), 'New telecommunication services for the private domain, technical potentials and needs of the German population', in *Tenth International Symposium on Human Factors in Telecommunications*, June, Tenth International Symposium, Helsinki

Hakim, C. (1984), Homework and Outwork: National Estimates from Two Surveys, *Employment Gazette*, January

Harkness, R. C. (1977), *Technology Assessment of Telecommunications/Transportation Interactions*, Stanford Research Institute

Harkness, R. C. (1983), 'Move information not people', in *Economic Impact*

Harkness, R. C. and Standal, J. T. (1982), 'Telecommunications alternatives to transportation', in *Communication and the Future*' edited by Dicksbury, H. F., World Future Society

Harvey, D. (1982), 'Waiting for the electronic postman', *International Management*, September

Hebenstreit, J. (1983), 'Training for future office skills', in *New Office Technology: Human and Organisational Aspects*, edited by Otway, H. J. and Peltu, M., Frances Pinter for the Commission of the European Communities

Hedberg, B. and Mehlmann M. (1981), *Computer Power to the People, Computer Resource Centers or Home Terminals? Two Scenarios*, Arbetslivcentrum, Swedish Center for Working Life

Heilmann, W. (1987), *Tele-programmierung*. Die Organisation der Dezentralen Software-Produktion, Forkel-Verlag, Wiesbaden

Heilmann, W. (1988), 'The organisational development of teleprogramming', in *Telework: Present Situation and Future Development of a New Form of Work*, edited by Korte, W. B., Steinle, W. J. and Robinson, S., North-Holland

Heilmann, W. and de Vittorelli, J. (1984), 'Teleprogrammierung in der Bundesrepublik Deutschland', in *Office Management*, **5**, 442–444

Heller, D. K. (1981), 'Industry taps productivity of part-time at-home programmers', in *Infoworld*, 7 December

Hilburg, M. and Monse, K. (1988), 'Home interactive telematics and new services: strategies and trends in restructuring the service sector', in *Concerning Home Telematics*, edited by van Rijn, F. and Williams, R., North-Holland

Hirschheim, R. A. (1983), 'Assessing participative systems design: some conclusions from an exploratory study', *Information and Management*, **6**

Hirschheim, R. A. (1985), *Office Automation: A Social and Organisational Perspective*, Wiley

Holden, L. (1984), 'Note on law and practice on restrictive covenants and town planning', in *Planning for Homework*, Conference Report, 2 May, Housing Associations Charitable Trust

Holti, R. and Stern, E. (1984), *Social Aspects of New Information Technology in the UK: A review of, Initiatives in Local Communication, Distance Working, Education and Training*, Tavistock Institute

Holti, R. and Stern, E. (1985), *The Origins and Diffusion of Distance Working*, Fast Distance Working Project, Working Paper No. 3, Tavistock Institute

Housing Associations Charitable Trust, (1984), *Planning for Homework*, August, Housing Associations Charitable Trust

Huws, U. (1983/84), 'Cable TV and women's work', *Emergency*, no. 1, Winter.

Huws, U. (1984a), *The New Homeworkers: New Technology and the Changing Location of White-Collar Work*, Low Pay Unit

Huws, U. (1984b), 'New technology and homeworking', *Newsletter of International Labour Studies*, April

Huws, U. (1984c), *Keying into Careers: Opportunities for Keyboard Operators*, Greater London Council Equal Opportunities Group

Huws, Ursula (1985), 'The global office', in *Conference Proceedings, Third World Information Network*, Greater London Council

Institute of Personnel Management (1986), *Flexible Patterns of Work*, edited by Chris Curson, Institute of Personnel Management

Judkins P. and West, D. (1984), 'A case history', in *Flexible Manning—the way ahead*, Institute of Manpower Studies

Judkins, P., West, D. and Drew, J. (1985), *Networking in Organisations: The Rank Xerox Experiment*, Gower

Kappus, M. (1984), Die Computerheimarbeit', in *Neue Juristische Wochenschrift*

Kawakami, S.S. (1983), *Electronic Homework: Problems and Prospects from a Human Resources Perspective*, University of Illinois at Urbana-Champaign, LIR 494

Kelly, M.M., October (1985), 'The next workplace revolution: telecommuting', *Supervisory Management*, October

Kilian, W., Bosrum, W., Hoffmeister, U. (1986), *Telearbeit und Arbeitsrecht. Forschungsbericht*, No 139, des Bundesministers für Arbeit und Sozialordnung, Bonn

King, John Leslie, and Kraemer, Kenneth L. (1981), Cost as a social impact of information technology in *Telecommunications and Productivity*, edited by Mitchell, Moss, Addison-Wesley

Klebe, T., Roth, S. (eds) (1987), *Information ohne Grenzen. Computernetze und internationale Arbeitsteilung*. Hamburg

Kleiman, C. (1983), 'Work-at-home trend could be two-edged sword', in *Chicago Tribune*, 27 December

Kordey, N. and Korte, W. B. (1989), 'Raumwirksame Anwendungen der Telematik. Beispiele, Potential und Entwicklungschancen', in *Geographische Rundschau*

Korte, W.B. (1986), 'Telearbeit—Status Quo und Perspektiven. Rasante Aufwärtsentwicklung oder unbedeutende Anwendungen?' *Office Management*, **3**

Korte, W. B. (1988), 'Telework: potential and reasons for its utilisation from the organisation's as well as the individual's perspective', in *Concerning Home Telematics*, edited by van Rijn, F. and Williams, R., North-Holland

Korte, W. B. and Robinson, S. (1988a), 'Telearbeit—Ein arbeitsorganisatorisches

Konzept zur effektiveren Gestaltung der Büroarbeit', *Office Management*, **12**

Korte, W. B. and Robinson, S. (1988b), 'Telearbeit als organisatorische Alternative. Anwendungspotentiale und Empfehlungen zur Vorgehensweise bei der Einführung', *Office Management*, **12**

Korte, W. B., Robinson, S. and Steinle, W. (1988), *Telework, Present Situation and Future Development*, North-Holland

Kraemer, K. I. (1982), 'Telecommunications/transportation substitution and energy conservation: Part I', *Telecommunications Policy*, March

Kraemer, K. I. and King J. L. (1982), 'Telecommunications/transportation substitution and energy conservation: Part II', *Telecommunications Policy*, June

Kravaritou-Manitakis, Y. (1987), *New Forms of Work and Activity: Their Repercussions on Labour Law and Social Security Law in the Member States of the European Community*, European Foundation for the Improvement of Living and Working Conditions

Kufner-Schmitt, I. (1986), 'Die Soziale Sicherheit der Telearbeiter', *Spardorf*,

Lallande, A. (1984), 'Probing the telecommuting debate', *Business Computer*, April

Lange, B. P., Kubicek, H., Reese, H. and Reese, J. (1982), *Sozialpolitische Chancen dei Informationstechnik*, Campus Verlag, Frankfurt

Lanier Business Products Inc. (1982), *Lanier Announces Immediate Availability of Telestaff*, publicity material

Larson, E. (1985), 'Working at home: is it freedom or a life of flabby loneliness?' *Wall Street Journal*, 13 February

Leighton, P. E. (1983), *Contractual Arrangements in Selected Industries*, Research Paper No 39, Department of Employment

Lewis, M. (1984), 'If you worked here, you'd be home by now', *Nation's Business*, April

Lie, M. (1985), *Is Remote Work the Way to the Good Life for Women as well as Men?* Institute for Social Research in Industry, Trondheim

Lohmar, U. (1984), *Die neue Heimarbeit mit Mikroelektronik und Telekommunikation Aspekte einer veränderten Arbeitswelt*, unpublished ms

Long, R. J. (1987), *New Office Information Technology: Human and Managerial Implications*, Croom Helm

Maggiolini, P. (1986), 'Office automation benefits: a framework', *Information & Management*, **10**, 75–81.

Manning, A. M. (1985), 'Control Data Corporation: alternate work site programs', in *Office Workstations in the Home*, edited by National Academy of Sciences, National Academy Press

Markusen, A. (1983), 'The lonely squandering of urban time', in *The Technological Woman: Interfacing with Tomorrow*, edited by Zimmerman, J., Praeger

Mason, R., Jennings, L. and Evans, R. (1984), 'A day at Xanadu: family life in tomorrow's computerised home', *The Futurist*, February

Mattera, P. (1985), *Off the Books: The Rise of the Underground Economy*, Pluto Press

Mazzonis, D. (1984), 'Telework in Italy', in *Telework: Impact on Living and Working Conditions*, edited by Craipeau, S. and Marot, J-C. (eds), European Foundation for the Improvement of Living and Working Conditions

McDavid, M. (1985), 'US Army: prototype program for professionals', in *Office Workstations in the Home*, edited by National Academy of Sciences, National Academy Press

McHale, J. (1976), *The Changing Information Environment*, Paul Elek

Meager, N. (1985), 'Temporary work in Britain: its growth and changing rationales', in *IMS Report no 106*, Institute of Manpower Studies

Medhurst, F. (1984), 'Planning considerations', in *Planning for Homework'*, Conference Proceedings, 2 May, Housing Associations Charitable Trust

Mehlmann, M. (1985), 'Commuting by cable', in *Chipping Away at Society*

Mehlmann, M. (1988), 'Social Aspects of Telework: Facts, Hopes, Fears, Ideas', in *Telework: Present Situation and Future Development of a New Form of Work*, edited by Korte, W. B., Robinson, S. and Steinle, W. J., North-Holland

Mertes, L. H. (1981), 'Doing your office over electronically', *Harvard Business Review*, March–April

Metayer, G. (1981), 'Les Possibilités télématiques', *Cadres CFDT*, July–August

Meyer, N. D. (1983), *The Office Automation Cookbook: Management Strategies for Getting Office Automation Moving*, Sloan Management Review Association

Miller, D. (1985), 'Overview', in *Office Workstations in the Home*, edited by National Academy of Sciences National Academy Press

Miller, T. (1986), 'Telecommuting benefits business with dp's help', *Computerworld*, 17 February

Mitter, S. (1986) *Common Fate, Common Bond; Women in the Global Economy*, Pluto

Monod, E. (1983), 'Le Télétravail: une nouvelle manière de travailler', *Datafrance*, 15 September

Monod, E. (1985), 'Telecommuting, a new word, but still the same old story?', in *Women, Work and Computerisation: Opportunities and Disadvantages*, edited by Olerup, A., Schneider, L. and Monod, E., North-Holland

Monod, E. and Metayer, G. (1982), *Télétravail: Premier Bilan*, CESTA

Moore, S. (1985), 'Telecommuting: today, tomorrow or never?', in *On Communications*

Morgenbrod H. and Schwärtzel, H. (1980), 'Informations- und Kommunikationstechnik verändern den Büroarbeitsplatz', in *Chip Technology and the Labour Market*, Ministerie van Sociale Zaken

Moss, M. L. (1984), *New Telecommunications and Technologies and Regional Development*, New York University Press

Müllner, W. (1985), *Privatisierung des Arbeitsplatzes*. Chancen, Risiken und rechtliche Gestaltbarkeit der Telearbeit, Stuttgart, München, Hannover

Müllner, W. (1986), 'Neue Arbeitsstrukturen unter besonderer Berücksichtigung der Telearbeit', *Personalführung*, **5–6**, **6**, 220–225

Mumme, C. L. (1983), 'La Renaissance du travail à domicile dans les économies développés, *Sociologie du Travail*, July–August, September

Musiol, A. (1986), *Vernichtet moderne Automatisierungstechnik Arbeitsplätze? Wird die Arbeit von den Büros in die Privatwohnungen verlagert?* Self-published pamphlet, Munich

National Research Council (1985), *Office Workstations in the Home*, National Academy Press

Nelson, K. (1986), *Automation, Skill, and Back Office Location*, Association of American Geographers

New Scientist, (1984), 'Plug into exploitation', *New Scientist*, 3 May

New York Times, (1981), 'Rising trend of computer age: employees who work at home', *New York Times*, 3 December

Nilles, J. (1982), 'Telework may soon make daily long-distance commutes obsolete while enhancing worker productivity and satisfaction', *Technology Review*, April

Nilles, J. M. (1985a), 'Commentary', in *Office Workstations in the Home*, edited by National Academy of Sciences, National Academy Press

Nilles, J. (1985b), 'Teleworking from home', in *The Information Technology Revolution*, edited by Forester, T., Basil Blackwell

Nilles, J. M., Carlson, F. R., Gray, P. and Hanneman, G.J. (1976), *The Telecommunications-Transportation Tradeoff*, Wiley

Olson, M. H. (1981), *Remote Office Work: Implications for Individuals and Organisations*, School of Business Administration, September, New York University

Olson, M. H. (1982), *New Information Technology and Organizational Culture*, School of Business Administration, July, New York University

Olson, M. H. (1983), 'Remote office work: changing work patterns in space and time', *Communications of the ACM*, **26**, No 3, March

Olson, M. H. (1985a), 'The potential of remote work for professionals', in *Office Workstations in the Home*, edited by National Academy of Sciences, National Academy Press

Olson, M. H. (1985b), 'Do you telecommute?', *Datamation*, 15 October

Olson, M. H. (1987), *An Investigation of the Impacts of Remote Work Environments and Supporting Technology*, Centre for Research on Information Systems, New York University

Olson, M. H. (1988), 'Organisational barriers to telework', in *Telework: Present Situation and Future Development of a New Form of Work*, edited by Korte, W. B., Steinle, W. J. and Robinson, S., North-Holland

Olson, M. and Lucas, H. C. (1982), 'The impact of office automation on the organisation: some implications for research and practice', *Communications of the ACM*, November

Olson M. and Tasley R. (1983), *Telecommunications and the Changing Definition of the Workplace*, New York University

Otten, K. W. (1984), 'Changes in business communications: innovative uses of new media technologies', *Journal of Information & Image Management*, September

Otway H. J. and Peltu, M. (eds) (1983), *New Office Technology: Human and Organisational Aspects*, edited by Otway, H.J. and Peltu, M., Frances Pinter for Commission of the European Communities

Park, M. (1982), 'Will new technology woman be a drudge?', *Computer Talk*, 13 September

Peles, S. (1985), *Travail à domicile: problèmes posés et ébauché de la rèponse syndicale: cas de la Belgique*, European Centre for Work and Society

Peltu, M. (1980), 'New life at home for office workers', *New Scientist*, 27 March

Pfarr, H. (1984), 'Schnelles Handeln des Gesetzgebers gefordert. DV-Fernarbeit bricht mit Arbeitstraditionen', *Computerwoche*, September

Phelps, N. (1985), 'Mountain Bell: program for managers', in *Office Workstations in the Home*, edited by National Academy of Sciences, National Academy Press, Washington

Pollack, A. (1983), 'Finding Home Computer Uses', *New York Times*, May 11

Postgate, R. (1984), *Home: A Place for Work?*, Calouste Gulbenkian Foundation, UK Branch

Posthuma, A. C. (1987), *The Internationalisation of Clerical Work: A Study of Offshore Office Services in the Caribbean*, Science Policy Research Unit

Pratt, J. H. (1983), *Home Teleworking: A Study of its Pioneers*, Allied Professionals Educational Consulting Service

Pratt, J. H. and Davis, J. A. (1985), *Measurement and Evaluation of the Populations of Family-owned and Home-based Businesses*, Joanne H. Pratt Associates

Pugh, H. S. (1984), *Estimating the Extent of Homeworking*, Social Statistics Research Unit, April, City University,

Pye, R. (1976), 'Effect of telecommunications on the location of office employment', *Omega, International Journal of Management Science*, **4**, No 3

Pye, R., Tyler, M. and Cartwright, B. (1974), 'Telecommunicate or travel?' *New Scientist*, 12 September

Raney, J. G. Jr (1985), 'American Express Company: Project Homebound', in *Office Workstations in the Home*, edited by National Academy of Sciences, National Academy Press

Renfro, W. L. (1985), 'Second Thoughts on Moving the Office Home', in *The Information Technology Revolution*, edited by Forester, T., Basil Blackwell

Revill, K. (1984), 'Future housing', in *Planning for Homework, Conference Proceedings*, 2 May, Housing Associations Charitable Trust

Rifkin, G. (1983), 'Working remotely: where will your office be?', *Computerworld*, 15 June

Robins, K. and Hepworth, M. (1988), 'Electronic spaces', *Futures*, April

Romero, D. (1983), 'The invisible employee: can you meet the challenge?' *Hardcopy*, January

Ryan, G. M., Wynne, R., Cullen, K., Ronayne, T., Dolphin, C., Korte, W. B., Robinson, S., Hopkins, M. and Ennis, B. (1988), 'Concepts, methodology and guidelines for understanding and managing IT-uptake processes in user organisations', in *Esprit 1988, Putting the Technology to Use, Part 2*, North-Holland

Sandiford, D. H. (1982) (unpublished), *Some Recent Developments in Working From Home*, British Telecom Long Range & Strategic Studies Division

Sarson, R. (1986), 'A blueprint for the new homeworkers?' *Computing*, 20 March

Saxon, R. (1984), 'Existing housing', in *Planning for Homework, Conference Proceedings*, Housing Associations Charitable Trust, 2 May

Schiff, F. W. (1983), 'Flexiplace: pros and cons', *The Futurist*, June

Shirley, S. (1979), 'The remote control of projects', in *EURO IFIP 79*, edited by Samet, P. (ed), North-Holland

Shirley, S. (1982), 'The distributed office', in *Integrated Office Systems*, Pergamon Infotech

Shirley, S. (1985), 'F International: twenty years' experience in homeworking', in *Office Workstations in the Home*, edited by National Academy of Sciences, National Academy Press

Shirley, S. (1987), *The Distributed Office*, presentation to the Royal Society of Arts, London, 16 February

Shirley, S. (1988), 'Telework in the UK', in *Telework: Present Situation and Future Development of a New Form of Work*, edited by Korte, W. B., Robinson, S. and Steinle, W. J., North-Holland

Siegel, L. and Markoff, J. (1985), *The High Cost of High Tech*, Harper & Row, London

Silver, H. (1985), 'Home work in Great Britain', in *Telecommuting Review: the Gordon Report*, 9 January

Smith, S. and Wied-Nebbeling, S. (1986), *The Shadow Economy in Britain and Germany*, Anglo-German Foundation

Steinle, W. J. (1988a), 'Telework: opening remarks on an open debate', in *Telework: Present Situation and Future Development of a New Form of Work Organisation*, edited by Korte, W. B., Robinson, S., Steinle, W. J., North-Holland

Steinle, W. J., (1988b), '"Weiche" Telearbeit als Unternehmensstrategie. Kann die traditionelle Büroorganisation noch bestehen?' *Office Management*, **12**

Stern, E. and Holti, R. (1986), *Distance Working in Urban and Rural Settings*, Tavistock Institute of Human Relations

Strassman, A. (1985), *Information Payoff: The Transformation of Work in the Electronic Age*, Macmillan

Trades Union Congress (1985), *Homework: A Trade Union View*, Trades Union Congress

Taylor, J. R., (1982), 'The office of the future: Weber and Innis revisited', *Search/En Quête*, **VIII**, No.3

Technology, (1984), 'Skilled outwork loses pay', *Technology*, 7 May

Tippmann, M. (1985), 'Telearbeit—eine sozialpolitische Zukunftsaufgabe', in *Die Betriebswirkschaft*

Toffler, A. (1981), *The Third Wave*, Pan

Toffler, A. (1985), *Previews and Premises*, Pan

Trade Unions Group (1984a), 'Evaluation report' in *Telework: Impact on Living and Working Conditions*, edited by Craipeau, S. and Marot, J-C., European Foundation for the Improvement of Living and Working Conditions

Trade Unions Group (1984b), 'Impact of teletravail on living and working conditions', in *Telework: Impact on Living and Working Conditions*, edited by European Foundation for the Improvement of Living and Working Conditions

Turoff, M. and Hiltz, S. R. (1983), 'Working at home or living in the office', *Information Processing*, September

US Congress, Office of Technology Assessment (1985), *Automation of America's Offices*, US Government Printing Office OTA-CIT-287

Upton, R. (1984), 'The "home office" and the new homeworker', *Personnel Management*, September

Vedel, G. (1984), *Just Pick up a Telephone!, Remote Office Work in Sweden*, Copenhagen School of Economics and Business Administration

Vedel, G. (1985), *Telematics and Remote Office Work*, Copenhagen School of Economics and Social Science

Vedel, G. and Gunnarsson, E. (1985), 'Flexibility in women's remote office work', in *Women, Work and Computerisation: Opportunities and Disadvantages*, edited by Olerup, A., Schneider, L. and Monod, E., North-Holland

Vitalari, P., Venkatesh, A. and Gronhaug, K. (1985), 'Computing in the home: shifts in the time allocation of households', *Communications of the ACM*, **28**, No 5, May

Voge, J. (1981), 'Les Téléphones sur les remparts', *Le Monde du Dimanche*, 15 March

Wall Street Journal (1984), 'No workplace like home', *Wall Street Journal*, 23 February

Walter, K., Evans, S. (1984), 'Telecommuting: an idea whose time has almost come', in *Management Technology*, January

Webb, M. (1983), 'Life in the electronic cottage', *Working Woman*, December

Whitehouse, F. (1981), 'Computer experts go to work without ever leaving home', *New York Times*, 28 June

Wiegner, K. K. and Paris, E. (1983), 'A job with a view', *Forbes*, 12 September

Williams, F. (1983), *The Communications Revolution*, Sage Publications,

Wilson, L. (1982), 'Chained to the kitchen computer', *London Standard*, 3 September

Wolfgram, T. H. (1984), 'Working at home: the growth of a cottage industry', *The Futurist*, June

Woodham, A. (1983), 'Who really wants to work from home?' *Company*, February

Zientara, M. (1981), 'Ten million telecommuters by 1990? Companies experiment with telecommuting', *Computerworld*, 30 November

Zimmerman, J. and Horwitz, J. (1983), 'Living better vicariously?', in *The Technological Woman: Interfacing with Tomorrow*, edited by Zimmerman, J., Praeger

Zismann, M. (1978), 'Office automation: evolution or revolution?,' *Sloan Management Review*

Index